NIHILISM:

A Philosophical Essay

NIHILISM:

A Philosophical Essay

by Stanley Rosen

New Haven and London, Yale University Press, 1969

This book is dedicated to
Françoise and Nicholas

Acknowledgments

Shortly after completing this manuscript, I learned of the untimely death of my friend and teacher, Alexandre Kojève. The present essay is a consequence of long reflections which were decisively influenced by that extraordinary man, whose memory I cherish, and whose absence cannot be replaced. I am equally indebted to another great teacher, Leo Strauss, who first set me on the longer way.

Once again it is a pleasure to acknowledge the assistance of Mrs. Jane Isay of the Yale University Press. The final version of this essay was written during a sabbatical granted by the Pennsylvania State University, and I am grateful to those who made this possible. Portions of Chapter 4 were published previously, in different form, in *Social Research* (Summer 1968), under the title "Philosophy and Ideology." In writing Chapter 6, I have adapted material first printed in the *Review of Metaphysics* (December 1962), under the title "Wisdom," and in *Man and World* (February 1968), under the title "Reflections on Nihilism." My thanks to the editors of these journals for permission to reprint.

Contents

"the Philosopher's Way in all Ages has been by erecting certain *Edifices in the Air;* But, whatever Practice and Reputation these kind of Structures have formerly possessed, or may still continue in, not excepting even that of *Socrates,* when he was suspended in a Basket to help Contemplation; I think, with due Submission, they seem to labour under two Inconveniences. *First,* That the Foundations being laid too high, they have been often out of *Sight,* and ever out of *Hearing. Secondly,* That the Materials, being very transitory, have suffer'd much from Inclemencies of Air, especially in these North-West Regions."

Jonathan Swift,
A Tale of a Tub

Preface

I.

Nietzsche defines nihilism as the situation which obtains when "everything is permitted." If everything is permitted, then it makes no difference what we do, and so nothing is worth anything. We can, of course, attribute value by an act of arbitrary resolution, but such an act proceeds *ex nihilo* or defines its significance by a spontaneous assertion which can be negated with equal justification. More specifically, there is in such a case no justification for choosing either the value originally posited or its negation, and the speech of "justification" is indistinguishable from silence. For those who are not gods, recourse to a creation *ex nihilo,* whether disguised by the intricacies of the axiomatic method or onto-poetic integrity, reduces reason to nonsense by equating the sense or significance of speech with silence. This book is a study of nihilism in the sense defined by Nietzsche, and subsequently elaborated by Heidegger, but which is also to be found in the teachings of philosophers like Wittgenstein and his various epigones. For the reason which has just been summarily stated, and which will be developed in detail in the following pages, what seem to be various forms of nihilism in fact reduce finally to just one form. Similarly, in the context of nihilism, the various forms of silence reduce finally to just one form, or rather to formlessness. Since silence is rendered articulate by speech, and receives its formal diversification from the reflexive shaping of discursive consciousness, it loses this articulateness when treated as the source of significance. Although I discuss a number of episodes in the history of philosophy, my book is not intended as history, but as a philosophical essay about the contemporary crisis of reason. The historical sections form an integral part of an analysis of this crisis, if only because one cannot understand contemporary opinions, and certainly not contemporary opinions about the past, without knowing the connections between the present and the past. Although philosophy seeks to replace opinions by truth, it cannot succeed unless it is able to make an accurate identification of opinions, past and present, and perhaps especially of past opinions presently masquerading as truths.

Every philosophical essay contains an unavoidable polemical component. Since my book is a defense of reason, it must necessarily be an attack upon what I regard as the enemies of reason. My claim is that, although the danger of nihilism is a permanent human possibility, the actual pervasive presence of nihilism today is due to a series of specific philosophical decisions in the past. The net effect of these decisions has been to produce a radical deterioration in our conception of what it means to be reasonable. More specifically still, the conception of "reason" has been detached from its traditional affiliation with the conception of "good." It has become a virtually unanimous article of faith, among the ostensible friends as well as the avowed enemies of reason, that one may speak reasonably about logical patterns of inference or "empirically verifiable facts" (a phrase which is a tissue of ambiguities), but not about what is good. The only exception of any contemporary consequence—and it is very influential indeed—is that of "historicism" in its various species. By this, and in this context, I mean the view that rational speech about the good is possible only with respect to the meaning of history. But the identification of "good" with "what happens" (whether in an ontological or an ontic sense) leads to a fatalism and subordination to the factic that is indistinguishable from positivism.[1] Rather, it is worse than positivism, which, since it denies rational significance to the good in any, and especially in any historical, sense, is able to resist tyranny and baseness by conventionally indoc-

---

1. Here and throughout, I use the distinction between "ontological" and "ontic" in the sense employed by Heidegger to distinguish between speech about Being and speech about beings. Similarly, the term "factic" is of Heideggerian origin and designates the radical contingency of temporal givenness.

trinated appeals to virtue—a nonsensical but salutary appeal to history in opposition to history.

By detaching "reasonable" from "good," the friends of reason made it impossible to assert the goodness of reason. Indeed, they made it all the more easy for the enemies of reason to assert the evil of reason. If reason is conceived exclusively on the model of mathematics, and if mathematics is itself understood in terms of Newtonian rather than Pythagorean science, then the impossibility of asserting the goodness of reason is the extreme instance of the manifest evil of reason. Reason (we are told) objectifies, reifies, alienates; it debases or destroys the genuinely human. It obscures the significance of human existence by superimposing the rigid, inhuman, and, in the last analysis, man-made categories of a mathematized ontology. Man has become alienated from his own authentic or creative existence by the erroneous projection of the supersensible world of Platonic Ideas, of an arithmological domain of beings, and so of an autonomous technology, which, as the authentic contemporary historical manifestation of "rationalism," will destroy us or enslave us to machines. Reason is a machine or machine-like; ultimately, a stultifying poem or human creation. Little wonder that so many are today searching for edifying poems in the regions of the nonsensical and the insane.

The link between modern rationalism and historicism lies ultimately in the separation between "reasonable" and "good." Thanks largely to the combined influence of mathematics and Christianity (in a positive and negative sense), the good was said to lie beyond the domain of the rational investigation of this world. The Cartesian *ego cogitans* has become the symbol of the process by which man sought to master the world by relying on himself and mathematics alone. Still, whatever may have been Descartes' own vision of the coherence of this project, it resulted in the famous problem of "subjectivism" or "subjectivity." If the ego independently perceives the independent mathematical order, that is, if the reason of the ego is essentially mathematical, then the question of the goodness of the order immediately arises. If, however, the ego projects or creates its mathematical definitions, the process of world-mastery would then seem to be simultaneously a project of world-creation. Mathematical order, on this alternative, is a poem—not merely a poem which excludes the issue of goodness, but whose own goodness is again a purely "subjective" or nonrational matter.

In its traditional form, the problem bequeathed by Descartes to modern philosophy is called "dualism." Dualism refers primarily to the difference between body and soul or mind. In order to free mathematical physics from the theoretical and practical obstructions imposed by Christianity, Descartes and his allies employed a Christian distinction, thereby preparing the way for a restriction of reason to God's creation, or the things of this world. Mathematical physics studies the body; metaphysics studies the soul. But the influence of mathematical physics led to the "secularization" of metaphysics by transforming it into the philosophy of history, whereupon the influence of history, together with the autonomous tendencies of the mathematizing ego, led to the historicizing of mathematical physics. Hence the great revolution of modern philosophy, carried out in the name of certitude against the mixture of superstition and empty speculation practiced by the ancients, ended paradoxically in a philosophy of radical historicity, of poetry rather than of mathematics. The "mathematicians," who fancy themselves as hard men, have attempted to avoid the softness and paradox of poetry by refusing to speak about the origins or foundations of their thought in any but meta-mathematical terms. No amount of technical genius can veil the philosophical emptiness of this effort, which even now gives itself away by praising itself in aesthetic terms: mathematical works of art hanging in the void between the two despised Platonic domains of sun and cave.

Thus the fundamental problem in a study of nihilism is to dissect the language of historicist ontology with the associated doctrine of human creativity. The hard men are soft at the core; whether among friends or enemies of reason, the difference between philosophy and poetry has today disappeared. The most important contemporary thinker is therefore without question

Heidegger, because he alone has stated with genius and exhaustive rigor the onto-poetic historicism that underlies contemporary philosophies of the most divergent appearances. If my book is considered in terms of its contemporary polemics, then *the* opponent is Heidegger; and I have attempted to show both how he states, better than those who presume to despise him, the nihilist implications of the post-Hegelian philosophical world, as well as why and how his statement is inadequate, or is itself an expression, rather than an overcoming, of nihilism. Heidegger can never be adequately "refuted" by those who are ignorant of his thought, and certainly not by those self-styled rationalists who are ignorant of the degree to which Heidegger states, more powerfully than they, the consequences of their own assumptions. One does not defend reason by refusing to speak of the unreasonable; neither does one defend it by refusing to speak of reason. The fashionable contemporary defense of reason amounts to silence. This must, of course, be discursively demonstrated. But far more important is the demonstration that Heidegger's "speech" itself is indistinguishable from silence.

II.

I have tried, then, to write a defense of reason from the perspective of the problem of nihilism. In so doing, I have not hesitated to attack, to the best of my ability, some of the most fashionable dogmas of the day. I ask the philosophical reader to honor his love of wisdom and to think through with me the arguments by which I claim to expose the inadequacies of some imposters to the title of truth. This book has not been written in a spirit of reactionary opposition to the modern or contemporary world. No one who loves philosophy will waste a moment in wishing for history to move backward, anymore than he will contribute to the destruction of the present by vain wishes for the future. The reactionary, exactly like the radical innovator, is a slave of history; and I write in opposition to just this enslavement. A genuine loyalty to the present is never restricted

by the chains of the *hic et nunc*. Today philosophy and historical existence are both threatened by the nihilistic consequences
of the denaturing of reason, which was ostensibly a purification
of its nature. There is no time for melodramatic posturing before the abyss of nothingness, but neither is there time for an
absurd refusal to take seriously the threat of absurdity. I trust
that I have not forgotten, in writing this book, that Socrates
laughed once but never wept. In that sense, I am a Platonist;
but a Platonist in that sense is one who sees no difference
between philosophy and the good life. A good life, let the reader
remember, can be lived only in the present.

If these remarks are sound, it follows that no polemic against
contemporary dogmas can be valid or valuable if it does not rise
above mere polemic. My book, taken in its entirety, contains a
reasoned discourse on the nature of philosophy and therefore,
as I suggested previously, on the problem of nihilism as implicit
in human nature. I realize very well that each chapter could
have been expanded into a volume. But if I had done so, this
specific book would never have been written; and I want to say
very frankly that this book, or one like it, needs to have been
written. I would ask those readers who agree with the need to
defend reason, or rather who agree with the need to state in a
coherent and synoptic manner *what reason is,* to join with me,
not in a facile communion with contemporaneity, but in a
detailed conversation wherein we may expand and improve the
introductory formulation contained in this book or replace it
with a more articulate statement.

Let me conclude this preface with a few words about the
structure of this volume. I begin my study with an analysis of
"ordinary language philosophy," or the most popular contemporary version of epistemology.[2] In order to engage the atten-

2. Some might contest this statement by citing the popularity in the
United States of linguistic analysis based upon mathematical logic (or
the study of "ideal" languages). However, the members of this school
seem to agree that their logic is determined by their ontology, and in the
present context, it is ontology with which I am concerned. An inspection
of the ontology in question normally shows it to reduce either to mathematical aestheticism or vulgar empiricism, buttressed by the prestige

tion of those members of the philosophical community who regard nihilism as a literary neurosis imported from continental Europe, I believe it is useful to spell out the nihilistic consequences of a mode of philosophizing that prides itself upon its rigor and Anglo-Saxon sobriety. The more serious justification for this procedure is that nihilism is in fact primarily a theoretical, and only secondarily a practical or cultural, phenomenon. Thus, in the second chapter, I turn to "fundamental ontology," the inverse of the Janus-coin of contemporary philosophy. The thesis of these two chapters is that, in each case, the principles of the teaching, when correctly and consistently formulated in the terms approved by their own masters, lead to the negation of those principles, or to silence. And speech that is indistinguishable from silence is nihilism. In the third chapter, I supply the historical framework needed to make intelligible the common origins of the modes of thought dissected in the first two chapters. Chapter 4 is a "sublation" of the first three, or an attempt to develop the political consequences of historicist ontologies. Chapters 1 to 4 thus move from epistemology to politics by supplying the substructure of ontology and history. In Chapter 5, I offer an alternative formulation of the connection between reason and the good to the one criticized in the preceding pages. This formulation is to be found in the dialogues of Plato. I concentrate on the image of the good discussed in the middle of the *Republic,* and argue that the teaching contained therein is valid for all times. To accept it is altogether compatible with fidelity to the best features of modernity, which are, after all, not so radically removed from the thought of Plato as to make my suggestion a reactionary one. In the sixth and last chapter, I discuss nihilism in conjunction with the dialectical structure of human nature, as well as with the dialectic of speech and silence in the heart of philosophy itself.

(which is left unexamined) of the physical sciences. In either case, it has no independent philosophical status of its own. It is a tragic fact in contemporary philosophy that "logic without metaphysics" too frequently means "epistemology grounded in ideology."

In a sense, then, the first four chapters are critical, and the last two more constructive. But this remark, if taken too seriously, is misleading, and in two different senses. The first is that a critical analysis of erroneous and dangerous doctrines cannot be successfully carried through unless it exhibits at each stage the doctrine which the author regards as sound or superior to those he is criticizing. The second is that I have not presumed to "solve" the problem of nihilism, if by a solution is meant a recipe for extirpating the unwanted phenomenon. Nihilism, to repeat, is a perennial human danger: it cannot be "solved" without the dissolution of human nature. But one can surely offer suggestions for mitigating the otherwise fatal results of this perennial pestilence. Since the disease is perennial but takes different forms at different historical epochs, protective inoculation must take into account both the permanent structures and the local infections of these structures. Such is the task of philosophical medicine, and such is the intention of the pages which follow.

State College, Pennsylvania
July 16, 1968

Chapter 1

Wittgenstein and Ordinary Language

I.

In this chapter, I shall be primarily concerned with the philosophical assumptions and procedures that are widely associated with the movement, or family of movements, known as "ordinary language analysis" or "ordinary language philosophy." My purpose is very specific: to show the sense in which this philosophical movement is a version of nihilism. Since the most important figure in the tradition under scrutiny is Wittgenstein, I shall introduce my argument with some general remarks about his two main works. The first thing to be said, and I ask the reader to bear it in mind throughout what follows, is this. Although I regard the claim that a philosophy terminates in nihilism to be a fundamental criticism, it does not follow from this that, if the claim is proven, one must repudiate all traces of the convicted teaching. A philosopher may have a defective conception of what he is doing generally, while nevertheless doing sound things in particular. It is also quite possible for a defective general conception of the nature of philosophy to serve useful ends in a given historical epoch. Many of Wittgenstein's strongest admirers have claimed something like this in his own case. They reject Wittgenstein's view that philosophy, or a general theory about philosophy, is impossible, and so reject the interpretation which he himself gave to his own work, while insisting upon the fundamental and lasting importance of the details of that work. My procedure is different but related to this. The details of Wittgenstein's teaching, the techniques employed by his disciples and successors, and the claimed results of that employment are of interest to me only as they illuminate his general conception of the nature of philosophy. The techniques and their results may or may not be of interest; my point is that whatever soundness or interest they possess cannot

1

be accounted for by the general conception of philosophy which underlies them. The results, if they are results, are necessarily silent about their own significance and merit.

The problem may be introduced by starting from Wittgenstein's contention that philosophical theory is impossible or nonsense. If we agree with Wittgenstein, we are immediately plunged into the night in which all cows are black. If we disagree with him, yet wish to retain his technical innovations and results, then a new interpretation of their significance is required. Many of Wittgenstein's successors have been fatally inconsistent in this crucial respect. Although convinced of the positive merits of Wittgenstein's work, they have been unable or unwilling to give it a general theoretical justification, taking refuge in the invocation to "do philosophy" rather than to talk about it. Because of the wide-sweeping consequences of "doing philosophy" in the ostensibly Wittgensteinian manner, this amounts to both asserting a positive "Wittgensteinian" doctrine about the nature of philosophy and denying that such a doctrine can be asserted. One cannot "do philosophy" unless one knows what one is doing, or what it means to philosophize (in the correct, Wittgensteinian manner). What counts as correct philosophical procedure is supposedly justified by recourse to the normative function of ordinary language. For the speaker of ordinary language, however, philosophy either never arises or, if it does, takes a variety of deteriorated shapes stemming from the whole panoply of traditional philosophical discourse. If one claims that ordinary language, because it is free of philosophical paradoxes or works efficiently in getting its jobs done, is the standard for adjudicating philosophical disputes, the results are contradictory. In the first place, if ordinary language is taken in its ordinary sense, then it might be said to include all of the puzzles and paradoxes which gave rise to the various traditional philosophical schools. If philosophies arise in order to dispose of grammatical puzzles, one cannot appeal to the source of the puzzles as the criterion for deciding when they have been correctly resolved. But apart from this, by raising ordinary language to the status of philosophical criterion, one engages in a mode of discourse which would never be uttered by an ordinary man. And this is equivalent to asserting an interpretation of philosophy, while at the same time denying that an interpretation of philosophy may be asserted.

The aforementioned contradiction is partly disguised by the appeal to the charms of common sense as embodied in ordinary use, but to submit to these charms is either to refuse to philosophize or to equate common sense with philosophy. If we refuse to philosophize, then we are at the mercy of interminable chatter or interminable silence, of sophistry or mysticism. If we equate common sense, as embodied in ordinary language, with philosophy, we offer a theory about the nature of philosophy which, since it could never be made by ordinary language, has not actually been made by philosophy. That is, however much talk has been generated by the "doing of philosophy," philosophy has not genuinely appeared or transpired. We are at bottom totally silent, mere farceurs or satirists of sobriety. The only alternative, within the horizon of Wittgenstein's teaching, is to seek a theory about the nature of philosophy which is implied by those parts of the teaching we wish to preserve. And this raises the question as to the criteria by which we select and reject the *disjecta membra* of the master's corpus. If the criteria are themselves derived from within the corpus, they must be free from the taint of Wittgenstein's negative convictions about the nature of philosophy. There must, as it were, be at least two Wittgensteins (by which I do not mean the early and the late), the positive and the negative. But the criteria by which we distinguish between the positive and the negative cannot be derived entirely from Wittgenstein; he himself made no such division within his teaching, and for us to do so requires that we invoke a standard external to his teaching. We must believe in the possibility of philosophy as a self-descriptive, theoretical enterprise, a possibility which is to some discernible degree rendered actual by Wittgenstein's own accomplishments. Nevertheless, the significance of these accomplishments is extra-

Wittgensteinian. To preserve the light from the dark within Wittgenstein, one must have recourse to instruments he did not entirely furnish.

It should be obvious by now that the only conceivable source of these instruments is philosophy, in the large, untrammeled, and traditional sense of the enterprise. In order to be able to take Wittgenstein seriously, one must first reject his claim, repeated and implied by countless disciples, that he "solved" the problem of the nature of philosophy, whether in a positive or negative sense. Wittgenstein did not expose "traditional" philosophy as nonsense, since it is just by philosophizing in the traditional sense that we have our only prospects for grasping and assessing his own teaching. Wittgenstein's work is significant only as an attempt to answer the traditional question: what is philosophy? The fact that he rejected the answers given by his successors is in itself merely a mark of his traditionalism. But whether we accept Wittgenstein's silence or the (contradictory) speech of his successors, our acceptance is worthless without philosophical argument, and this means polemical disputation with other answers to the traditional question. Philosophy is necessarily dialectical and eristic because it seeks to account for the whole, even in the negative sense of specifying the limits of rational speech. No account of the whole is complete unless it refutes or sublates its rivals. Thus, my objection to the polemical aspects of ordinary language philosophy, or to their attacks upon "metaphysics" and "traditional philosophy," is not that they are polemical, but rather that they are incompetent.

In these preliminary remarks, I have tried to establish an essential point in an elementary way. Either ordinary language philosophers know what they are doing, or they do not. If they do not, we may altogether disregard them. If they do know what they are doing, they must be able to tell us what it is in terms that go beyond the mere assertion of their presuppositions. One does not go beyond the assertion of these presuppositions by appealing to ordinary use, if only because every account of what use counts as "ordinary" is already an instance of the extraordinary use of language. In order to discriminate among rival instances of extraordinary use, an extraordinary criterion is required. That extraordinary criterion, as I shall argue throughout this book, is *wisdom,* or at least the claim by someone to have given a complete rational speech. Such a claim cannot be fulfilled, but that takes nothing from its validity as the end and standard of philosophy.

II.

The charge of nihilism has already been leveled against Wittgenstein's earlier teaching as contained in the *Tractatus Logico-Philosophicus.* Gustav Bergmann identifies this nihilism as the denial of philosophical propositions. "Those passing for such are neither true nor false but, literally, nonsense." [1] For Bergmann, the crucial point is the denial of ontological status to logical form, or the assertion that "a sentence expressing a tautology (logical truth) really says nothing and is therefore not really a sentence." [2] If no proposition can say anything about the logical form of any proposition, then, of course, the propositions of the *Tractatus* are themselves nonsensical. The truth is that there is no truth, that is, no speakable or rational truth; hence, not even the absence of rational truth can be spoken. It is as though the early Wittgenstein shared the view of the later Heidegger that Being (i.e. truth) is rendered invisible by the very manner in which it presents itself. This comparison with Heidegger can be extended. For example, the world of the *Tractatus* is a process of facts, analogous to Heidegger's conception of facticity, empty of value or significance, except perhaps as the manifestation of nothingness or silence, as the occasion for our insight into the inadequacy of speech. More precisely, the silence toward which the *Tractatus* points is Wittgenstein's analogue to what Heidegger calls "ontological" speech. For the moment, however, let us put to one side this comparison with Heidegger. My question is rather this: does the later

1. "The Glory and the Misery of Ludwig Wittgenstein," in *Logic and Reality* (Madison, The University of Wisconsin Press, 1964), p. 226.
2. Ibid., p. 228.

teaching of Wittgenstein, as adumbrated in the *Philosophical Investigations,* escape the reduction of speech to silence and so the charge of nihilism?

As Anthony Quinton, among others, has pointed out, the thesis of the impossibility of philosophy is still present in the *Investigations* in the form of "the philosophical theory that it was no part of philosophy to propound theories but only to describe facts about language that were perfectly familiar already, arranging these familiar descriptions in a fashion designed to break the hold on our minds of philosophical confusions and paradoxes." [3] Quinton's language suggests that there is something paradoxical about a theory that excludes the possibility of theories of the type it instantiates. Still, Quinton is one of many who hold that this negative or (as I should say) self-canceling view of the nature of philosophy may be separated from the positive aspects of Wittgenstein's work. I myself am very dubious that this is so. In my opinion, all of Wittgenstein's writings are permeated by what one may call the yearning for silence, which took explicit form in the last half of the *Tractatus,* but which is visible in the *Investigations* as well. This yearning arose from dissatisfaction with a conception of reason as equivalent to logical calculation plus the scientific verification of facts. Wittgenstein saw clearly that such a conception of reason, essentially prepared by the scientific philosophers of the seventeenth century, was unable to assert its own value or the reasonableness of being reasonable in any but an instrumental, and so contingent, sense. The ends toward which reason is directed cannot themselves be certified as reasonable. They are contingent facts, what happens to be the case or, even worse, what some men hope or believe to be the case. As a result, the use of reason is itself a contingent fact, the nonrational consequence of a subjective desire, inclination, or convention. Unfortunately, Wittgenstein was convinced of the accuracy of the mathematico-scientific theory of reason; his dissatisfaction could be overcome only by a transcendence of reason. Reason

3. "Excerpt from 'Contemporary British Philosophy,'" in *Wittgenstein,* ed. G. Pitcher (Garden City, Doubleday, 1966), p. 9.

is in effect speech; that is, it is the discursive representation of form. Wittgenstein's initial solution to the inadequacy of (discursive) reason is to regard it as a ladder taking man up, namely, above speech to the silent intuition or vision of logical form. Presumably, once man has attained to the domain of silent intuition, he will be in a position to satisfy his ethical and religious longings as well, to find in silence the silent exposition of "the sense of Being."

In traditional language, the Wittgenstein of the *Tractatus* aspires to *noēsis* without *dianoia,* or vision without speech. The purpose of the *Tractatus* is not to fulfill the Leibnizian (and Russellian) dream of a universal rational language, but rather to show the limits of language, the impossibility of universal reason. In order to do this, Wittgenstein develops his theory of logical form, but the theory, considered as a contribution to logic or epistemology, has only secondary importance. To see it in those terms is, as it were, to look into Wittgenstein's world from the perspective of its interior. It is thus not altogether adequate, although certainly helpful, to speak of Wittgenstein's enterprise as "Kantian." [4] For Kant, although one can have no knowledge of the noumenal, there is such a thing as practical reason, or rational participation in the ultimate meaning of life. For Wittgenstein, although reason is "practical" in the sense of being an activity, this activity functions to preclude our participation in the source of meaning or value of the whole. That is, the activity of reasoning is the immanent surface of man's yearning for truth and fulfillment: the transcendental surface is silent vision.

Wittgenstein thus initially presents himself by no means as a unique instance of a type that aspires to mysticism by means of a logical asceticism. It would seem that the Wittgenstein of the *Investigations* is in an entirely different, even opposite, situation. And yet, I believe, the appearance is deceiving. There is, of course, a difference between the *Tractatus* and the *Investigations,* which might be expressed as follows: the later Wittgen-

4. As does Stenius in his commentary on the *Tractatus.* The best commentary on the *Tractatus* that I have seen is by Favrholdt.

stein seems to have surrendered his earlier yearning for silence, and so denied the very possibility of noetic vision in the traditional sense of the immediate apprehension of form. The goal of the philosopher now seems to be to immerse himself entirely in dianoia. It is easy to understand the epistemological shift from "ideal" to "natural" language in these terms. The doctrine of noēsis is from the beginning associated with a bias for mathematics as the paradigm of reasoning. Although the *logos* of Plato is of course not the logic of Russell, we may remember that, in the *Republic,* mathematics is closest to the noetic perception of, and reasoning exclusively with, the Ideas. Mathematical (and logical) form seems to give us the best example of the always steadfast, perfectly accessible foundation for rational form in general. If there is nondiscursive or immediate intuition, must it not be of what is preeminently unmoving, unchanging, and self-identical?

One may compare the dianoetic obsession of the later Wittgenstein, not with the dialectic of Socrates, which always points toward the Ideas, but with the procedures of Aristotle in his ethical, political, and rhetorical writings. As a linguistic therapist, the later Wittgenstein attempts to replace in every case the claim to an immediate (and so private) intuition or psychic experience by a mediated, discursive (and so public) account of speech or behavior within a given context of custom, of *nomos* or *doxa.* Part of what this means has been well expressed by P. F. Strawson in his review of the *Investigations:*

> It is true that having a thought is not to be identified with any particular outward process of speech or writing or action; nor with inner speech or other imagery. The having of a thought is not the occurrence of any of these; but nor is it any other occurrence. It is the occurrence of one of these in a certain context, in certain circumstances. To see what sort of context, what sort of circumstances are relevant here, one must consider what criteria are used in ascribing thoughts to people.

And a paragraph later, "The concept of thinking demands such a general pattern as a setting for the occurrence of thoughts. In this, which I shall call his hostility to the doctrine of immediacy, Wittgenstein is surely right." [5]

This "hostility to the doctrine of immediacy" corresponds to what I mean by the apparent rejection of noēsis; the interpretation of thinking as dependent upon "a general pattern of actions and events," which are in turn given determinate significance by use or agreement, corresponds to the identification of thinking as dianoia in the sense of nomos or doxa. What it means to think, and hence to mean, is decided within the context of an already understood language, more specifically a language in a given historical stage, an all-encompassing horizon of intentions which must be accepted as the basis for analysis or use-specification—a *Lebensform*. The Lebensform is Wittgenstein's equivalent to the nineteenth-century conception of Weltanschauung, a word he uses once to ask whether it is not what "earmarks the form of account we give, the way we look at things." [6] The inaccessibility of the Lebensform to theoretical evaluation replaces the earlier impossibility of speaking about logical form. In the present case, the Lebensform is equivalent to the language or language game,[7] that is, to custom or use. In both stages of his teaching, Wittgenstein denies the possibility of a logos or theoretical account of speech, in both cases because he identifies the horizon of speech as that about which one must remain silent. Formerly, however, one had to remain silent about logical form, or what may be called the natural order of the world. Now one must be silent about the foundations—because there is no natural order of the world. There is no *physis,* so far as philosophy is concerned, but only nomos.

It is therefore correct to say that the change in Wittgenstein's teaching amounts to a rejection of "noēsis without dianoia" in favor of "dianoia without noēsis." But it would be wrong to say that the resultant replacement of silence by infinite chatter is complete or consistent. Noēsis continues to lurk in the background in the shape of the intelligence of activity. Take for

5. "Review of Wittgenstein's *Philosophical Investigations,*" in Pitcher, pp. 50–51.

6. *Philosophical Investigations,* I, par. 122.

7. Ibid., I, par. 19, 23; II. xi, p. 226.

example the crucial conception of "language game." We are presumably always able to identify a game, and, wherever speech is possible, an appropriate game, but we are presumably always unable to utter a rational speech about the form common to all games. Wittgenstein's denial that there is such a common form is contradicted in practice by the visibility of games as games. The common form is present, very much like a Platonic Idea.[8] Every speech, however, is an instance of *a* game, not of *the* common form; hence, every speech veils the common form which allows a speech to stand forth as what it concretely is: again, the similarity to Heidegger is unmistakable. Being (*Sein*) is defined in a given case by the relevant language game. Hence, one can neither attribute nor deny Being to the language game itself or to the paradigm case in the language game.[9] The language game is the source of Being, i.e. the source of meaning. And man, the speaking animal, is the source of the language game. Again, as in Heidegger, man, the "house of language," bestows Being. The pre-linguistic horizon of meaning or Being is for both philosophers human activity. "Doing" is equivalent in the *Investigations* to noetic intuition.[10]

III.

The teaching of the *Philosophical Investigations* suffers from two fundamental and closely related defects which are sufficiently pervasive to infect the entire enterprise of ordinary language philosophy. The first is the attempt to ignore the derivation of speech from the prior intelligence of doing; Wittgenstein seems here to insist upon not understanding the consequence of his own words. He is in fact advocating the view, typical of post-

8. Cf. the essay by R. Bambrough on "Universals and Family Resemblances," in Pitcher.

9. *Investigations,* I, par. 50.

10. Cf. *Investigations,* I, par. 620: *"Doing* itself seems not to have any volume of experience. It seems like an extensionless point . . . etc." I very much doubt whether Wittgenstein would have explained this passage as I do, but in it, he seems to me to have had approximately the insight which I develop in the text.

Hegelian German philosophy, that man *makes* meaning, and so that there is no basis, external to human agreement, by which to distinguish between sense and nonsense. As Hobbes and Locke, the ancestors of this view, put it, we understand only what we make. It remained for thinkers of a later age to make explicit the corollary to this proposition: whatever man does not make is meaningless. Wittgenstein, as the *Tractatus* shows, understood the self-vitiating character of this doctrine. For, to be meaningful, it too must be a human construction. But by that token, there is no way in which to certify the meaningfulness or value, in a rational sense, of man's construction of reason. It is a contingent, arbitrary fact, engulfed in the silence of nothingness. No doubt what prevented the early Wittgenstein from developing an "existentialist" philosophy of absurdism was his conception of logical form as independent of human constructive activity. Like Husserl and Frege, Wittgenstein was an opponent of psychologism. But since, unlike the traditional rationalists, he regarded logical form as inaccessible to speech, the result was mysticism.

The *Investigations* does not repudiate mysticism, but illustrates a new response to the question of silence. Whereas, in the *Tractatus,* silence was the goal of philosophy, it is now something to be avoided at all cost. Whereas speech was previously understood as pointing toward, and pointing out (exhibiting), the silence of logical form, the same logical form is now conceived as one of indefinitely many kinds of speech, all emerging from the silence of human praxis, in the contingent but insurmountable and radically unquestionable shape of a Lebensform,[11] the historicist's decomposed version of the Kantian transcendental ego. Why this change in Wittgenstein's thought? If truth and meaning are discursive, and discourse is factic contingency, then it is out of the question for human beings to "see" the truth of logical form as independent of discursive thinking. The entire visual dimension of the *Tractatus* is nothing but an optical illusion. Even an invocation to silence is a speech

---

11. *Investigations*, II. xi, p. 226. This is what it means to say that philosophy leaves everything as it is (I, par. 124).

about silence. If the teaching in the *Tractatus* were correct, it could not even be uttered. But only discursive thinking can pronounce a teaching to be "correct"; it is altogether inconceivable that the teaching of the *Tractatus* is correct. The real consequence of the *Tractatus* is that one can say nothing of the shortcomings of speech altogether, either to oneself or anyone else. To man as speaker, speech has no shortcomings. As Wittgenstein later put it, "ordinary language is all right."

This brings us to the second pervasive defect of the *Investigations*. By demoting logical form to the status of product of speech, Wittgenstein destroyed the last vestige of "nature" in the classical sense of the standard or end of speech. The term "nature" appears infrequently in the *Investigations,* either in a sense actually equivalent to "custom"—what happens normally in human affairs, what we habitually do—or in the unexamined sense of "natural science" and "laws of nature." But the meaning which scientists attribute to "nature" must itself, as a product of speech, be a matter of conventional agreement. The "facts of nature" have sense only because people talk about them in a customary way; hence one cannot verify the sense of the way we are accustomed to talk by pointing to the facts of nature. Linguistic conventions, not the facts, are normative.[12] Thus Wittgenstein observes that "we are not doing natural science; nor yet natural history—since we can also invent fictitious natural his-

12. The problems faced by an ordinary language philosopher who attempts to defend this aspect of Wittgenstein's teaching are well exhibited in an essay by Stanley Cavell, "Must We Mean What We Say?" in *Inquiry, 1* (1958). According to Cavell, no question may be raised about normal action. The reason is presumably that "normal" is a "categorial" term, part of a statement about how we use our language, "about the concept of an action *überhaupt*" or a part of transcendental rather than formal logic. Transcendental logic is thus the same as empirical or contingent *facticity* (cf. pp. 81–86). Some of the embarrassment that ensues from the assertion of this thesis is apparent in the following statement: "The claim that in general we do not require evidence for statements in the first person plural does not rest upon a claim that we cannot be wrong about what we are doing or about what we say, but only that it would be extraordinary if we were (often)" (p. 87).

tory for our purposes." [13] The same must be said with respect to human desires, volitions, or purposes. Their meaning is determined discursively, within a specific context of behavior and speech which is itself determined by, or rather is an application of, the Lebensform. But the Lebensform, as we have already seen, is the verbal incarnation of history.

The absence of "nature" in any sense other than as a linguistic convention or construction reduces Wittgenstein's later teaching to historicism or conventionalism. This may be illustrated by a brief inspection of Gilbert Ryle's well-known distinction between "use" and "usage." The point of the distinction is precisely to rescue Wittgenstein from conventionalism without referring to "Platonic entities" external to things referred to by the words themselves.[14] An unwillingness to refer to Platonic entities is no proof of their absence. This reticence on the part of Wittgenstein's successors merely reflects the master's silent injunction to "keep talking," or never to refer to those entities about which discursive speech is ostensibly impossible. In any case, Ryle defines "usage" as "a custom, practice, fashion, or vogue," in other words, as a linguistic convention. "Descriptions of usages presuppose descriptions of uses, i.e. ways or techniques of doing the thing, the more or less widely prevailing practice of doing which constitutes the usage." And again:

> Perfectly mastering a use is not getting to know everything, or even much, about a usage, even when mastering that use does causally involve finding out a bit about a few other people's practices. We were taught in the nursery how to handle a lot of words; but we were not being taught any historical or sociological generalities about employers of these words. That came later, if it came at all.[15]

13. *Investigations,* II. xii.
14. G. Ryle, "Ordinary Language," in *Ordinary Language, Essays in Philosophical Method,* ed. V. C. Chappell (Englewood Cliffs, N.J., Prentice-Hall, 1964), p. 29.
15. Ibid., pp. 31, 32.

One must reply to Ryle that ignorance of history is no excuse. The question is whether what we were taught in the nursery was itself a historical or sociological generality. Wittgenstein himself is quite clear about the fact that the sense or meaning of a word or phrase lies in its use within a particular circumstance of the Lebensform.[16] But the way a word or phrase is used depends precisely upon its linguistic history. Summarizing I. 84–87 of the *Investigations,* Strawson, in a previously cited essay, says: "What determines whether there is enough precision in the rules, or a sufficient explanation of them, is whether the concept is used successfully, with general agreement." [17] The use which underlies usage is a summation or general agreement, or a linguistic convention that is the result of widespread resemblance (if not identity) in hermeneutic habit. Hence the only way in which Ryle and Wittgenstein can escape the charge of conventionalism is precisely by referring to some kind of Platonic entities or natural standard of normal use. Benson Mates says in his criticism of Ryle's paper that the discussion "appears to indicate that for him there is some sort of normative element in assertions about ordinary use. If the opposite of use is misuse, then use must be somehow right, proper, or correct." [18] This point, while well-taken, may be sharpened. Ryle tacitly appeals to the pre-linguistic intelligence of doing as the source of the orderliness, sense, or intelligibility of pre-technical speaking. As pre-linguistic, however, it is inaccessible to discourse; we have nothing but discourse as its own justification. And this is why meaning depends upon agreement; Wittgenstein is a proponent of the "social contract" theory of epistemology, because to him the "state of nature" affords no basis for human existence. In fact, the state of nature is itself a linguistic convention: nothing can be said about nature that is

16. See esp. passages like I, par. 208, 421, and 430 (the usually cited passage is I, par. 43).

17. Pitcher, p. 33.

18. "On the Verification of Statements about Ordinary Language," in Chappell, p. 67.

not a consequence of previous agreement by speakers in a given Lebensform.

The distinction between "use" and "usage" makes only a limited or temporary kind of sense: "use" is the latest and best approximation to intersubjective certitude as crystallized from "usage." We cannot point to the facts because there are no facts prior to linguistic agreement and, so, no pointer. Wittgenstein's conventionalism thus prevents him from developing, or in my view from recognizing that he has tacitly developed, a theory about speech. Even when he points to "natural" causes of speech like pain, desire, or other modes of behavior, he has altogether stepped outside of the skin of his own doctrine. If behavior in the sense of physiological response to the natural environment is the source of speech, then ordinary language, contrary to Wittgenstein's quoted assertion, is a branch of, and dependent upon, natural science. Fidelity to Wittgenstein's own pervasive and explicit teaching, however, leads instead, or ought to lead, to the interpretation of natural science as a linguistic convention. What we *say* about physiological response is the relevant factor for philosophy, and *what* we say is a fact—a contingent linguistic "happening." The facticity of the world in the *Tractatus* continues to be present in the *Investigations,* only now it is extended to include logical form. In sum, use is either by rule or by nature. If by rule, it is conventional; and this is so regardless of whether the conventions are formalized. But if use is by nature, whether in the sense of Platonic entities or logical forms, then ordinary language philosophy is reduced to the status held by rhetoric or certain operations of political prudence in Aristotle, which is to say that it must be rendered obedient to traditional philosophy (in which I include all serious theoretical justifications of an "ideal" language).

If nothing can be said that has not been said before, how can we begin to speak at all? Wittgenstein would appear to be an Aristotelian in physics as well as in politics. The objections leveled by Wittgenstein against a private language serve equally well to destroy the possibility of a public language. A private

language is excluded because it depends upon noetic intuition—
the immediate apprehension of form about which, although it is
itself silent, we speak. Thus Wittgenstein repeats at length the
charge that, in a private language, there is no criterion by which
I may decide that a given use of a word in that language is
correct. I cannot confirm it by remembering an agreement with
myself to call a given experience or sensation by the word
"X," because there is nothing to guarantee the correctness of
my memory. And my decision to call an experience "X," e.g.
"the same," is an arbitrary one, because it is dependent entirely
upon my pleasure. But if I can call things whatever I please,
then again there is no criterion for distinguishing between correct and incorrect names, rules, or interpretations.

These, I believe, are the two central points in Wittgenstein's
rejection of private language. Both beg the question by assuming that there is no basis for certifying rules and remembering
names, except intersubjective certitude. If this were the case,
however, by what criterion could I know that the linguistic
conventions embodied in the dictionary's definitions are themselves based upon correctly learned and formulated rules? If I
check the definitions in the dictionary with the "living speech"
of my neighbors, how do I know (a) that I have correctly
remembered what they said, one minute after they stop speaking
to me, and (b) if I do remember or, what amounts to the same
thing, can follow and retain their conversation as it is taking
place, that what they (we) are saying correctly mirrors the
standard responses to experience or procedures for constructing
linguistic rules? There is no answer to "a"; the situation is even
worse than Wittgenstein suggests when he observes that careful
attention can discover only "what is *now* going on in *me*." [19]
For what is going on has temporal extension and can therefore
be retained only in the memory. Otherwise "now" must refer to
the nontemporal instant, accessible only to immediate intuition
despite Wittgenstein's distrust of the immediate. As for "b,"
either we are at the mercy of what people say, a kind of gossip;
or else we must check what they say against the facts. But there

19. *Investigations*, II. xi, p. 219.

are no facts independently of what people say. In sum, there is no more reason to trust our memory of a public discourse than of a private one. And even if we do trust our memory of the words, the public evidence of a public speech itself amounts to a public speech, to an infinite regression that transforms public speech into the logical equivalent of nonsense or silence.

IV.

Wittgenstein and his philosophical progeny are nihilists because they cannot distinguish speech from silence. And so we come to what is for me the crucial case. If reason is discursive, there is no reason to speak rather than to be silent. If we arbitrarily begin to speak, simply because "this is what we do," it is impossible to speak reasonably about the value or *goodness* of what we do. To the question, what good is reason? reason would appear to have nothing to say. It is pointless to distinguish and collect the various senses of the word "good" if the enterprise itself can only be called "good" in a conventional or nonrational manner. In this section, I want to reconsider the conclusions drawn above about Wittgenstein, but with specific respect to the relationship between reason and goodness.

Ordinary language philosophers claim to identify the fact of use with the philosophical soundness of that fact. And yet, it is easy to see that this cannot be true. To say that X is a sound use is not to use X but to generalize upon the difference between X and non-X, and therefore to refer to a universal framework or theory of signification.[20] The philosophical analyst and the ordinary speaker of ordinary language do not mean the same thing when each asks, "what do we mean when we say 'X'?" To the ordinary speaker, however rich and ambiguous the linguistic scope of X, its meaning is always determined in a specific case by specific circumstances, which determine the scope of X to achieve a specific instance of linguistic satisfaction. If we ask

20. This is the real consequence of Wittgenstein's cryptic remark, "What I am looking for is the grammatical difference" (*Investigations,* II. viii, p. 185).

the ordinary speaker to reflect upon the scope of X by posing
the aforementioned question, "what do we mean when we say
'X'?" he will begin with a series of specific examples, using
statements from ordinary language to cast light upon the statement whose meaning we are interrogating. This is the procedure
which the ordinary language philosopher believes himself to be
following when he conducts his own analyses of the meaning of
a statement. But such is not the case.

Suppose that someone has said, within earshot of an ordinary
language philosopher, "John is a good man." If the philosopher
asks, "what do you mean by 'a good man'?" the speaker may
say something like this: "I mean that he is honest," or "good to
his family," or "a real man," or "someone you can go to the
well with in the middle of the night," and so on. As long as the
ordinary speaker is using ordinary language in an ordinary way,
he does not ask about, or refer to, "the logic of 'good' "; that is,
he does not go beyond the ordinary significations of "good" to
give a logical definition of the concept—unless he is corrupted
by the linguistic impurities of his philosophical interlocutor. The
result of such corruption is to arrive at a definition of "good"
which is not itself good in the sense that John is a good man.
Consequently, no matter how good the definition of "good" may
be for providing an agreed sense to various uses of the term, it
is *bad* from the viewpoint of the speaker of ordinary language in
all cases in which his intentions are not syntactic or lexico-
graphic. The ordinary speaker, in calling John a good man, is
not referring to a logical concept, but to goodness. If the logical
concept of "good" is itself good, this cannot be simply because
the use of the concept provides us with a serviceable interpretation of uses of the concept "good."

The man who asks, "what good is 'good'?" is not suffering
from a confusion of ordinary language that may be removed by
linguistic therapy of the Wittgensteinian type. On the contrary,
the question arises because the speaker has understood the ter-
rible significance of accepting this type of linguistic therapy as
an *interpretation* of ordinary speech, namely, as an interpretation which has not accurately distinguished itself from the use

of ordinary speech. What the theoretician calls "fact of use" contains a tacit theoretical interpretation of the meaning of "use," and so of the meaning of "meaning." This can be easily seen in the following example. Within ordinary language, men frequently observe the different senses given to words like "good," and they conclude from this observation something that looks like a colloquial expression of a statement in the discourse of ordinary language philosophy. I refer to the common conclusion by ordinary persons that "good is whatever we say it is." But there are also many ordinary persons who condemn statements of this sort as "moral relativism" or even as "nihilism"; and they reply with contrary assertions that may be summarized as "good is X," where "X" means "something other than 'whatever we say it is.' " Can this dispute be settled on the authority, that is, within the perspective, of ordinary language? Certainly not if the meaning of ordinary language is the same as its use, since "good" is used in contrary and even contradictory ways. In practice, this difficulty is solved by linguistic therapists only through a transcendence of ordinary language. The empirical description of distinctions in use is transcended by a decision as to the goodness (soundness, validity) of a specific use or set of uses; this decision is not and cannot be justified by an empirical observation on ordinary use. That in itself of course is not objectionable; or if it is, then all philosophical or meta-utilitarian reflections are objectionable. What is objectionable is the lack of self-awareness concerning the theoretical presuppositions of the decision about goodness of use.

In terms of the present example, nihilism may be defined as the view that it makes no difference what we say, because every definition of "difference" is itself merely something that we say. A correct speech is one that obeys the rules of the game, but if we ask why we ought to play the game, or why this game is better than another, then we will be treated to analyses of the logic of "ought" and "better" or disquisitions which, while denying on logical grounds the validity of self-predication, nevertheless reflexively assert their own excellence by use of a language of silence. Thus, we will be told, given two uses of "better," b_1 and b_2, b_1 is "better" than b_2 if it conforms more closely with the conventions of use (euphemistically entitled "the logic of the concept"). Since the conventions of use determine the significance of "better," the concept by which we distinguish between b_1 and b_2 is self-certifying. It is better to speak conventionally or in the usual way because "better" means "conventional or usual speech." To the question, "why is it better to speak conventionally than unconventionally?" the answer is, "because 'better' and 'conventional' are the same." It is then nonsense to appeal to a standard beyond convention for determining the rightness or goodness of convention. "The law is the law," as W. H. Auden put it in a somewhat similar argument. To ask for a justification of the use of "better" in a way other, or ostensibly better, than how we use "better" is impossible (in a rational sense or manner). It would be like asking, "why is 'better' better than 'worse'?" In sum, the exposition of the logic of "better," or how we use the word, is itself better than an exposition of "better" which adjudicates its uses by criteria other than themselves. There are no other criteria, if what you want is a rational, discursive analysis or certification of the concept.

So in fact there *is* an answer to the question, "why is 'better' better than 'worse'?" It is this: "better" is better than "worse" because by "better than" we mean "more in conformity with conventional use," and "better" means "more conventional." Therefore, what is more conventional is more in conformity with conventional use than what is less conventional. And so, a rational, discursive analysis of proper speech leads to the advice to say what is usually said. Even if we assume that there is, again self-reflexively, widespread agreement on what is usually said, some dangerous radical may be tempted to ask, "what *good* is what we usually say?" This person has somehow and regrettably fallen off the merry-go-round; we can get him back on by repeating the incantations just recorded, that is, by reducing goodness to "good," or what we say. He who refuses to participate in *la ronde* is manifestly unreasonable, because "to be reasonable" means "to speak in the usual way," and so on,

and so forth, to infinity. I note in passing that the political implications of this epistemological theory are enormous but have
not to my knowledge been adequately recognized and formulated by proponents of ordinary language philosophy, just because they believe that "the problems of epistemology are
mainly academic. Their practical causation and effects, therefore, are unimportant." [21]

This, in brief, is the *absurdisme* of ordinary language philosophy, or the linguistic branch of contemporary existentialism. The
linguistic absurdist denies the possibility (knowingly or otherwise) of a rational justification of reason, or of the claim that
reason is good, in any sense that does not identify "good" with
the "logic of the concept." For to say that reason is good because
we like it, or because it makes life possible, or enables us to
satisfy our desires, is to use "good" in a different way from the
one employed in statements like "a rational assertion is good."
In the latter case, as we have found, "good" means "in accordance with the rules of conventional use." But in the former
case, its meaning is not at all clear; on the conventionalist interpretation of meaning, one would be led to doubt whether the
term has any meaning at all. Take the statement that "reason is
good because I like it." "Reason" by hypothesis means "speech
in accord with conventional statements about how to assert
what is the case," whereas "good" will be assumed to have its
ostensibly usual meaning in this context, or "in accordance with
the rules of conventional use." By means of appropriate substi-
tutions, we then obtain the following statement: "speech in accord with conventional statements about how to assert what is
the case is (speech) in accordance with the rules of conventional use because I like it." If we reduce this statement by
striking out the tautologous repetition, we obtain "speech
accords with conventional use because I like it." But whether or
not we perform this reduction, statements of this kind are still

21. Margaret Macdonald, "The Language of Political Theory," in
Logic and Language, ed. A. Flew, *1* (New York, Philosophical Library,
1951), p. 170. Cf. my article, "Political Philosophy and Epistemology,"
in *Philosophy and Phenomenological Research, 20* (June 1960), 453–68.

tautologies. This follows from an analysis of what it means to say "I like it."

"I like it" can refer either to what counts as rational speech or to the factual situation about which we speak. In the first case, "I like it" can only mean "I recognize it to be in accordance with the rules of conventional use." For if I like a speech that does not so conform and yet offer it as an answer to the question why reason is good, I violate the rules of the game and am talking nonsense. I am saying in effect " 'sense' because 'nonsense' " or "N → S." But this is equivalent to saying "S v S." I can say anything I wish as a foundation from which to deduce what counts as "sense." The evidence for "sense" is "nonsense" and for "nonsense" is "sense." This is what I mean by nihilism.

In the second case, "I like it" refers to the factual situation about which we speak. This situation cannot by hypothesis be linguistic or rational but is made up of my physiological or psychophysical responses: the sugar level in my bloodstream, moods of contentment or discontentment, sexual desire, boredom, love of honor, and so on. We can bring these responses into the domain of rational discourse, but only as facts about which it is convenient to speak, and in a conventional way. The conventional way to speak of this or any other fact is to assert it, correctly, of course, which means in accordance with what is the case. Now what is the case? A physiological response is intended, e.g. "I have a high blood-sugar level." Hence, using this example, "I like it" has no rational significance except as a conventionally appropriate way of saying "it raises (lowers, maintains) my blood-sugar level." "I like it" has no rational significance in any sense other than as a code for a set of responses, which is to say that we cannot *rationally* discuss whether the responses are good or bad, because "good" means "I like it," and "I like it" means "I respond as follows," and so once again the circle is complete.

V.

I have begun my study of nihilism with epistemological themes, because it seems important to me to emphasize that the problem of nihilism is only secondarily one of morality. Second is indeed very high; I do not mean to trivialize morality but to suggest that what counts as moral is a derivative of our conception of reason. For even if we should insist upon the altogether nonrational character of morality, this would depend upon our conception of reason as nonmoral. Thus, for example, in contemporary philosophy the question of the relation between reason and goodness is frequently discussed in terms of "ethical naturalism," or the view that nature provides a criterion for distinguishing between bad and good. But "nature" is usually understood, by both parties to the dispute, to be the domain of scientific or empirical fact and so visible to reason only in the sense of the faculty that ascertains what is the case, namely, by the use of logic, mathematics, observation, experiment, and the like. A rational statement is one which asserts a fact; facts are either by nature or by convention, or rather, it is conventionally agreed that a natural fact is the object of a statement about "what is the case" as established by empirical science. Since the ethical naturalist usually shares the theory of meaning held by his opponent, that is, since a scientific fact has no "value" beyond its facticity, since, like Jaweh, the fact is what it is, little wonder that the ethical naturalist has so much difficulty in making a persuasive case.

When the contemporary anti-naturalist, as I shall call the critic of the above view, is told that X is a fact and X is good, he wisely insists that "good" is here an unanalyzed term, or that given a fact, nothing logically follows as to its moral goodness or preferability to another fact. The criticism is final because (or for as long as) both parties to the dispute agree upon the meaning of "fact," and so actually upon the meaning of "reason." Let me try to illustrate the issues involved here by reference to the work of R. M. Hare. Hare makes two kinds of assumptions which are pertinent to the present discussion, both of them questionable, to say the least. First, Hare regularly assumes that moral terms are visible prior to philosophical analysis as characteristically moral and, so, as not factual. This enables him (and presumably us) to select certain words or sentences as moral utterances, as for example when distinguishing between moral and nonmoral imperatives.[22] Thus Hare says:

> Value-terms have a special function in language, that of commending; and so they plainly cannot be defined in terms of other words which themselves do not perform this function; for if this is done, we are deprived of a means of performing the function.[23]

In a word, we have to know a moral term before we can assess its logic. We have to know the moral phenomenon *before* we speak about it, and this is something about which Hare does not speak.

But the pre-analytic status of our knowledge of moral terms is altogether ambiguous. If this knowledge is merely conventional, then so too is the resultant analysis, however technically proficient; we return to the dilemmas of the previous section. If the knowledge is not conventional, but (by hypothesis) pre-analytical, then it can only be intuitive, namely, a direct mental apprehension of the natural moral situation. In that case, the claim of ethical naturalism has been reestablished, with the correlative demand that we redefine the previously analyzed operative terms—"reason," "fact," "good." Naturalism itself is then not reestablished, but rather the need to develop a more reasonable conception of nature if we are to avoid reducing moral language to the status of nonsense. In other words, Hare himself is implicitly testifying as follows: barring a return to conventionalism, the *fact* is that it is our nature to intuit moral imperatives, i.e. we intuit their significance as the necessary basis for subsequent clarifying analyses. Unfortunately, Hare does not say this, because despite his "analytic" concern with ordinary experience, he pays no attention to the pre-analytic situation in its own extraordinary complexity. Instead, he begins with a reduced version of ordinary experience, one which fits comfort-

22. *The Language of Morals* (Oxford, Oxford University Press, 1952), p. 36.
23. Ibid., p. 91; cf. p. 12 and Hare, *Freedom and Reason* (Oxford, Oxford University Press, 1963), p. 89.

ably into the theory entailed by his conception of analysis. He is not analyzing ordinary experience, but experience as it is ordinarily understood by analysts in their professional guise. Hence, the only way in which he might legitimately refute ethical naturalism is by replacing it, not with conventionalism, but with a different conception of nature.

Hare has not managed to say anything significant about the relation between reason and goodness. This becomes evident in the following passage:

> Thus a complete justification of a decision would consist of a complete account of its effects, together with a complete account of the principles which it observed, and the effects of observing these principles . . . . Thus, if pressed to justify a decision completely, we have to give a complete specification of the way of life of which it is a part. This complete specification it is impossible in practice to give; the nearest attempts are those given by the great religions . . . . Suppose, however, that we can give it. If the inquirer still goes on asking "But why *should* I live like that?" then there is no further answer to give him, because we have already, *ex hypothesi,* said everything that could be included in this further answer. We can only ask him to make up his own mind which way he ought to live; for in the end everything rests upon such a decision of principle.[24]

By "way of life" Hare means something very much like what Wittgenstein intended by Lebensform. In both cases we find ourselves at the edge of rational speech. Hare's second assumption is this: morality is a matter of principle, and nothing can be said about a choice between principles, which is for Hare equivalent to denying the rational character of such a choice. But, instead of acknowledging this assumption, he proceeds immediately to deny it:

24. *The Language of Morals,* p. 69; cf. *Freedom and Reason,* pp. 89, 151, 224.

> To describe such ultimate decisions as arbitrary, be-
> cause *ex hypothesi* everything which could be used to
> justify them has already been included in the decision,
> would be like saying that a complete description of the
> universe was utterly unfounded, because no further fact
> could be called upon in corroboration of it.[25]

By "description" Hare means "factual description" in the sense
of "account of what has been ascertained to be the case." This
account may be divided into two parts: things or events, and
human assessments of things and events. Things and events,
when correctly described, have no moral character; they are
what they are. Thus the moral content of a complete description
could come only from human assessments. But human assessments are themselves linguistic interpretations, or intuitive, pre-
verbal apprehensions of natural moral forms, or some combination of the two. Hare never mentions moral intuitions, although
he neccessarily, if unconsciously, uses them. Like Wittgenstein,
he is more or less explicitly committed to dianoia. The moral
discourse sanctioned by Hare terminates in a list of all the facts
in the universe and the moral principle which the individual
"infers" from that list. But no rational basis is provided for
making the "inference" in question. As rational, it would rest
on facts, and facts not only are not principles, but are logically
distinct from them. In Hare's own terms, then, a complete description of the universe, if it is rational, makes no claim to be
good or, alternatively, to describe a good universe (no real
difference here, since the description would necessarily have to
be a "fact" in the universe). In these terms, there is in principle
only one complete description of the universe. But there are
many moral principles, each claiming to be good or to define
good action. The facts cannot allow us to decide rationally
which principle is best, unless the principle is assumed as a
proposition in a moral syllogism; and therefore, despite Hare's
rejoinder, his moral philosophy terminates in absurdisme.

A completely factual description, whether of the universe or

25. Hare, *The Language of Morals,* p. 69.

a human action, makes no claim to define "good," whereas this is precisely the claim of a moral principle. Either, then, moral principles are not rational, or "to be rational" means something more than "to assert what is the case," or finally, there are more things that are the case than is currently dreamt of by spokesmen for reason. Thus the question of the relation between reason and goodness goes much deeper than the question of the nature of morality. For unless reason is good, I venture to say that morality has no nature, but is mere conventionalism, or an arbitrary attribution of sense to nonsense. Even worse, the "choice" of reason, however resolute or sincere, is itself the certification of nonsense as the basis for the significance of sense, and this is nihilism.

Chapter 2

From Ordinary Language to Ontology

I.

I have introduced the problem of nihilism with a discussion of Wittgenstein for several reasons. To begin with, Wittgenstein's thought is still the basis for most philosophical discussion in English today. I count among his descendents those whose work, however critical of the master, remains within the horizon either of the *Tractatus* or the *Investigations*. The descendents of Wittgenstein tend either to ignore or to be scornful of the theme of nihilism. For the most part, they exclude it from the domain of genuinely philosophical topics, which are in effect identified with the topics of epistemology. Nihilism would then seem to be an egregious product of "continental nonsense" or, at best, a concern of cultural historians, litterateurs, and psychiatrists. It was therefore essential to demonstrate the nihilistic consequences of the epistemological presuppositions of ordinary language philosophy. Caveat emptor: if nothing can be done to moderate the sangfroid of professors of ordinary language philosophy, one may at least hope to show the potential philosopher something of the difference between sobriety and naïveté. Ordinary language philosophy is incompatible with ordinary language, or is unable to distinguish between speech and silence. Since man is a speaking animal, if ordinary language philosophy were assiduously practiced, it would make human life impossible. As an academic enterprise, it is, if not impossible, a fatality, in a way similar to the sense in which Nietzsche spoke of himself. The ordinary language philosopher teaches us to philosophize, not with a sledgehammer, but with a nail-file. He does not say, "I am dynamite," but rather, "I am a kitchen match." The tools are different, but the historical pattern is the same. In both cases, the remark of Leopardi is apposite: "Reason is a

28

light; nature wishes to be illuminated by reason, not set on fire." [1]

In recent years, it has become rather fashionable to point out the resemblances between Wittgenstein and Heidegger, and so to speak of their common *ontological* concern. I have already indicated some striking similarities between the two thinkers and, somewhat obliquely, the sense in which Nietzsche is an important ancestor of both ordinary language philosophy and fundamental ontology. The essence of the relationship turns upon the "valuelessness" of facts and the high status of history as the expression of human creativity. A detailed analysis of the historical development that culminates in the movements best represented by Wittgenstein and Heidegger would require several volumes. In order to understand the philosophical problem of nihilism, we shall have to consider later some episodes from that historical development. In this chapter, however, our task is more specific, namely, to complement the preceding treatment of ordinary language philosophy with an exemplary analysis of the nihilistic consequences of "the language of Being." It is true that Wittgenstein and Heidegger have a common defect, namely, the elaboration of a theory about speech which is itself a denial that such a theory may be stated or fully formulated. The result of Heidegger's distinction between the "ontological" and the "ontic," to use his early terminology, is silence.

Let us begin with a brief inspection of the etymological significance of "ontology." This word, which seems to have been invented in Germany about two hundred years ago, is a compound of the Greek words λόγος τοῦ ὄντος. At first glance, this phrase might be translated into English as "speech about being." Unfortunately, such a translation conveys nothing of great clarity or significance, and besides, we might quarrel about whether the translation is the best possible one. For example, is λόγος to be rendered by "speech," "reason," "science," or some other term? Again, I wrote "about being" rather than "of being" or even "of Being." Is it being (or Being) that speaks,

1. G. Leopardi, *Zibaldone di Pensieri,* ed. F. Flora (Opere, Mondadori, 1949), *1,* 32.

or is something else speaking about being (or Being)? If it is not being (Being) that speaks, what else is there? Can nonbeing (Being) speak? Is τοῦ ὄντος the genitive of a singular being, or does it designate the Being of beings? It would seem that a definition of the word "ontology" must be equivalent to an ontology or speech about being. Yet how can one begin to speak about being when one does not know the meaning of "being"? And so we find ourselves immediately in the famous ontological circle. If ontological speech is possible, then it must be on the basis of pre-ontological awareness or, in other words, ordinary language.

The defects in ordinary language philosophy arose from a failure to engage in ontology, or to offer a speech about the whole. We seem now to have discovered that ontological deficiencies follow from a failure to engage in ordinary language. Ordinary language philosophers confuse their philosophical interpretation of ordinary language with the use of ordinary language because they are committed to discursive, as independent from intuitive, reasoning. Since for them philosophy begins in and as discourse, ordinary speech, if it is reasonable, must be in essence the same as philosophical speech: "in my beginning is my end." This essential sameness is not and cannot be overcome by technical distinctions like use and mention, language and meta-language, and the like, because the rationale for the techniques is identical with the reasonableness of ordinary discourse. At the same time, it is not ordinary discourse which pronounces its reasonableness, but technical discourse which certifies ordinary language. This confusion is very far-reaching. Despite the fact that philosophical analysis is by hypothesis *of* ordinary speech, the conception underlying the significance of philosophical analysis makes a sharp distinction between it and ordinary speech impossible. The "of" in the phrase "philosophical analysis of ordinary speech" is then exactly as ambiguous as the "of" in "speech of being," and in exactly the same way. It necessarily functions as both a subjective and objective genitive. Philosophical analysis is not the speech of philosophers, but it is ordinary speech speaking, and in a way in which ordinary speech cannot speak.

With these salutary warnings in mind, we resist the temptation to avoid ontology altogether as a *niaiserie* induced by the ghost of nihilism itself. Let us instead have another look at the Greek phrase λόγος τοῦ ὄντος. Ontology, in the first and simplest approximation, is "speech about being." In this translation, which must be illuminated by our pre-ontological awareness, the word "being" is more troublesome than "speech." Not only do we have a pre-technical understanding of what it means to speak, but even in the technical sense, ontology is much more plainly a speech by certain kinds of beings, called "ontologists," than it is an explanation of the word "being." Many people, including some philosophers, recognize that speech is transpiring when they hear ontology, yet they persist in their inability to understand the "being" about which ontology claims to speak. On the other hand, if we do not understand what "being" means, or if we are right in supposing that it means nothing, then we may be mistaken about the kind of speech we are hearing, or the meaning of "speech" in "speech about being." Thus, whether "speech" is perspicuous or specious, it would seem advisable to begin our study of ontology with "being" or, rather, τὸ ὄν.

The Greek word ὄν is the neuter singular participle of the verb εἰμί, "I am," infinitive εἶναι. It stands normally for "being" in the sense of "thing," or individual of any kind about which we care to speak. A thing is identifiable by a shape or form which holds it together by holding it apart from things of other shapes; in addition, the binding function of the shape is at least one factor in the separation of the thing from others of the same shape. The shapes in which things come may themselves be collected and divided by various criteria: for example, man, monkey, and dog are things quite different from stone, star, and gas. Both kinds differ again from things like baseballs or airplanes. And then there are things like justice, number, relation, and so on. Thus far, plain sailing: there is a tremendous number of kinds or classes, and another tremendous number of members of these classes. "Thing" would then seem to mean "anything at all." Technically, this is a circular definition, since "thing" recurs in the definiens. But what this suggests is just what ontologists have insisted upon, that we have a pretechnical or pre-ontological awareness of the meaning of "thing": something like an intuition, not by any means totally sundered from speech, yet as the basis for, prior to technical, analytic, interpretive speech. The latter kind of speech must deal with such vexing questions as the structures of shapes, the exact relation between the shape of the thing and the stuff that is shaped, the connections between shapes of various kinds, and the like. But none of this would be possible if we did not "see" what a thing is, in a sense preliminary to, and adequate for, analysis.

II.

The first hasty inspection of "being" would seem to belie our earlier impression as to the ambiguous meaning of ὄν or "being." A "being" is a thing, and a "thing" is anything at all, of which all of us have pre-ontological awareness. "Ontology" then is the speech that discusses the properties common to things; it makes statements which are (hopefully) true of "anything at all." But this hastily achieved clarity disappears with equal celerity. If "ontology" is speech about being, and "being" is "thing" qua individual, then is "anything at all" an ὄν in the same sense as a stone, a man, a god, an artifact, or a moral principle? Let us reconsider. Speech about man, we may say, is "anthropology"; about god, "theology"; about stars, "astronomy"; and similar words might be found for speech about each kind of thing. Given the specificity of things, must there not be a similar specificity of speeches? What kind of thing is "anything at all," and what kind of speech is "speech about anything at all"? If an utterance is true of anything at all, then how can it ever be false? And if an utterance can never be falsified, there is no difference, with respect to it, between true and false, or sense and nonsense. Is this not nihilism?

The problem, then, is to find statements that are true of anything at all. Perhaps the first candidate that springs to mind is this: "things have being." As it stands, of course, it is unacceptable, since "being" has been defined as "thing." It surely makes no sense to be told that "things have thing." But this abortive exercise (which might also have been performed on such candidates as "things exist" or "things are") suggests to us that perhaps we mistranslated ὄν in our initial reflection upon the meaning of "ontology." Let us rather proceed as follows. Whereas the normal use of ὄν is to designate "thing," in philosophical literature, τὸ ὄν may be interpreted to stand for that which things have in common, or what makes a thing a thing. And so we must boldly assert, despite admonitions to the contrary, that ordinary language is not all right, and we must translate τὸ ὄν as *thinghood*. Our error was to ignore the definite article τὸ in our first translation. Τὸ ὄν may mean "the thing," but in ontology it means "being qua thinghood." Differently put, we must, in ontology, say "Being" rather than "being."

On this revised assessment of the situation, a statement true of all things is "things have thinghood" or, alternatively, "things have Being." This statement could never be false, yet it conveys a kind of sense. One would be inclined to say that statements which are never false must be analytically true, or tautologies. If ontology is a speech whose statements are all tautologies, then what use does it serve? Every tautology has the logical form $A = A$ and so is itself identical to the assertion of A. If "things have thinghood" is a tautology, why not just say "things"? At this rate, we become ontologists merely by uttering words or by making words into names: "man! star! orange! thing!" Ontology would then be a kind of Dadaism, and the deepest or most systematic speech would be an assertion of nihilism. Or else it would be mathematics, that is, the articulation of tautologies, or the unending pursuit of equations having the form $A = A$. In this case, as a pure symbolic representation of tautology, it would be, with respect to concrete things as well as its own significance, the same as silence. Perhaps then ontological statements, although universally true, are not tautologies, but what Kant called "synthetic a priori propositions," or something analogous to these. Perhaps when we say "things have thinghood," we are adding new information to our awareness of "thing" in the sense of "anything at all" and, so, saying what is always true but not reducible to $A = A$. To make the same point in a different way, perhaps we are mistaken in assuming that $(A = A) = A$. Does not the left-hand side of the equation actually say more than the right-hand side?

And so we return to "things have thinghood." The question is now: what does "thinghood" mean? Of course, we cannot give a complete answer to this question, since to do so would be to possess the complete and true ontological speech. Our task is much simpler. Since every speech can be uttered only one sentence at a time, we should like to begin with the (or an) initial ontological statement. The statement "things have thinghood" has been presented as a candidate for the title. But at most this can be only *an* ontological statement; it cannot be the first because it is dependent for its meaning, not simply upon our pre-ontological awareness of "things," but upon our understanding of "thinghood." We must know enough about the meaning of this word to be able to use it in the statement under analysis, i.e. to assert a universally true fact about things, which the assertion of "things" alone does not convey. Hence, our statement is itself dependent at least upon the priority of a statement something like this: " 'thinghood' stands for what all things have in common." We now seem to be in the midst of ontology. Our pre-ontological awareness tells us what things are, more or less, but not what they are exactly. It tells us, so to speak, that things have "things" in common, but not what these "things" are, or not what the difference is between things and "things." If we take "are" and "things" as incomplete symbols referring to what ontologists call Being, then the result of this is the following. Ontology is the study of what things have in common, which we may designate as thinghood or Being. The way to conduct this study is by studying things, since if we do not know the things themselves, we can scarcely say anything about their common properties.

But now, just as light seems to be breaking in a decisive manner, we suddenly find ourselves in the midst of the central difficulty. The results just stated, although they might hold for "traditional" ontology, would be rejected by contemporary fundamental ontologists, following Lukacs and Heidegger, but more specifically the latter, as an objectification or reification of Being. Let us first see the situation in general terms. Despite our rectification of "being" to "Being," we carried over to the latter term the essential nature of the former. Being is not a thing (the ontologists say), but the *source* of things. To speak of this source as the sum of properties common to things is to reduce the source of things to an abstraction derivative from things. It is to make things the source of Being, an absurd reversal of the truth! Speech about things is ontic speech and, as such, diverts our attention away from Being: seduction by ontic speech thus makes fundamental ontology impossible. Being is not an abstraction, because abstractions are derived or constructed from concrete particulars; Being is not a construction, but the source of all possible constructions, hence not abstract but most concrete. Finally, an abstraction is still itself a particular thing, whereas Being, as the origin or ground of particulars, is not. Being is not a thing; rather than call it "anything at all," we would be better advised to say that Being is nothing. Ontology is speech about no thing, and so about nothing. But even further, since human speech is necessarily of, and in terms of, things (and so ontic), ontological speech is also the speech of nothing: it is nothingness speaking about itself, or a gift from nothingness to man, whose own ontic speech obscures the gift even in the act of acknowledging, receiving, or attempting to dis-cover it.

An interpretation of ontology that began from our pre-ontological awareness of τὸ ὄν has terminated in nothingness. And yet contemporary ontologists have been motivated by an explicit desire to return "to the things themselves." The ultimate

fate of the intention to do justice to the things themselves is
prefigured in Husserl's failure to combine successfully a Platonic
or mathematical conception of the visible noetic forms of things
with a Cartesian or Kantian doctrine of the transcendental ego
or subjectivity. Husserl defined noetic form as appearance or
presence before, and so as presence within, subjectivity. In a
way reminiscent of the historical fate of the Cartesian conception of the clear and distinct idea, Husserl's phenomenon very
soon became permeated by the temporality of the subjectivity in
and to which it is present. The crucial passage from eternity to
temporality occurs in Heidegger's *Being and Time*. In ostensibly
transcending both the Platonic (objective) and Cartesian (subjective) dimensions of Husserl's thought, Heidegger excluded
eternity altogether from the horizon of human existence. Consequently, the identification of the phenomenon with Being was
for Heidegger simply the assertion of a more radical version of
historicism than had hitherto been formulated. The phenomenon
is not the factically apparent thing of everyday temporal life, but
the hidden Being, the sense or ground of the thing. This hidden
ground is accessible to man only within, indeed if not as, the horizon of temporality.[2] In this context, the question of what Being
is in itself is replaced by the question of what Being is as it
presents itself to man. From the very beginning, Heidegger
identifies the radical temporality or historicity of Being with its
hiddenness or nonpresence. A genuinely ontological speech
would therefore be, not of things, but of what is hidden by
things, namely, the horizon of temporality itself. The discussions
of existential structures which take up the bulk of *Being and
Time* can only be transitional speeches preparing us, on the
basis of our pre-ontological awareness, for the final ontological
speech. But this final ontological speech never transpired, and
in the context of Heidegger's thought it never could transpire.

Thus the second half of *Being and Time,* or the discussion of
temporality, is radically less satisfactory than the existential
analytic of the first half. It becomes steadily more apparent that

2. *Sein und Zeit* (7th ed., Max Niemayer Verlag, Tübingen, 1953),
pp. 17, 34–36.

Heidegger will not and cannot achieve the goal he has set for himself. The so-called turn in Heidegger's thought may be most simply understood as his tacit recognition of this impossibility. The hidden phenomenon of *Being and Time* will not and cannot appear or, what amounts to the same thing, cannot be spoken. The nothingness of Heidegger's earlier teaching thus comes more and more to merge with the silence of absent Being. Hence, too, the gradual transformation of Heidegger's own idiom of speech from ontological to what one can only call prophetic. Heideggerean prophecy is the attempt to transcend verbal speech, or to evoke the silent process of Being itself. Verbal speech, whether pre- or post-ontological, consists of things or particulars, namely, words which are not merely themselves individuals, but which designate individuals, whether these be understood as meanings or "real" objects. The most compelling interpretation of speech is that it is ontic: thus the chapters in ontological treatises dealing with the nonontic character of Being are all written in what linguists call "natural" languages, consisting of words ordered by syntactical rules or of things designating things. If this is a merely ontic and so inadequate interpretation of the linguistic situation in ontological speech, it is obvious that no rectification can be made simply by the replacement of one ontic speech with another.

If X is an ontic and so erroneous speech of or about Being, I cannot remove the error by another speech, Y, and say "X is an ontic and so erroneous speech of or about Being because Y." In order to correct X, Y itself must be ontic. The negation of determinations, if it is conveyed in speech as normally understood, must itself be determinate. If one wishes to negate X, Y, and Z, one must say non-X, non-Y, and non-Z. Must it not be the case that speech about nothingness is always ontic, i.e. proceeding discursively with determinate statements like "nothingness is not-X" or "nothingness is Y"? If, on the other hand, ontology is the speech of nothingness itself, then must it not be silence? Ontology, or nonontic speech, does not seem to be speech at all. If then it is silence, or silent speech, or nothing about (of) nothing, is it not nihilism? The affirmation of this negative conclusion would seem to be a version of mysticism, or the repudiation of rational speech, together with the possibility of a relation between reason and goodness. But, to repeat, treatises on fundamental ontology are written in verbal, not silent, speech. If they are not self-negating speeches, one of two alternatives must hold. Either these speeches prove the impossibility of ontology, as Wittgenstein in effect claimed in his *Tractatus,* or ontologists have discovered a new kind of speech, as Heidegger in effect claims for himself.

III.

I am well aware that the principal claim of ontologists is to use ontic speech to elicit pre-verbal experiences of Being. They do not seem to appreciate, or at least to state, the full implication of this claim so far as their own speech is concerned. The implication is that ontology, a mode of speech, is in fact *ontics,* whereas pre-ontology, in the sense of pre-verbal experience, is genuine ontology. This is what I take to be the true meaning of the following passage in Sartre's *Being and Nothingness,* which, as a vulgarization of Heidegger's *Being and Time,* makes certain themes more visible than the original: "The only knowledge (*connaissance*) is intuitive. Deduction and discourse, improperly called kinds of knowledge (*connaissances*), are merely instruments that lead to intuition." [3] In other words, fundamental ontology, within the school we are examining, is the attempt to achieve noēsis without dianoia, although by means of dianoia.[4] However, noēsis is here understood in the existential, experiential sense, and not in the traditional sense of the intuition of determinate form. Discursive reason is both the instrument for

3. *L'être et le néant* (Paris, Gallimard, 1955; orig. pub. 1943), p. 220. The idea is essentially Nietzschean; cf. *Götzen-Dämmerung* in *Werke,* ed. K. Schlechta (Munich, Carl Hanser Verlag, 1955), *2,* par. 26, p. 1005.

4. To a certain extent, it resembles the Neoplatonic effort to achieve pure contemplation of the divine *parousia,* just as the emergence of beings from Being resembles the emanation of the many from the One in Neoplatonic thought.

eliciting intuition and the obstacle to its discovery. This is Heidegger's claim, and up to a point it fairly states the difficulty in his own enterprise. But one cannot leave it at that. Since the claim is stated in ontic speech, it not merely "obscures" the uncovering of Being but guarantees the impossibility of such an uncovering. There is not and cannot be any such thing as fundamental ontology. At most, there can only be fundamental ontics, or the proof of the impossibility of fundamental ontology.

It must be emphasized that claims made for a new kind of speech are made in the old kind of speech, indeed, in the oldest kind of exalted speech—poetic prophecy. It is claimed that preverbal (pre-ontic) or ontological experience "speaks" to man of Being in a way that verbal speech cannot, as for example in the experience of nothingness. What is in one sense an attack on speech is in another an extraordinary identification of speech as the "house of Being." Heidegger and his disciples are not saying, as does Plato indirectly, that whereas noēsis is the preverbal intuition of silent forms themselves, we are nevertheless enabled to, and in fact must, say what we have seen in discursive speech. Instead, they claim that what we "intuit" is itself speaking pre-verbally, and that "intuition" (the new kind of thinking) is pre-verbal listening or apprehending of that "speech." Verbal speech is an ontic manifestation of the preverbal speech of Being. If properly apprehended, it enables us to "hear" the Being within it. But if we listen to the verbal speech qua verbal or ontic, we do not hear Being; the voice of Being is "silenced" or distorted by the voice of things.

According to Heidegger, the voice of things "silences" the voice of Being in that it prevents us from hearing the silence of the voice of Being. Thus Heidegger can also say that it is Being which "silences" or covers itself in the misleading tones of ontic (verbal) speech. The essential point is the ontological priority of silence. This is very well illustrated by the following passage from a late work:

Die Sage versammelt als das Be-wëgende des Welt-geviertes alles in die Nähe des Gegeneinander-über und

zwar lautlos, so still wie die Zeit zeitigt, der Raum
räumt, so still, wie der Zeit-Spiel-Raum spielt.
Wir nennen das lautlos rufende Versammeln, als
welches die Sage das Welt-Verhältnis be-wëgt, das
Geläut der Stille. Es ist: die Sprache des Wesens.
In der Nachbarschaft zum Gedicht Stefan Georges hörten
wir sagen:
    Kein ding sei wo das wort gebricht.
Wir beachteten, dass in der Dichtung etwas Denkwür-
diges zurückbleibe, dies nämlich, was es heisse: ein
Ding *ist*. Denkwürdig zugleich wurde uns das Verhältnis
des verlautenden, weil nicht fehlenden Wortes zum "ist."
Nunmehr dürfen wir, in der Nachbarschaft zum dich-
terischen Wort denkend, vermutend sagen:
    Ein "ist" ergibt sich, wo das Wort zerbricht.
Zerbrechen heisst hier: Das Verlautende Wort kehrt ins
Lautlose zurück, dorthin, von woher es gewährt wird:
In das Geläut der Stille, das als die Sage die Gegenden
des Weltgeviertes in ihre Nähe be-wëgt.
Dieses Zerbrechen des Wortes ist der eigentliche Schritt
zurück auf dem Weg des Denkens.[5]

I have left this passage in German because no gain in clarity
would ensue from a translation, which, if it captured Heidegger's neologisms, would simply require another translation into
"ordinary" English. Let me instead try to interpret the passage.
    Being is for Heidegger the silent process by which the world
differentiates itself into the four dimensions or regions, Earth
and Heaven, God and man—*"das Weltspiel."* [6] It is the process
of emergence of things, the process which, as the source of
things, is also the origin of their essence. However, as process,
Being gives to things, not an essence in the sense of traditional
metaphysics, but what Heidegger calls elsewhere *wësen* and here
das Be-wëgende. These neologisms are intended to convey the
temporality of the presentation of Being. The essence is not a
motionless form or nature, but a moving way—a way of emer-

5. *Unterwegs zur Sprache* (Pfullingen, G. Neske Verlag, 1959), pp.
215–16.
6. Ibid., p. 214.

gence. Within the speech of things is the "silent calling gathering" of Being as way. This notion of Being, not dissimilar to the Chinese Tao, may be metaphorically called Heidegger's unified field theory of Being. But in order to apprehend the unified field, one cannot capture its form in equations or discursive speech: there are no formulas of Being because Being is the source of the emergence of forms. Hence one must instead "shatter" ontic words or move *within* verbal speech toward unification with "the sound of stillness" by means of foundational thinking. The way of ontological thinking is into the "bewaying" of the Being-process. This need to shatter verbal speech is the reformulation in Heidegger's later terminology of what in *Being and Time* he called the need for a fundamental destruction of the tradition of western metaphysics.

We shall return in subsequent chapters to the nihilistic consequences of Heidegger's destructive project. At the moment, he serves as an example of an example. The task of the present chapter is to show in a general way that the distinction, introduced by Heidegger, between the ontological and the ontic is impossible. It is impossible because, whatever the nature and revelatory capacities of pre-verbal experience, the significance of such revelations can only be expressed discursively. If the voice of Being is silent or pre-verbal, then the teaching of ontology has no significance for the ontic world of things. Despite its own condemnations of "spectatorial" conceptions of theory and its insistence that it transcends the ontic distinction between theory and practice, foundational thinking, like positivism, amounts to a celebration of "what is the case." This celebration is positive rather than negative, or active rather than passive, in the sense that the revelatory identification with the emergence-process is conceived as dependent upon human thinking. Man is that being in and to whom Being reveals itself as the process of emergence. But what man does, or "ought" to do, is to let Being be. As we shall see later in some detail, ontological *Gelassenheit* means an acceptance of or submission to history, now called Historicity. Since Being "speaks" to man in the shape of Historicity, man must not interfere with the gift of Being or impose his ontic prejudices onto the ontological flow of emergence. The ontic consequence is to counsel resignation to whatever forces dominate in human history; Nietzsche's creative superman is transformed into the passive spectator, not of the eternal return of the similar, but of temporality.

The distinction between the ontological and the ontic is therefore itself the precise incarnation of the dualism it purports to have overcome—the split between the two worlds of Being (Historicity) and historical (ontic) existence. Whatever the faults of the traditional dualism, the new ontology is infinitely more dangerous because it is unconscious of its own nature. This lack of consciousness is the result of a deeper or inner monism; the two worlds of Being and beings are the same as Time and its moments. Since form itself is conceived as a consequence of temporality, however, no radical distinction can be maintained between Time and its moments. Speech about form is then not speech about Time; as we have seen, there can be no speech about Time. In sum, fundamental ontology is nihilism because it makes the ostensible speech of Being irrelevant to human action. Of course, its practitioners tell us that for moral and political advice one must turn to clergymen, political scientists, and the like, but not to authentic philosophers, a view identical to that held by ordinary language philosophers. The result is to urge man to return to the conventionalism and positivism of contemporary ontic speech, or to sever the connection between "thinking," the new and higher form of reason, and the good. Ontology, which knows what *is,* tells man as a moral and political animal to make do with what *is not,* and in two senses: first, by resignation to the silence of nothingness, and second, by obedience to ontic speech. It tells man that, if Historicity should so dictate, he must even surrender ontology. There is no ontological reason why man as an ontic being should prefer ontological to ontic speech.

IV.

"Reasons for . . ." are discursive statements, or verbal and hence ontic interpretations of things. If ontology is not speech about things, then there is no such thing as ontological speech. The same point follows from the ostensible transcendence by fundamental ontologists of the limitations and distortions of rationalism. People who give reasons appeal both to "things as they are" and words as a logically coherent bridge between things and thoughts. However rapid the mental transition from evidence to inference, and even if the evidence is intuitive, reasons are statements having the general form "Y because X." The need of ontologists for reason-statements can be seen in the self-negating character of Humean criticisms of causal inference. "Because" cannot be challenged except *because* of observations, discursively expressed, on the rational pattern of noetic inference. In any event, the phenomenological school of ontologists are to a considerable degree derived from Hume's own metaphysical epistemology; crudely expressed, to say what one sees, or what presents itself, is to say nothing about "real" or ontic connections between things. The difficulty of the ontologist lies instead in the internal structure of "Y because X." Suppose that "Y because X" is an ontological statement and hence expresses the situation of Being rather than of beings. Since Y and X are things or concatenations of things, the ontological character must reside in the nature of the statement as a whole. The force of "because," or whatever is substituted in its place, must be such as to shatter the ontic shell of X and Y, and so to allow us to hear the voice of Being within. This would seem to be possible only if "because" is already the voice, and hence the percussive capacity, of Being. Now here is the difficulty. If "Y because X" is ontological because of "because," then why are Y and X needed? Since "because" is already the voice of Being, may we not simply attend to it? Even further, if we cannot so attend, but "because" needs Y and X in order to make clear both its own sense and their relative senselessness, then clearly ontological speech is impossible. If Y and X are not ontic, they cease to be distinguishable either from each other or from "because." If they are ontic, then ontological statements are always of and about things. If "because" is ontological, whereas Y and X are not, then "because" has no internal structure; I mean that its sense cannot be reproduced discursively, or replaced by statements having the form Y or X. Consequently, it is discursively meaningless or silent, whatever its ontological force. Since "Y because X" is, through the nature of Y and X, within the ontic domain—the only one in which ontologists can communicate, whether with friend or foe—"because" has no value and may be omitted. The effective result of an ontological statement is then (Y,X), and such statements are less meaningful than ontic statements, since they cannot explain the relation between Y and X, whereas ontic speech can furnish "because" with ontic significance. Finally, if Y, X, and "because" are all ontological, then ontological statements are indistinguishable from ontic statements, because Y, X, and "because" are all words, or sequences of words, and so things, each of whose significance derives from some other thing it names or symbolizes.

The significance of any ontological speech is dependent upon, and rendered determinate by, its inexpugnably ontic constituents. This is the same as the statement, which frequently occurs in the writings of Plato and Aristotle, that "to be" is to be "something." It should then be clear that the ontologist gains nothing by insisting that the example be changed to "X is Y." If ontology, as speech, is something more than saying "is," all of the difficulties just mentioned remain. In addition, if "is" gives voice to Being and carries the meaning that "X is" and "Y is"—i.e. that within the ontic shells of X and Y is "is"—then the ontological speech may be translated by " 'X is' is 'Y is.' " Now what does this mean? I can see only three possibilities. The first amounts to the assertion of "is" as all that the voice of Being cares to say in its own persona, given the vulgarity of its ontic environment. But the universal affirmation of what is the case is just a peculiarly inarticulate version of positivism, or one in which "is" is indistinguishable from "isn't." The second possibility is that " 'X is' is 'Y is' " is a tautology and can be reduced to "X is Y and Y = X", or "X = X," or "X," which is about as instructive as "is." Of course, if we maintain that the point about tautologies is to express them in as many different ways as possible in order to shed light upon the ultimate monadicity of the Being-process, then ontology is simply an incompetent surrogate for mathematical logic. And if the ultimate ontology is the speech of mathematical logic, this is a negative version of the third possibility I want to mention. That is, " 'X is' is 'Y is' " is an incompletely articulated and so *unreasonable* imitation of a rational theoretical speech about the fundamental or general properties of things. To spell out the meaning of "X is Y," we need to rely upon X, "is," and Y as all having an internal structure or rational form, one which, even if initially intuited, can be discursively described both to ourselves and our interlocutors; otherwise, we just do not know what we are talking about. But if we do know what we are talking about, or at least can give a discursive account of what we think we know, then ontology is ontical, or, as its name asserts, "Speech about things."

I have been arguing that ontological speech, in the sense attributed to it by those who follow Heidegger's distinction between the ontological and ontic, is in fact silence. Ontologists of this type wish to talk about Being as distinct from beings, and speech will simply not permit this. If this is a defect of speech, and the significance of speech is in the deepest and final sense relative to silence, then there is no reason for what we say or for whether we speak at all, other than the mere fact, although there is equally no reason to keep silent. The result is absurdism or nihilism. Therefore no reason can be given which would justify our falling into such desperate straits. Every fundamental ontological speech of the type in question is not just self-refuting but self-canceling. It is exactly as if the fundamental ontologist had never spoken (except, unfortunately, for the practical effects of his speech). And yet, of course, the fundamental ontologist does give reasons for his beliefs. I have now discussed at some length the main reason—that Being is not a being, but also neither an abstraction nor a syncategorematic expression. A somewhat different way to express the fundamental ontologist's controlling intuition is to say that Being is process. This formulation has the added advantage of showing the affiliation between the new ontology and one of the two oldest philosophical traditions. It is not necessary here to enter into a historical survey of the various kinds of process philosophy. Suffice it to say that fundamental ontology takes its bearings from a criticism of Platonic Ideas, or the view (attributed to Plato since the time of Aristotle) that there are two kinds of reality—the spatio-temporal world of genesis, and the separate, eternal, unchanging world of archetypical forms. But one need not be a Platonist in this arbitrary and problematic sense in order to insist that intelligible speech is speech that explicates the formal structures of things.

It is not difficult to construct a definition of λόγος as rational thing-speech which is neutral with respect to the most perplexing features of Platonism in its traditional version. For example, a λόγος is a discursive account, and so one which possesses a discursively analyzable structure, of some thing or things, each of which is visible and accountable by virtue of an internally articulated structure; the account, then, thanks to its own structural heterogeneity, attempts to exhibit the structure of the thing or things in question, namely, how these things "hang together" or show themselves in the way they do. One might easily write a lengthy volume explicating this definition. For my purposes, I believe it will be enough just to say a few additional words about "structure." This word is especially useful for giving a non-Platonic analysis of the concept of form. It comes from the Latin *"struo," "struxi," "structum"*—to join together, build, arrange, or order. Struo is related to *"sterno"* and thence to the Greek στόρνυμι, to spread smooth or level. A structure is an "orderly spread," an arrangement of connected parts, constituting a smooth or level unity of a manifold. And nothing has been said about the principle of unification. It might be the creative faculty of God, the synthetic apprehension of the transcendental ego, or, for that matter, the voice of Being articulating itself into units of internal complexity. The structure, whether joined together by God, man, nature, or history, as a unified manifold, is held together, and so apart from all other structures, by the specific shape, pattern, or order of its arrangement. This order is its μορφή or εἶδος, its form. A λόγος exhibits (thanks to its own structure) the εἶδος of a structure and so may contribute to the task of rendering explicit the thinghood of the thing in question. This account of λόγος is not incompatible with the main features of the interpretation of Heidegger, except that it emphasizes the dependence of "gathering together" or "revealing" upon determinate shape. Heidegger, as it were, "reduces" the act of speech to existential activity (such as gathering in the harvest); [7] he does not make clear that the visibility of what is gathered together depends upon its structure. Thus he does not distinguish clearly between the structuring of speech and the structure of what is spoken.

Obviously many difficulties are raised by the account just sketched. The main difficulty lies in the relation between the structure of speech and that of things. Ontologies of language, whether derived from Heidegger or Wittgenstein, desire to overcome the dualism inherent in the thesis of two structures, but the price they pay is to return to monism and so to silence. It may be that the problem can never be solved, or perhaps three structures rather than two or one are necessary. In any event, such a problem is beyond the scope of this study. My point is rather this: *if* there is to be rational speech, one must distinguish radically between the structure of speech and the structure of things, or, more simply, between speech and things. Speech cannot be identified as the Being from which things emerge. Man does not bespeak Being because he is not a god, and hence he must give a reason (λόγον διδόναι) for what he says. If reasons have no external "objective" reference but are altogether self-certifying, then they are arbitrary utterances, lacking in rational justification or human value. What passes as the creative freedom of human autonomy may then be described with equal justice as the absurd chatter of self-deception.

The only intelligible sense to be given to "ontology" is, in my opinion, that of speech which explicates the structures (forms) of things. It is by speech of this kind, and only of this kind, that

7. Cf. *Vorträge und Aufsätze* (Pfullingen, G. Neske Verlag, 1954), pp. 207–30.

men give an account of what they know, or have seen, or heard; and only by giving such an account do they show themselves to possess knowledge or insight that we can *count on*. I use this phrase in its moral as well as its mathematical-epistemological sense. Here I note in passing what will later be discussed more thoroughly; the connection between mathematics and political or moral virtue is rooted precisely in the nature of structure—in the fact that things hang together and thereby provide a framework upon which we may hang speech. It is this distinction between nonverbal and verbal structure, not firmly made by either ordinary language analysts or fundamental ontologists, that enables us to give a sensible interpretation to "ontology." We may now point to at least a conceivable reconciliation between the two kinds of speech inadequately sundered in the distinction between the ontological and the ontic. Ontology both speaks and does not speak about things. True, speech *is* thing-bound, both because words are things and because they speak of things. But ontological speech uses thing-words to refer to the formal structures of things rather than to the things as mere instances of their forms.

I have mentioned three separate but related domains of reality—speech, nonverbal things, and formal structures. Ordinary language analysts are unable to distinguish between speech and formal structure; fundamental ontologists carry this defect one step further. They are unable to distinguish between speech and nonverbal things. In both cases, although there are some differences in the itinerary, the destination is the same: a process from which things emerge, but whose visibility cannot be explained; and again, an account of process which cannot be justified because there is no way to distinguish the account from the process. A name, not without ambiguities, that has been traditionally applied to this consequence is *historicism*. In the last section of this chapter, I shall summarize what has been said thus far and shall prepare for the next chapter, by trying to formulate the most evident sense in which ordinary language analysis and fundamental ontology are two different versions of historicism.

V.

At first glance, the two movements in question would seem to be incompatible. As I myself expressed their difference, ordinary language analysis is committed to dianoia without noēsis, whereas fundamental ontology strives for noēsis without dianoia. But the result in the first case is the absence of any criterion for "ordinary" in the sense of "regulative" that is not subject to contradiction by another interpretation of "ordinary." Ordinary language philosophy is misnamed because, if I may employ this metaphor, its numbers are cardinal rather than ordinal. The most massive consequence of this fact is that there exists no coherent theoretical interpretation of the foundations, or justification of the procedures, of ordinary language analysis. Its practitioners are like men who have had a divine intuition about the function of language, but who refuse to admit the possibility of intuition. An infinite number of particular analyses will never discharge the need for an account of the intuition that is not ostensibly another totally discursive, and so particular, analysis. Either ordinary language analysis is a form of conventionalism, which owes more than it cares to admit to the mathematical sciences but lacks the daring of axiomatization, or else it is an unselfconscious gift of Being.[8]

In the case of fundamental ontology, dianoia is employed only in order to express its own irrelevance. Since nothing discursive can be said about Being, the discursive formulations of this impossibility must themselves be irrelevant or, rather, distortions of the need for silence. Verbal speech of any kind may be understood as an inauthentic response to a gift of peculiar

8. With the last sentences above, cf. J. Urmson's remarks in *La Philosophie analytique,* Cahiers de Royaumont, Philosophie, No. IV (Paris, Les Éditions de Minuit, 1962), p. 39: a language analysis practiced according to the Pure Oxford method could never be completed. "Fut-elle achevée pour l'Anglais, il resterait encore à déterminer dans quelle mesure ses conclusions pourraient s'appliquer à d'autres langues . . . ." And this is totally impossible for some, like ancient Greek.

inaccessibility. And yet, perhaps because of the inaccessibility of Being, ontologists discourse more copiously than even the ordinary language analysts (and, I might add, are also more aware of the connections between the two movements). Since only Being can provide a standard for the measurement of the relative excellence of speeches, and since Being is absent, one speech becomes as good as another—exactly the case in ordinary language analysis. In both cases, we have a continuum of speech, articulated internally by happenstance. I must say more precisely what this means.

Ordinary language analysis begins from the heterogeneous continuum of speech, or the "natural" medium of human thought. I put "natural" in quotation marks in order to indicate from the very beginning the insuperable difficulty it poses. If man is by nature a speaking animal, then the science of human nature is not simply a matter of use, but of fact. The fact of nature must then regulate speech, or be accessible to speech in a way that is not a matter of linguistic use. If the fact of nature is a function of linguistic use, then the facts can change as does use, which is, after all, local or historical. But this means that man can change his nature by changing his speech habits: to give the decisive example, he can become a consistent fundamental ontologist by refusing to speak at all, at least verbally. In this case, the speech continuum is no longer the medium of significance. Nor can one avoid this problem simply by taking the truth of science as an established fact of ordinary language. Not only is scientific language extraordinary, but for that reason it demands an extraordinary justification—namely, a vision of the fact that regulates speech. But I mention this in passing. Granting that speech is in some sense the medium of thought and meaning, the analyst sorts out particulars from the language continuum by recourse to human purposes. What we say depends upon which game we are playing. As we saw in the first chapter, this doctrine of human purpose emerges in Wittgenstein as the notion of Lebensform and Weltanschauung; to this one may add that the subordination of linguistic construction to purpose is also a characteristic of positivism, at least in some of its formulations.[9]

But Wittgenstein (like the positivists) gives us no coherent discussion of "purpose" or "intentionality" as a characteristic of mind or consciousness. This is no doubt because he wishes to avoid the dualism of mind and body; the result, however, is that there is no explanation of the difference between speakers and speech. Dualism is avoided, if at all, by recourse to monism. Consciousness, like its objects, is treated as a modification of the language continuum, which must then be conceived as somehow differentiating itself. The heterogeneity of the continuum is paradoxically made dependent upon purposes which can themselves arise only *after* the pattern of heterogeneity has been established.[10] Let us consider a brief grammatical analysis of the term "analysis" as implicit in the conception of a self-differentiating or self-analyzing continuum. The word "analysis" is Greek in origin: ἀνάλυσις means a "spreading out" by means of a loosening or dissolving, which may be characterized as an "upward" motion, but perhaps rather by a pervasion into all directions or dimensions. It is thus apparent that the word "analysis" is closely related to the word "structure," which we found previously to mean "to join together, to arrange," and so "to spread smooth, to level." I said that a structure is an orderly spread, or arrangement of connected parts, constituting a smooth, finished, level unity of a manifold. The arrangement or orderly way of any given spread is its shape or form, its εἶδος. "Analysis" spreads out or dissolves what has been spread

9. E.g. by R. Carnap in his essay "Empiricism, Semantics and Ontology," in *Semantics and the Philosophy of Language,* ed. L. Linsky (Urbana, University of Illinois Press, 1952), p. 219: we decide to accept linguistic frameworks on purely practical grounds, that is, on the basis of "being more or less expedient, fruitful, conducive to the aim for which the language is intended." Cf. Wittgenstein, *Investigations,* I, par. 16, 17, 19, 23, 122, 199, 241, 655.

10. Cf. Plato, *Philebus* 18b6 ff., where articulations (letters) internal to the monad "sound" are differentiated out by the god Theuth. For Wittgenstein and Heidegger, no god is available.

smooth or joined together. A "logical analysis" is thus the attempt to give an account (λόγον διδόναι) of the arrangement of a form, or to put into speech what would seem to be an imitation of a silent structure. In any event, "analysis" is posterior to the intuition of form (if only in the Husserlian sense of an intuition "founded upon" but not reducible to a perception).

An essential aspect of any account of a form is clearly an explanation of its internal articulation, or the manner of conjunction of the elements that make up its way of presentation. Are they given by nature, synthesized by the transcendental ego, or brought together by historical flow? We do not opt for any of these in posing the question, what is the principle of the "standing together" or *synthesis* of that which lends itself to analysis? I would risk the observation that, on this point, Wittgenstein's *Philosophical Investigations* is an unconscious continuation of German Idealism, except that, instead of the absolute ego, we have the language continuum. The language continuum conducts a self-analysis by a process of self-differentiation, in terms of its own projects or purposes. Here, no doubt, the analogy with Idealism breaks down, since the purposes are linguistic contingencies, or *how things happen to be*. In any case, since different purposes produce different loosenings, or dissolutions of what was previously posited by synthesis, whereas the different purposes themselves arise from different loosenings of the continuum, thanks to the synthetic "fixing" or "positing" of what has been loosened, it is evident that the fundamental notion of ordinary language analysis is *difference*. To repeat a previous citation from Wittgenstein, "I look now for the grammatical difference." [11]

The notion of difference combines within itself both affirmation and negation, and despite the unreflective preference of analysts for affirmation, our grammatical consideration has shown us that the name "analysis" is closer to the negative than to the positive pole of mental activity. What is loosened loses its shape, and so spreads out like water, and consequently evaporates, or moves "upward" in the sense of disappearing, like

11. *Investigations*, II. viii.

steam. The process of analysis, or differentiation of ("of" in the subjective and objective genitive) the continuum into heterogeneous particulars, is in fact just a reassertion of the homogeneity of the continuum. The "logic" of ordinary language analysis tends to dissolve into chatter, or silence. The continuum is essentially the Parmenidean monad; nothing can be said about its apparent heterogeneity, because nothing can be said about its underlying unity. Exactly as in the case of fundamental ontology, the speech of analysis is an aural illusion. The negativity within difference has triumphed over the affirmative. For what I call here the language continuum is the analogue to what in Heidegger has been named "the lighting-process of Being." In both cases we have an immanent continuum of motions which negate themselves as they are performed or projected. In both cases, self-moving speech (a descendent of the *Selbstbewegung* of Hegel's Absolute) becomes the medium from which men and things emerge, so that in both cases it is impossible to distinguish between the speaker and his speech. In both cases, there is no real difference between analysis and synthesis, but rather only difference loosening as it fixes.[12]

In sum, the continuum, whether we call it language or Being, is identical with temporality or historicity. The "difference" or "otherness" of temporality is in both cases primarily negation. One may express this by observing that possibility is made prior to, or more fundamental than, actuality. In other words, the facticity of difference-as-temporarily-visible has no ground or principle, except that of self-presentation or creation *ex nihilo*. This may be emphasized by a brief contrast with Aristotle, whose conception of ἐνέργεια is to some extent the preparation for Heidegger's conception of Being. In Book VIII of the *Metaphysics,* Aristotle discusses "difference" in conjunction with τήν ὡς ἐνέργειαν οὐσίαν τῶν αἰσθητῶν, the being-at-work

---

12. Cf. Heidegger, *Identität und Differenz* (Pfullingen, G. Neske Verlag, 1957), pp. 62–63: "Sein im Sinne der entbergenden Überkommnis und Seiendes als solches im Sinne der sich bergenden Ankunft wesen als die so Unterschiedenen aus dem Selben, dem *Unter-Schied* . . . etc."

of sensible things. He concludes that "it is" is spoken in as many different ways as there are differences among genera and species within genera. That is, matter is differentiated by forms, which are in turn distinguished from each other by διαφοράς.[13] This is analogous to the differentiation of the language continuum by purposes or linguistic contexts, which are in turn identical to the ontological notions of projects or existential–historical situations. But for Aristotle, the genera of differences are the principles of being, or ways in which οὐσίαι are.[14] Οὐσία in the primary sense is form, which is *different from difference*.[15] I mean by this that differences, as pointing out the "ways" of forms, are correlative and subordinate to form.

Aristotle can speak about being (which I leave lowercase to distinguish it from the fundamental ontological "Being") because he maintains the priority of actuality to possibility, or the (partial) determination of the possible by the differences of form, and the accessibility of form to speech by way of noetic intuition. Without suggesting that Aristotle would accept my formulation, I would rephrase the point as follows. The central difficulty faced by contemporary monistic philosophies is to give an account of difference (heterogeneity). The only way in which this can be done without surrendering monism is to make the monad (language, Being) self-differentiating, and this in turn requires the monad to be defined as process or a processive field. The emergence characteristic of process is then indistinguishable from the regression, dissolution, or disappearance, since there can be no recourse to a principle of emergence external to, or transcending, the processive field itself. As a result, the monad is conceived, consciously or unconsciously, as temporality, or the process wherein position is identical to negation. One of course can avoid this consequence by refusing to discuss

13. 1043b10 ff. I can only mention here that the passage under discussion shows a distinction between the "principle of individuation" or matter and the "principle of differentiation" or form. The terminology is mine, but it corresponds to the argument of Aristotle, which has not been given full justice by commentators.
14. 1042b31. Cf. 1043a2 ff.
15. 1043b10 ff.

it, either through linguistic conventions or the more or less explicit identification of Being as nothingness. In either case, the result is nihilism, or the denial of the possibility of thought to reason with and about itself. In what one may call the Aristotelian heritage, nothingness is a component of difference, or a structural component of the noetic, formal domain, visible in the difference of one form from another, but as different from these forms, because each form is self-identical or fixed as what it positively presents itself to be; whereas "difference" has no positive or self-identical fixity but is essentially visible only as an absence of identity. The visibility of nothingness is dependent upon the visibility of what I can only call somethingness, although the significance of the two is the result of their being inseparably intertwined. As a consequence, silence is similarly dependent upon, while significatively correlative with, speech. Nothing can be said, whether meaningfully or meaninglessly, without the differentiating function of silence. On the other hand, nothing *can* be said, and its meaningfulness is audible thanks only to that which in itself is indifferent to difference.

Chapter 3

History and Nihilism

I.

Thus far I have tried to show, in general but fundamental terms, the nihilist implications of what are perhaps the two most influential philosophical movements of our time. These movements share a grave defect, which I called historicism, or the inability to distinguish between being and time. In this chapter, I should like to make a new start and concentrate upon the link between history and nihilism as it emerges in the thought of Nietzsche and Heidegger. Whereas the two preceding chapters were dedicated to epistemology and ontology, the theme of history necessarily leads us to more practical considerations. As I have already indicated, I did not begin with these practical considerations because I wanted to suggest how they are forced upon us by purely theoretical decisions. In the movements which served as illustrations, the crucial decision was to neglect practice in favor of theory, while at the same time conceiving of theory as a kind of practice. This twofold decision is typical of modern philosophy altogether and is responsible for the main *aporiai* that characterize philosophical teachings of the past three hundred years. Reason has been conceived as a human project or the instrument of a human project, but in either case it emerges from the pre-rational stratum of desire, basically, the desire to master nature. However successfully we have satisfied this desire in some ways, there has been a complete failure in another, more important way. We are unable to explain to ourselves in a rational way the *point* to our success, and consequently the difference between success and failure.

Contemporary man desperately needs a rational interpretation of reason. Instead, he has been furnished with epistemologies, or technical discussions of how reason works. Even these technical discussions, for all their genius, have been theoretically compromised by the inability to ask *why* reason is working. We are faced with the absurd spectacle of spokesmen for reason who do not understand, or refuse to acknowledge, the extraordinarily complex web of theoretical and practical presuppositions underlying the axiomatic method, the scientific experiment, or the logical construction of reality, to give only three examples. It is simply absurd to suppose that techniques like these are self-certifying, or that they can be certified by the exposition of further epistemological techniques. To say that these techniques "work" is to say nothing at all, until it has been explained whether the work in question is good or bad, reasonable or unreasonable. Knowledge may well be power, but power can be used wisely or stupidly. Man's natural love of wisdom, which is to say, his need for it, together with the unnatural scorn which contemporary rationalists usually show to statements of this need, has led to the perversion of ideology as a substitute for "metaphysics" or comprehensive thinking. In concrete political terms, the result is both curious and depressing. Having lost the enthusiasm and confidence of the founders of modern rationalism, their contemporary descendents can no longer be distinguished, once they emerge from the cave of epistemology, from their irrational neighbors.

Let me emphasize this point. What today passes for rational discussion in the political sphere must be sharply distinguished from the discussion of politics by professors of philosophy who regard themselves in their professional guise as rationalists. At some points, of course, the two discussions may be one and the same, but there is no necessary connection between them. It is impossible to understand the force of romantic irrationalism in contemporary society without being equally aware of the failure of modern rationalism. When reason cannot speak of its own goodness but must have recourse to convention, sentiment, or ideology, it strengthens the indictment of reason as evil. If good and evil are equally unreasonable, then it is impossible to discriminate among the various senses in which reason may be said to be "beyond good and evil." And the result is nihilism.

In order to place the discussion of historicism in the proper perspective, it is necessary to say a few words about the development of the modern conception of reason. We may take our bearings by noting two main characteristics of this conception, which would be accepted by both friends and foes of reason. The first is the belief that reason is identical with, or modeled after the paradigm of, mathematics. To "be reasonable" is thus something like to count, to measure, or to intuit numerical and geometrical forms; or it is to perceive the presence and absence of deductive structures, to carry out "logical inferences." The second characteristic belief about reason today is that it is identical with, or a creature of, historical consciousness. This may be understood to mean that the rational capacity is either a subjective production or project of the historical individual, or a more general determination of the total historical process. These two characteristics, the "mathematical" and the "historical," are by no means mutually exclusive. On the contrary, modern philosophy is the consequence of the progressive integration of the conceptions of "mathematics" and "history." Differently stated, modern philosophy is the result of new conceptions of "mathematics" and "history," and therefore of a new conception of reason. The specific feature of this new conception with which we are concerned is the widespread opinion that reason is incompetent to guide us in choosing the ends or values by which we live and in terms of which we find coherence, integrity, or wholeness in our lives.

In simple terms, this opinion takes three main forms. The first states that reason is restricted to drawing inferences, clarifying meanings, and establishing the truth or falsehood of propositions. The second states that although reason is involved in the choice of ends or values, the entire process is a function of the historical situation; in the non-Marxist world at least, this is normally taken to mean that no reason can be given for the workings or process of history. The third states that reason, even in the tasks assigned to it under the first form of the general opinion, is a slave, employee, tool, or derivative of more fundamental modes of apprehension, such as the passions, moods, biological or physiological inclinations, and the like.

These three forms of the general opinion may combine with each other to produce a wide range of philosophical positions. Within this variety, however, is a basic unity, stemming from the aforementioned integration of the characteristically modern conceptions of mathematics and history. For example, some contemporary thinkers insist upon a distinction between "facts" and "values," following in effect the Humean distinction between the "is" and the "ought." Others would deny this rigid distinction, but at the price of making facts values or values facts. I refer here to the descendents of Nietzsche, on the one hand, and to the various forms of positivism or scientific behaviorism, on the other. The feature common to these cases is an inability to sustain the contention that one end or value is intrinsically more reasonable than another.

Modern confusion about the relative status of facts and values results from a misunderstanding or exaggeration of the classical distinction between theory and practice. One finds very clearly in Aristotle, and more ambiguously in Plato, recognition of the difference between an attempt to see mentally "how things are" (theory) and an attempt to ascertain the relative degrees of excellence of the various modes of human conduct (practice). For both thinkers, however, these two kinds of mental activity are related precisely by what one could call "the logical structure of the world." Of course, "logical" here means something quite different from the meaning attached to the term by its contemporary admirers. The Greek word *logos* means both speech and reason. To the Socratic philosophers, the world is "logical" or "reasonable" because it provides us with a basis for speaking meaningfully about the relative merits of the various human activities. The link between theory and practice, then, is not an abstract argument in epistemology or an imagined developing pattern in world history, but the nature of man as the animal who both speaks and acts. There is then a reasonable basis in nature for distinguishing and responding to the *unreasonable*. The Aristotelian tradition, still alive in our ordinary language, refers to reasonable speech in this sense as the consequence of prudence or practical intelligence.

The classical conception of reason is inseparable from the notion of "good." This notion in turn contains two dimensions
which we may call "noble" or "beautiful," and "useful." Modern philosophy generally, and its empiricist branch particularly,
tends to begin with a radical separation of these terms (although
sooner or later the "beautiful" is redefined as the "useful").
This is to say that the unity between theory and practice in
human nature is disregarded; it is replaced by a new division between the two dimensions of man's practical nature. The useful
is separated from the noble or beautiful for two reasons which
seem themselves to be opposed to each other—the influence of
Christianity, on the one hand, and mathematics, on the other.
For the Christian, the "good" refers finally to God and therefore
to an other-worldly or *trans-rational* dimension, whereas the
"useful" refers primarily to this-worldly calculation of essentially selfish interests.[1] In other words, "utility" has primary reference to man's fallen condition and is therefore implicitly associated with sin rather than with goodness. For the seventeenth-
century, mathematically oriented philosopher (with the out-
standing exception of Leibniz), however noble or beautiful he
may regard mathematics to be, "reason" is the activity of discerning geometrical and logical form, or the intelligible struc-

1. This distinction is perhaps most clearly stated in the Kantian
ethic, for the very reason that Kant attempts to give a "reasonable"
formulation to the Christian teaching without transforming it into a
species of rationalism. Kant's identification of the most important (a
good will) as grounded in the trans-rational (or in his distinction between *Vernunft* and *Verstand*) is as much an ancestor of contemporary
irrationalism as Kierkegaard's emphasis on paradox. For the Christian
emphasis on the superiority of the good will to the good intellect, cf.
Saint Thomas, *Summa Theologiae, Prima Pars,* Q. V, 4. In the following Question (VI, 4), St. Thomas asserts, not without ambiguity, that
the goodness of a thing inheres in it by assimilation from the divine
good. The significance of this is in turn evident from the subordination
of the "other sciences" to the sacred science (I, 6). For the Christian
demotion (by Augustine) of the pagan notion of *utilitas* (Cicero), cf.
H. Blumenberg, "Kosmos und System," in *Studium Generale, Heft 2*
(1957), p. 68, esp. n. 33. See also the discussion of the separation of
reason from *inclinatio* (the moral law stamped in man's heart) by
Cusanus, in F. Borkenau, *Vom feudalen zum bürgerlichen Weltbild*
(Paris, Librairie Félix Alcan, 1934), pp. 43 ff.

ture of "this" world. The "useful" is then the rational extension of man's power, thanks to an understanding of the mathematical order which underlies experience.[2] By the extension of his own power, man makes himself, in the famous phrase of Descartes, "master and possessor of nature" and thereby inevitably reduces the mastery and power of God.

In a very deep sense, modern philosophy accepts the Christian association of "utility" and "sin," with the radical difference, of course, that it repudiates the religious significance of "sin," which it calls instead "freedom," whether as "self-interest" or "self-fulfillment." The turn to this world, although part of the rebellion against the sovereignty of the next world, also provides us with the link between mathematics and history. It now seems possible to change, and not simply to know, the order of this world by careful attention to its particular events. Thus Machiavelli inaugurates modern political philosophy by distinguishing between the theory and the practice of the ancients. The former is erroneous, the latter praiseworthy; in order to understand ancient practice, one must turn to the study of history. Nor is this study merely academic; the lessons of the past may be applied directly to the present, and the future modified in accord with human power. Machiavelli thus anticipates the attitude taken toward nature by the experimental scientist:

> it is better to be impetuous than respectful, because fortune is a woman, and it is necessary, if you wish to keep her quiet, to beat her and hit her. It is evident that she lets herself rather be conquered by such men, than by those who proceed coldly. Therefore, like a woman, she is always the friend of the young, because they are less cautious, more ferocious, and command her with more audacity.[3]

2. Although the initial impetus for the conception of order in mathematical terms came from the influence of Plato, the transformation in the understanding of the nature of mathematics as applicable to the study and manipulation of the sensible world was the most important factor in the seventeenth-century revolt against the "ancients."

3. *Il Principe,* p. 101, in *Il Principe e Discorsi* (Milan, Feltrinelli, 1960), *1.*

As his student and scientific propagandist, Sir Francis Bacon, puts it, to understand nature, we must put her to the torture or restrain her "in the trials and vexations of art." In the same work, Bacon writes that "knowledges are as pyramides, whereof history is the basis." [4] In this conception, we see already the seeds of post-Kantian philosophies of history. But the connection between science and history must be joined to a deeper, and in itself anti-historical, conception of theory as praxis.

This deeper conception takes place in the thought of Descartes. We need remind ourselves of only one or two aspects of this much-discussed situation. The first has to do with the connection between "order and measure" and mind. In *Principles* II, 64, Descartes identifies the "universal," symbolically exhibited and grasped object of universal science with the substance of the world, with corporeality or extension. In other words, the essential structure of the world consists of abstract, symbolical mathematical objects. The study of order and measure is at once the study of mathematics and of physics, but it is also the study of thinking or *ratio*. Symbolic number, multiplicity as such, is called by Descartes an *ens rationis,* a "being of reason." Its being comes from pure intellect alone; the figures or shapes of extension are reproduced in the imagination, and from this "picture," the symbolic idea of number is abstracted. If we combine passages from the *Regulae* and *Principles,* then, Descartes teaches that thought is intuition, or a viewing of primary forms and properties of extension through the mediation of the imagination.[5] These primary forms, although creations of the human mind, are dependent upon (in a Husserlian sense, *founded* in) the apprehension of natural forms by sense and imagination.

4. *Advancement of Learning,* ed. Spedding, Ellis, and Heath (Boston, Brown and Taggard, 1860–64), *6,* 188, 221. Cf. R. F. Jones, *Ancients and Moderns,* Washington University Studies (Saint Louis, 1961), p. 56: "More than any other element in his philosophy Bacon's conception of natural history and its importance influenced the seventeenth century . . . the most prevalent motive animating scientists in the third quarter of the century was the desire to contribute data to such a history."

5. *Regulae* IV, V; *Principles* II, 64.

Still more specifically, Descartes distinguishes between three forms of ideas—innate, adventitious, and *a me ipso factae*.[6] We may disregard adventitious ideas as irrelevant here. The ideas made by myself are the forms and concepts of mathematical physics, generated by the ratio in conjunction with an operation by imagination upon the external world. But these abstract constructions are themselves subject to verification by innate or general ideas, by which we understand what a thing is, or truth.[7] Descartes seems to qualify his definition of thinking as intuition by a definition of the subordination of intuition to the inspection of innate or divinely created ideas. This "theological" version of his teaching makes rational or mathematical order dependent upon God's will. Granted the inaccessibility of God's will to man, we are forced to conclude, with Leibniz, that such a teaching defines God as an arbitrary tyrant.[8] The least one could say is that our conception of God, as well as of the rational order, is actually derived from an inspection of clear and distinct ideas, that is, from a reflection upon our own powers of reason. So long as God chooses not to exercise his tyrannical authority, man is in effect his agent. A cynic might restate this teaching as the assertion that man is a god whose only limitations are those imposed by fate.

Fortunately for us, who are concerned exclusively with Descartes' historical influence, there is no need for a final decision concerning his theological position. Whatever his ultimate intentions, Descartes defines (or seems to define) thinking as a combination of mathematical intuition, imagination, and the inspection of "innate" ideas dependent upon the will of God or man. If we unite this ambiguous conception of thought with the emphasis upon experiment and history illustrated by means of Machiavelli and Bacon, the result is the basis for the modern interpretation of reason. Ratio is the "will to power," still articu-

6. *Meditationes* III (Adam-Tannery, 7), pp. 37–38. Cf. Second Responses to Objections, A-T, 7, pp. 160–61.

7. Ibid., pp. 38, 44, and VI, p. 73.

8. Cf. the opening paragraphs of Leibniz' *Discours de métaphysique* and Werner Conze, *Liebniz als Historiker* (Berlin, 1951), pp. 47 ff.

lated in a mathematical vocabulary, but one which is spoken, and to some extent created, by the *ego cogitans*. The noetic or purely rational content of the soul's activity is, if not created, at least produced from the mind itself by an act of the will more noble than all other thoughts because upon it depends the order and certitude of the world.[9] The nobility of this act of the will consists in the assertion of man's freedom; and, insofar as man is free, he is like God. That is, man becomes like God in mastering himself, or his desires.[10] As masters of our desires, we are masters of our will and so too of the thoughts which are produced by the will.[11] We achieve *generosité,* or the modern version of the pride of the great-souled man.[12]

It is not necessary to insist upon an extreme interpretation of the passages just cited from Descartes in order to understand their significance for our own inquiry. Man is free and divine to the extent that he generates nature from his own mental processes and can force nature to submit to his will. The "mathematical" conception of theory is in fact a theory of praxis. Reason is, or is on the verge of, being defined as construction in accordance with human will. For Descartes, history might be said to be a human creation, depending only upon the effective force we are able to apply upon fortune. In the subsequent development of modern philosophy, fortune, reconceived as the historical consciousness, will wreak its vengeance upon the human will. This development takes two parallel paths, which I can only mention here. The first is the gradual temporalization of the ego cogitans, culminating in the teaching of Rousseau that the human mind, or reason, is itself a product of history. The second is the transformation of Christian eschatology into the philosophy of history, culminating in the teaching of Hegel

9. *Les Passions de l'ame,* I. 19. Cf. *Meditationes* IV, p. 57.

10. *Passions,* I. 19, III. 152.

11. Ibid., I. 17.

12. Ibid., III. 153. Cartesian *generosité* is in effect the assertion of man's independence or, as I would suggest, an atheistic version of Stoic morality. The connection between the desire for independence and pride, or the philosopher's wish to be God, is well brought out by the "Cartesian" Malebranche, who criticizes Descartes on this point without mentioning his name. Cf. *La Recherche de la vérité,* Bk. II, Ch. 4.

that the human mind is essentially identical with the rational order of history, and so with God.

II.

Our sketch of the transformation from the classical to the modern conception of reason was intended to suggest the inner relationship between the two main, and apparently conflicting, branches of modern philosophy. If this suggestion has been fairly stated, many inferences may be drawn from it, each the subject for a chapter or volume in itself. In terms of my own intentions, I must content myself with the following brief remarks. In order to understand the force of the historicist attack upon reason, one must bear in mind how the modern conception of reason was formulated by its advocates. If "to reason" is "to know," and "to know" is to discern numerical and geometrical order, then there is no rational significance to statements about the "nobility" or "baseness" of numbers and shapes, no knowledge of God's intentions in creating those numbers and shapes. Whatever we may *hope* or *believe* about the eschatological significance of the mathematical order, there is no rational evidence or demonstration of these hopes and beliefs. In this sense, mathematically inspired philosophy confirmed the "fundamentalist" contention of Christianity that faith is extra-rational and, indeed, *absurd*. What one may call the "theological" consequences of seventeenth-century mathematical philosophy were thus radically less rational than the consequences of the teaching of such great medieval men as Maimonides, Averroes, and Saint Thomas. The new philosophy led or contributed strongly to the force of the view that *all* expressions concerning the "good" in any sense other than the "useful" are empty of cognitive or rational content, however necessary for human existence. In a word, it played a decisive role in establishing the view that one may speak rationally about utility, but not about nobility or beauty.[13]

13. For the separation of the beautiful from the good, and the identification of the good as the convenient (internally sensed by reason, whereas the beautiful is sensed externally), see Descartes, *Passions,*

The great founders of modernity believed that their mathematically oriented science also explained with precision and objectivity the nature of man. The difference between physics and anthropology is indicated by the fact that the principle of motion in man was understood by them in such contrary ways as pride and fear, love of glory and desire for material comfort. There is a disjunction between the number of motion and the significance attached by man to number that can never be supplied by mathematics or physics. The basic confusion in seventeenth-century philosophy with respect to the nature of man is shown by the fact that he was interpreted simultaneously in the light of God and in the shadow of the beast. Not the least element in the origin of contemporary nihilism is that, when the pride and confidence in the project to master nature evaporated, the light of God was extinguished, and man saw himself altogether in the shadow of the beast. It could well seem that the power of reason, as defined and exercised by the most reasonable and powerful of men, has as a necessary consequence the destruction of man's humaneness. From this perspective, the problem of modern philosophy up to Kant was not dualism, but rather its intrinsic inclination toward monistic nihilism.

This inclination is dramatically visible in the thought of David Hume, who must be counted as one of the ancestors common to empiricism and existentialism, as those terms are used in contemporary discussion. It is not possible to do justice to Hume's historical significance by treating him as an epistemologist or precursor of twentieth-century linguistic analysis. In strict accuracy, there is no epistemology in Hume because he denies the possibility of giving a *logos* or complete account of knowledge. Hume takes his bearings, not by the Platonist mathematical physics of Galileo, Descartes, and Newton, but by the sense impressions of the individual, or what is today called the "lived body." According to Hume, ideas are caused by sense impressions, which are in turn preceded by physical sensa-

---

Lxxxv; cf. Cxlv, Cxlvii. For the distinction between truth and falsehood, on the one hand, and the good and bad, on the other, see *Meditationes* (Adam-Tannery, 7), p. 15.

tions or generated by the imagination.[14] In fact, since reasoning from impressions depends upon the memory, which is merely a weak form of the imagination, and since there is no "natural order," no constancy and invariableness of impressions by which the imagination is restricted, reason is subordinate to the imagination.[15] All reasoning is as good as false, for "we have . . . no choice left but betwixt a false reason and none at all." [16] We are saved from melancholia, the precursor of existential dread, to which our reason leads us, by the passionate, physical, concrete character of everyday life.[17] The absence of stability and identity in the world as accessible to reason means that philosophy, or "calm passion," is a specious inference of rest from motion—a matter of custom, habit, feeling, and so of taste or preference.[18] Reason is the slave of the passions.[19]

These themes, introduced with relative calmness by Hume, are to be found in a more passionate (and so, perhaps, more reasonable) form in Nietzsche's doctrine of creativity and the will to power. For Hume, freedom turns upon the imagination, as in a sense it did for Descartes. But the power attributed implicitly by Descartes to the imagination as the bridge between man's will and the world of extension is missing in Hume. One way to understand this is in seeing that Hume accepts Locke's criticism of innate ideas. Hume takes the Cartesian turn, it would seem, by engaging in an introspective analysis of the ego cogitans, but he can no longer find its structure or principle of unity. In Descartes, it is not quite clear whether the necessity of mathematical reasoning is dependent upon, or the guarantor of, the clarity and distinctness of rational evidence. In Hume, it is perfectly clear that

> the necessity, which makes two times two equal to four,
> or three angles of a triangle equal to two right ones, lies

14. *A Treatise of Human Nature* (Oxford, Oxford University Press, 1955), pp. 4, 8 ff.
15. Ibid., pp. 265–67, 251.
16. Ibid., pp. 268–69.
17. Ibid., p. 270.
18. Ibid., pp. 437, 103, 115.
19. Ibid., p. 415.

only in the act of the understanding, by which we consider and compare these ideas; in like manner the necessity or power, which unites causes and effects, lies in the
determination of the mind to pass from the one to the
other.[20]

In beginning with the thinking subject, Hume terminates in
skepticism because he finds nothing within the subject but individual impressions and ideas. That is, he finds nothing but the
temporal flux of experience, or a preliminary version of the historicity of the individual. One could say with Kant that Hume
arrived at this result because he failed to appreciate the significance of the validity of mathematics. But not even Kant was
able to rescue the individual from mere historical flux simply by
citing the validity of mathematics. Instead, it was necessary for
him to account for these two dimensions of experience by transcending both. Without such a transcendence, and given the
priority of the thinking individual (as apparently sanctioned by
Descartes) Hume's conclusion is sound and perhaps inevitable.
Why *should* mathematics have any validity beyond what my
imagination and will, inflected by habit, lend its objects? The
imagination, presumably helped or hindered by the passions, is
free to generate any order of impressions it pleases. Therefore,
assessments of the relative worth of these generated orders,
which we may call "world-views" in anticipation of nineteenth-
century historicism, are a matter of mood or aesthetic taste.
They are projects of the human will, as conditioned by the
"stuff" of the historical situation.

For Hume, then, happiness is dependent upon chance, or as
Heidegger later calls it, our historical fate (although he speaks
of "authenticity" rather than of "happiness"). What we make
of ourselves will depend upon whether we are fortunate enough
to have the proper moods (Heidegger) or a sufficiently fertile
imagination (Nietzsche). Hume does not speak of "history"
(for which he later prophetically abandoned philosophy) in this
connection, but of habit and custom. Here we see the theoreti-

20. Ibid., p. 166.

cal and practical principle of twentieth-century empiricists, especially those who combine an admiration for Hume with the influence of the later Wittgenstein. Happiness, goodness, and the practical virtues in general, lacking all rational content or justification, depend upon habituation in accordance with generally accepted tastes. The significance of the world is how the world looks to man. Of course, Hume claims to have laid bare the general shapes of the process of "looking" or appearing. Even if one abstains from criticizing this claim by citing evidence internal to Hume's teaching, the most that could be said for it is that it is descriptive or "phenomenological." [21] In other words, Hume does not entirely jettison the mathematical model of reasoning but follows it in the version of the empirico-historical sciences—the study of "what is" in the sense of the individual fact. For Hume, no less than for Nietzsche or Heidegger, existence is characterized by *facticity*.

So much for our brief but necessary survey of modern rationalism. It is, as I hope we agree now, no accident that Nietzsche, Heidegger, and the existentialists, in attributing nihilism to the consequences of rationalism, accept without quarrel the rationalistic definition of reason. That definition was doomed from the outset on two main counts. First, the reduction of reason to ratio in the sense of counting, ordering, intuiting geometrical shape, and drawing inferences made it impossible to describe the activity of reason in reasonable terms. Second, the activity of reason, regardless of the divine powers initially attributed to it, was rooted in man's imagination, will, and passions. The application of ratio to the passions of the soul did not give a basis for pride but melancholia. Since the values attributed to human passions are but facts, and the pattern of the facts is a matter of chance, man has been revanquished by fortune. Contrary to Machiavelli's advice, fortune, even though put to the torture, has triumphed in the midst of her defeat.

Not all modern rationalists have succumbed to melancholia.

---

21. Consider the observation of Merleau-Ponty on the "positivism" of phenomenology, in *Les Sciences de l'homme et la phénomenologie* (Paris, Les cours de Sorbonne, n.d.), p. 9.

This, however, may be a sign of their thoughtlessness rather than of their strength of soul. Is the currently fashionable "scientific humanism," for example, anything more than an uncritical vulgarization of Nietzsche's interpretation of science as a free creation of spirit, and so as an expression of the will to power? Even an admirer of science might be forgiven for preferring Cartesian pride or Nietzschean creativity to the spectacle of positivism wedded to romanticism. However this may be, the net philosophical result of modern rationalist epistemology is to have created a situation which cannot be distinguished from Nietzsche's teaching, so far as the reasonableness of reason is concerned. Let us close this section of our study with a brief analysis of the crucial contemporary example of rationalist nihilism. Suppose we believe, as do so many scientific humanists today, that all psychic or mental phenomena may be reduced to biochemical processes and thereby to mathematically computable energy distributions. What is the status of this belief itself, and finally of the self who believes it?

To begin with, if the belief is true, it is itself an instance of a biochemical process, an electrical excitation of the physical organ known as the brain, and so a pattern of extension, matter, or energy. As such, it has no "value" in any sense other than the numerical. Thus, the mere fact of its truth (supposing it to be true) carries with it no rational or scientific recommendation, not to say obligation, that it be believed or, if believed, that it be regarded as a *reasonable* belief. If the reasonable is the useful, it is almost certainly unreasonable, because harmful, to accept a doctrine that obliterates the difference in dignity between man and dirt. On the other hand, if "reasonable" means "true," and the doctrine in question is true, then we accept it in tacit or explicit deference to the principle, "one ought to accept what is true." Now what status has this principle? If it is true that one ought to accept the truth, then it cannot be true that truth is always at bottom a mathematical description of energy patterns, since such patterns, if taken to be the final stratum of reality, into which all superficial or illusory strata are to be reduced, provide no basis for the reconstruction of moral or psychological imperatives. If it is not true that one ought to accept the truth (because of the assumption that "true" and "ought" are incompatible), but merely that we sometimes have a propensity to do so, then truth, and so reason, must be distinguishable from motives determining what we accept or believe. In other words, there is no *reason,* no *reasonable* reason, for believing the true rather than the false. The mere fact that proposition X is true is insufficient to command the allegiance of a reasonable man to that proposition, especially if it certifies that, qua man, or conscious being who is deliberating whether to accept X, he is an illusion and so does not exist in those terms which alone make rational the debate concerning the acceptance or repudiation of proposition X.

On this alternative, then, the *fact* that proposition X is true is paradoxically transformed into a *value,* namely, something which we may believe or not as we see fit, or depending upon whether we regard it as worthwhile to believe it. And the transformation is paradoxical because X in effect asserts the radical distinction between facts and values. This self-transformation of the assertion of the principle of contemporary rationalism into a value is equivalent to the transformation of philosophy into poetry by Nietzsche and others. In the first case, a distinction is made between facts and values which renders values unreasonable. In the second case, facts are redefined as a special kind of values, which means that facts are rendered unreasonable. The contemporary nihilist situation is a synthesis of these two (basically equivalent) processes: the total effect is to make both facts *and* values unreasonable and valueless. And so there is no real difference, in this context, between scientists and humanists. If it is fatuous to assume that nihilism will be overcome by knowledge of the second law of thermodynamics, it is equally fatuous to assume that it will surrender to an appreciation of poetic style. What then are we to say of the view that man's salvation lies in the union of such knowledge and such appreciation?

III.

The modern project to master nature begins in Cartesian pride and ends in the pessimism of Schopenhauer and the nihilism of Nietzsche. I speak here of the philosophical vision that has illuminated or obscured the human significance of scientific discovery and technical invention. The shift in mood from pride to nihilism corresponds in a deeper sense to a historical interpretation of mathematics; more specifically, it corresponds to the youth and old age of the philosophy of history. Thus, the pride taken by the twentieth century in its scientific and technological accomplishment has been largely negated by anxiety and nausea of spirit or, what is perhaps even worse, by the blinking of the last post-nihilist men, as Nietzsche prophetically called them. In the context of a discussion of Goethe, Nietzsche asks: "Is not the nineteenth century, especially at its end, an intensified, *brutalized* eighteenth century, that is, a century of *decadence?*" [22] In terms of what Nietzsche himself calls *Geist,* one might add: is not the twentieth century, at least thus far, a diluted, *vulgarized* nineteenth century, and for that reason a century of global convulsions? However inclined we might be to regard this question about our own age, it is clear that Nietzsche speaks for a commanding proportion of the discerning spirits of the nineteenth century. As Goethe himself remarked to Eckermann in 1831, a year before his death: "Niebuhr was right when he saw the coming of a barbarous age. It is already here, we are already in its midst; for in what does barbarism consist but in the failure to recognize the excellent?" [23]

Quotations of this sort, taken from observers of the most diverse theoretical and practical perspectives, might be multiplied indefinitely. But the evidence is well known, indeed, notorious —from Leopardi, Tocqueville, Burckhardt, Renan, Herzen, and

22. "Streifzüge eines Unzeitgemässen," in *Götzen-Dämmerung,* ed. Schlechta, par. 50, p. 1025.
23. *Gespräche mit Eckermann,* 22 März 1831, ed. E. Beutler (Zürich, Artemis Verlag, 1948), p. 487.

Dostoievski, to Kierkegaard, Marx, and Nietzsche himself, to say nothing of a dozen others.[24] The nineteenth century produced, again in Nietzsche's words, as "a total result, not Goethe, but a chaos, a nihilistic sigh, and ignorance as to where or whence, an instinct of fatigue." If we inspect this result from a Nietzschean perspective, how can it be most fundamentally understood? I believe that two ideas are paramount—the link between chaos and creativity, and the fatigue induced by historical consciousness. The modern project, as a radical manifestation of the will to power, is a human creation, a new world or perspective upon the chaotic elements from which worlds are generated.[25] But every new creation necessarily rises from the ruins of its predecessors, as the phoenix rises from its own ashes—a symbol of the constancy of the will to power throughout its historical transformations.[26] Hence the link between the artist and the warrior, and Nietzsche's high estimation of hardness and courage. The great creator must also be a great destroyer; in destroying or accelerating the natural decadence of the past, he also destroys his own historical consciousness and becomes like a child, freed from loyalty to and vengeance against the old world, able to create new values in the innocence of his playful strength.[27]

24. See Karl Löwith's essay, "The Historical Background of European Nihilism," in *Nature, History and Existentialism* (Evanston, Northwestern University Press, 1966), for relevant citations. Löwith has devoted a lifetime of scholarship to the study of the post-Hegelian period, much of it invaluable for our present theme.

25. The clearest formulations of Nietzsche's perspectivism or doctrine of creativity are to be found in the fragments called *Der Wille zur Macht,* regardless of the authenticity of the traditional arrangement.

26. *Also Sprach Zarathustra,* Vorrede, par. 2.

27. *Zarathustra, Werke,* ed. Schlechta, *2,* 294, 297–98, 305–06, 311–13, 358–59, 394–96, 407–08, 460; *Der Wille zur Macht,* ed. A. Baeumler (Stuttgart, Alfred Kroner Verlag, 1959), par 796–97, 983. The importance of play has been transmitted from Kant to Nietzsche through the intermediary of Schiller. For a post-Heideggerian formulation, cf. E. Fink, *Nietzsches Philosophie* (Stuttgart, W. Kohlhammer Verlag, 1960), p. 189: "Aber der spielende Mensch, der ekstatisch offensteht für den gestaltlosen-gestaltenden spielenden Gott Dionysos, lebt nicht in einer

Thus Nietzsche distinguishes between a noble and a base nihilism. The noble nihilism purifies and strengthens man by accelerating the destruction of the base nihilism, of the sickness, weakness, or decadence of an old world.[28] Hence the noble teaching of Zarathustra is compared to arson: the decadent cities of men must be burnt to the ground in order for the superman to rise from their ashes.[29] Since the modern project has terminated in the nihilism of decadence, a more radical nihilism of creativity, a "destruction of western metaphysics," is necessary in order to open the horizon for the possibility of a future revelation. We see here the pride and will of Descartes, stripped of Cartesian prudence, with poetry having replaced mathematics. Zarathustra is no longer a physicist, but the solitary promenader of Rousseau, whose aesthetic sensibility has been intensified by the lightning of Zeus, and whose isolation has been overcome by the possibility of a new historical epoch. But the need to destroy is implicit in the process of overcoming, as Descartes, beginning a previous epoch, has already taught us:

> It is true that we never see all the houses in a city being torn to the ground, for the sole purpose of rebuilding them in another way, and making the streets more beautiful. But one often sees that many tear their houses down in order to rebuild them, and even sometimes that people are constrained to tear them down, when they are in danger of falling by themselves, and the foundations are not genuinely secure.[30]

Descartes goes on to say that it would not be reasonable for a private citizen to reform a state from the foundations or to reform the body of sciences in the same way. Nevertheless, it is just this which he has decided to do with his own "opinions";

---

schweifenden Willkür der unbedingten Freiheit; er ist Mitspieler im Spiel der Welt und will zutiefst das Not-wendige."

28. *Der Wille zur Macht,* par. 39–47, 55, 62, 110, 112.

29. Cf. n. 26, above.

30. *Discours de la méthode,* ed. E. Gilson (Paris, J. Vrin, 1947), Pt. II, pp. 13–14; see also Gilson's commentary, pp. 169–70.

namely, to live his life by building upon new foundations, however cautiously he expresses himself.

Descartes' prudence, necessitated by the religious and political situation of his time, is in implicit contradiction to the spirit of the Enlightenment which his teaching symbolically originates. Man cannot become master and possessor of nature without usurping the authority of God. In these terms, the *Meditations,* beginning as they do with the untrustworthiness and possibly evil origin of the visible natural order, together with the emphasis upon self-reliance or subjective certitude, may be read as a manual for revolutionaries. As Descartes wrote to Mersenne,

> and I tell you, between us, that these six meditations contain all the foundations of my physics. But one must not say so, if you please, because those who favor Aristotle would perhaps make more difficulty in approving [the meditations]; and I hope that those who read them, will accustom themselves insensibly to my principles, and will recognize the truth in them before perceiving that they destroy those of Aristotle.[31]

The Cartesian revolution may be said to terminate in two nineteenth-century programs for a radically more direct and violent enterprise—Marx's revolution of the proletariat and Nietzsche's radicalization of nihilism in preparation for the superman. In both cases, mathematical physics is transformed by the engine of history into a doctrine of human creativity. In both cases, albeit in different terms, Hegel's doctrine of historical completion is modified by a conception of the decadence of nineteenth-century European society, from whose ashes a new age, if not the end of history, will emerge. Therefore, despite many differences between the two thinkers, a study of the forces which shaped the teaching of Nietzsche is also a study of the forces shaping Marx.

For the present, however, let us continue to see the situation

31. Adam-Tannery, *3,* 297–98.

with a view to Nietzsche. We recall once more that the Cartesian ego cogitans served as the link between the mathematical
and historical elements in the modern conception of reason.
There is an ambiguity in the relationship between the ego and
God, on the one hand, and between one ego and the rest, on the
other, which may be briefly restated as follows. The traditional
doctrine of two worlds, or the teaching of salvation (whether by
theory or practice) in the next world, obvious in Christianity
and apparently present in Plato, is replaced by an invocation to
create man's salvation by action in this world. However, since
the locus of activity is the solitary ego, the problem of two
worlds is replaced by the problem of solipsism. If mathematical
physics is a historical project of the human mind, if the "scientific world view" is merely a Weltanschauung, then there is a
radical separation between those who understand the truth
about history and those who are altogether dominated by it.
This becomes evident in the culminating phase of Rousseau's
complex teaching. The simple patriotism of the virtuous citizen
is impossible for the solitary promenader, whose reveries constitute the highest form of spiritual existence.[32] In what I have
previously called Rousseau's aesthetic sensibility, we have the
continental counterpart to Hume's "phenomenalistic" skepticism. Reason is impossible, or unsatisfactory to the highest man,
whether this defect be expressed in historical or mathematical
terms.

Hume's skeptic escapes solipsism (and nihilism) by escaping
from philosophy into the *Lebenswelt.* No such avenue is open to
the solitary promenader, who cherishes his uniqueness too
highly to submerge it in the general will of the social contract.
Nevertheless, Rousseau also prepared the solution to the problem of the "alienation" of the highest man from the body poli-
tic.[33] In the *Second Discourse,* he develops the conception of

32. For representative texts, cf. *Confessions* (Paris, Garnier, 1952),
1, 9, 218 ff., *2,* 179; *Les Rêveries du promeneur solitaire* (Paris, Garnier,
1949), pp. 1, 5–6, 18, 68, 83; *Émile* (Paris, Garnier, n.d.), p. 238.

33. In *Du Contrat social* (Paris, Garnier, 1954), Rousseau uses the
word "aliénation," destined for so notorious a future, to summarize the

man as a product of history, who evolves from his natural or animal condition because of the interplay of his desire for self-preservation, pity for his own kind, and a superiority to other animals in *"adresse"* or *"la faculté de se perfectionner."* [34] Stated somewhat more precisely, although man changes or evolves within history, the motion by which *"réflexion"* or human reason is separated from the merely animal is itself natural.[35] Thus, although man is a historical animal, history, and so man too, is a product of nature. Many, if not all, of the apparent contradictions in Rousseau's writings could be overcome, I believe, once we see this basic thesis: from the original motion of nature comes history, and so both human perfection and corruption. This is *a fact of nature* and not a contradiction in Rousseau's teaching. The purpose of political philosophy is to slow down the motions leading to corruption; yet precisely in so acting, it obstructs the motions leading to perfection. A similar situation exists within the motions leading to perfection. Reflection seems to begin as reason in the sense of ratio (e.g. calculations concerning self-preservation). But as it develops,

---

clauses of the social contract: "Ces clauses, bien entendues, se réduisent toutes à une seule: savoir, l'aliénation totale de chaque associé avec tous ces droits à toute la communauté: car premièrement, chacun se donnant tout entier, la condition est égale pour tous" (pp. 243–44). Thus, alienation is a departure "sans reserve" from the state of nature into an egalitarian political society. This alienation is later called "un échange avantageux d'une manière d'être incertaine et précaire contre une autre meilleure et plus sûre, de l'indépendence naturelle contre la liberté" etc.; in other words, it is advantageous for self-preservation (pp. 255–56). One could scarcely say the same, without serious qualifications, so far as solitary revery is concerned. Sparta, and neither Athens nor the Alps, is the paradigm of political virtue. In Marx, the proletarian is alienated from society, whereas among contemporary ideologues, one hears constantly of the alienated intellectual. The original force of the term is of an alienation from nature *into* society. We cannot understand what this implies for Rousseau if we remain within the Marxist perspective.

34. Crucial passages: *Discours sur l'origine de l'inégalité parmi les hommes,* in *Du Contrat social,* pp. 43, 48, 58, 67 ff.

35. Cf. ibid., pp. 67–68 and 91.

reflection bifurcates into scientific reason and aesthetic revery; and these two are again largely, if not completely, incompatible.

Reason is associated with power and utility; revery, with the beautiful and the good in the highest, not the political sense. Again we see the split between the useful and the noble which developed in the seventeenth century. The highest things are beyond reason, which concerns itself with the order of nature, or the laws of motion. But natural motion transcends itself, so to speak, in the form of man's self-consciousness. The stage is set for German philosophy, which, inspired by the rediscovery of Spinoza, will attempt to resolve this dualism of nature and Geist.[36] This resolution proceeds in two basic stages, which we can merely summarize here. It is followed by a third stage, the dissolution of the synthesis, culminating in the exhaustion of the historical consciousness as portrayed by Nietzsche. The first stage is the Copernican revolution of Kant, who was awakened from his dogmatic slumbers by Hume and set straight by Rousseau. The question here, of course, is not whether Kant under-

36. The pantheistic interpretation of Spinoza, the "god-intoxicated philosopher," which is still predominant among contemporary scholars, stems from Goethe and the Idealists. For a different view, closer to that of the seventeenth century, it is helpful to consider the words of Jacobi, apparently the first to use the word "nihilism" in a philosophical context, and who fell into disrepute because of the powerful attack leveled against him by Hegel. Jacobi points out that, at bottom, for both Spinoza and Leibniz, "eine jede Endursache eine wirkende voraussetzt . . . Das Denken ist nicht die Quelle der Substanz; sondern die Substanz ist die Quelle des Denkens. Also muss vor dem Denken etwas Nichtdenkendes als das Erste angenommen werden; etwas, das, wenn schon nicht durchaus in der Wirklichkeit, doch der Vorstellung, dem Wesen, der inneren Natur nach, als das Vorderste gedacht werden muss": *Ueber die Lehre des Spinozas,* in *Werke: Vierter Band, Erste Abtheilung* (Leipzig, G. Fleisher, 1819), p. 67. Jacobi goes on to claim that Spinozism and Idealism are atheism and nihilism (*Jacobi an Fichte,* in *Werke, Dritter Band,* p. 44). The result: "Alles löset sich (for man) allmählich auf in sein eigenes Nichts (when he tries to ground himself not in God, but in himself). Eine solche Wahl aber hat der Mensch; diese Einzige: das Nichts oder einen Gott. Das Nichts erwählend macht er sich zu Gott; das heisst: er macht zu Gott ein Gespenst" (p. 49).

stood Rousseau accurately, but how he transformed him. Kant tends to exaggerate the moral and political strands in Rousseau and to ignore the reveries of the solitary promenader, which may have impressed him unfavorably as a kind of *Schwärmerei*.[37] In any case, the dualism between nature and Geist underlies Kant's own distinction between the phenomenal and the noumenal. The human spirit is preserved from the mechanistic necessity of Newtonian physics, but at a heavy price. Kant resolves one form of dualism only to create another, one in which nature is no longer the source of reason or spirit, as in Rousseau. As a result, reason in the sense of the faculty of knowledge is redefined (as *Verstand*) and restricted in its operations to the phenomenal world of nature. There can be no knowledge of the highest things, namely, god, freedom, and immortality. Reason (*Vernunft*), as distinct from understanding, is the source of these regulative ideas, and the expression or determination of the good will in the categorical form of the moral principle amounts to an identification between the willing person and the rational order, or, in effect, God.[38] But the concepts of practical reason, although indispensable for the possibility of the summum bonum and therefore practically necessary, are useless from "a theoretical point of view." [39]

The highest function of reason is, then, empty of cognitive content but grounded finally in the fact of moral conscience, or man's sense of his own dignity.[40] Just as the phenomenal world

37. Cf. Kant's remarks on Plato in "Von einem neuerdings erhabenen vornehmen Ton in der Philosophie," in *Werke,* ed., W. Weischedel (Wiesbaden, Insel Verlag, 1958), *3*.

38. Adequate support for this statement would require a detailed interpretation of Kant's moral writings. Here I can only refer to the discussion of the good will as universal legislator, and of man as an autonomous member of the kingdom of ends who is nevertheless, as such, formally identical with the universal law. Cf. *Grundlegung zur Metaphysik der Sitten, Werke,* ed. Ernst Cassirer, *4* (Berlin, Bruno Cassirer, 1922), esp. pp. 285 ff. and 289 ff.

39. *Kritik der praktischen Vernunft,* ed. K. Vorländer (Hamburg, Felix Meiner Verlag, 1952), p. 154.

40. The autonomous will acts in accord with a duty to its own dignity: cf. *Grundlegung,* pp. 291 ff.

is finally a "project" of the synthetic productivity of the transcendental imagination, so the noumenal world might be regarded as a project of man's will:

> the righteous man may indeed say: I *will* that there be a
> God, that my existence in this world be also an exis-
> tence beyond the natural chain [of causes] in a pure
> world of the understanding, finally also, that my dura-
> tion be endless; I persist in these beliefs and will not let
> anyone take them from me. For this is the only case in
> which my interest, because I may not relax anything of
> these beliefs, inevitably determines my judgment, with-
> out paying any attention to sophistries (*Vernünfte-
> leien*), however little I am able to answer them, or to
> oppose them with others more apparent.[41]

Kant transforms the empirical view of men like Hobbes and
Locke, that we know only what we make, into the doctrine of
the synthetic production of the transcendental ego.[42] This in no
way changes, but rather emphasizes, the superiority of practice
to theory.[43] The Cartesian revolution, essentially pagan in
spirit, is translated into a kind of secularized or enlightened
Christianity (not, to be sure, in complete disagreement with the
spirit of Cartesianism): mathematical physics is altogether subordinated to morality. But the split between the "is" and the
"ought," or the motions of nature and Geist, has not yet been
overcome. Rational knowledge rests finally upon belief, a fragile
foundation that history will dissolve into mood and sentiment.
  In the third *Critique,* Kant develops a doctrine of purposive-

41. *Kritik der praktischen Vernunft,* p. 164. With respect to the
"project" of the transcendental imagination, cf. *Kritik der reinen
Vernunft,* B103 ("Die Synthesis überhaupt ist . . . die blosse Wirkung
der Einbildungskraft") and B130 ("dass wir uns nichts, als im Objekt
verbunden, vorstellen können, ohne es vorher selbst verbunden zu
haben").
42. *Kritik der Urteilskraft,* ed. K. Vorländer (Hamburg, 1954), par.
68, p. 248: "denn nur soviel sieht man vollständig ein, als man nach
Begriffen selbst machen und zustande bringen kann."
43. *Kritik der praktischen Vernunft,* p. 140.

ness and teleology in an effort to integrate the two domains of knowledge and belief, but without moving radically beyond what he had already accomplished: the primacy of morality and practical reason, and so of faith, or "the moral mode of thought of reason in holding that to be true, which is inaccessible to theoretical knowledge." That is, it is a "free belief" in "what we assume on behalf of a design in accordance with laws of freedom." [44] Two points emerge, however, which are of crucial importance for our subject. The first is the partial reappearance of Rousseau's aesthetic sensibility in the form of the perception of the beautiful and the sublime. The perception of the sublime results from recognition of the conflict between the imagination and the reason, or the inaccessibility of nature to the ideas of human reason.[45] This perception, which is higher than the perception of beauty, thus emphasizes the disjunction between nature and Geist, and so, although it leads to pleasure, begins in pain.[46] In perceiving the sublime, we transcend reason, or cognition based upon sensation, and hence, too, nature. That is, we are ourselves the source and model of sublimity, and not nature.[47] Through the exercise of our supersensible faculty, the divine character of order and intelligibility is manifested as an immanent transcendence of nature. We discern here the ancestor of Nietzsche's doctrine of cosmogonical poetry, as well as of Heidegger's conception of the revelation of the sense of Being through the existential self-meditation of *Dasein*.

The second point is the retention of what I called in the case of Rousseau the bifurcation of spiritual motion. This is strikingly visible in the section of the third *Critique* entitled "Of the ultimate purpose of nature as a teleological system." [48] Accord-

44. *Kritik der Urteilskraft*, par. 91, pp. 346–47.
45. Ibid., par. 27, p. 103; par. 29, pp. 114–15.
46. Ibid., par. 26, p. 99. We see here a decisive deviation, not yet present in Rousseau, from the classical doctrine of the natural pleasantness of existence: an "existential" revision of the need to master nature. In Nietzsche, this will become the suffering of the creative artist; in Kierkegaard, dread before sin.
47. Ibid., par. 28, p. 110.
48. Ibid., par. 83, pp. 298 ff.

ing to Kant, man may be understood as the ultimate purpose
of nature in two respects: first, with respect to his happiness,
and second, in terms of his culture. The first, however, is defective, and for two reasons: man's own vacillations concerning
the nature of happiness, and nature's inability to secure happiness as naturally understood. We must look instead to man's
aptitude for activity, to "what he himself must do, in order to be
an ultimate purpose." [49] In essence, this is his "ability to pose
purposes in general to himself, and . . . to use nature as a
means, in general conformity with the maxims of his free purposes." [50] Thus, as in the previous point, man is the instrument
by which nature, with respect to its highest purpose or ultimate
significance, is shown to transcend itself. Whereas previously
this occurred as an epiphany of the sublime, in the present instance it is a matter of human "culture." And just as culture
was distinguished from happiness, so it too admits of a bifurcation into the culture of skill, or unequal development of man's
faculties, and the culture of the whole civil community, or the
political reflection of the kingdom of ends. Even further, there is
a dualism within the development of skill; for, since it depends
upon inequality, or the suffering of the many in order to provide
leisure for the few, human progress is effected by a "splendid
misery." [51] This motion from inequality to equality, thanks to
the misery which is the precondition of human perfection, is the
basis of Kant's philosophy of history.

One may apply the notion of "project" in a fourfold sense to
the philosophy of Kant: epistemologically (the phenomenal
world is a project of the transcendental ego),[52] ontologically

49. Ibid., p. 300. Kant's criticism of eudaemonism is part of his rejection of the classical "aristocratism" of the proud philosophers in
favor of a philosophically modified version of Christian ethics. When
culture is also rejected as an inadequate mark of perfection, we are
ready for the exaltation of "authenticity."

50. *Kritik der Urteilskraft,* par. 83, p. 300.

51. Ibid., pp. 300–01.

52. This theme is incisively presented by Heidegger in his various
discussions of modern rationalism; cf. esp. *Nietzsche, 2* (Pfullingen,
G. Neske Verlag, 1961).

(the noumenal world is a project of moral conscience or sensibility), aesthetically (the perception of the beautiful and the sublime), and, as we now see, historically. These are obviously four different ways of looking at the same situation, suggested by Kant's own articulation. Although Kant's treatment of the historical way is the briefest and least satisfactory in terms of the development of his own teaching, it is the most important so far as the theme of the present chapter is concerned. In the case of Rousseau, the motion of the spirit is said to produce history and, as its inseparable concomitant, reason. This production results in both the splendor and the misery of the human race, in its genius as well as its moral corruption. In the passages just surveyed, Kant projects a hypothetical unification of splendor and misery by suggesting that history possesses an inner dialectical structure. In its surveyable stretch, history seems to expose the unresolved conflict of intelligence and moral virtue, as Rousseau so subtly showed. But if this is the final message of history, then there is a still deeper contradiction between nature and spirit, which in turn reflects upon the identity of reason and goodness in God. Unless the completion of progress, and so the elimination of war, misery, and political injustice, or the end of human striving, is at least visible in the Idea of man, "the natural dispositions must be seen for the most part as vain and endless, which destroys all practical principles." Hence nature, which must be regarded as wise in all its other forms, will be suspected of a "childish game with man alone." [53]

Kant's solution is to look for a clue to the inner plan of history, or the method it has selected to allow man the free development of his faculties as well as of his political condition. In brief this method is the aforementioned dualism of spiritual motions, or what Hegel later calls the "cunning of reason." Man's own selfishness, his antagonism toward his fellow humans, his desire to overcome their resistance to his private desires and in-

53. "Idee zu einer allgemeinen Geschichte in weltbürgerlicher Absicht," in *Kleinere Schriften zur Geschichtsphilosophie, Ethik und Politik* (Hamburg, Felix Meiner Verlag, 1959), p. 7.

tentions, leads first to society, then to rivalry and war among
societies, and finally, if our feeling about the future, our hypothesis as to the clue of history, is correct, to universal peace, or a
world state.[54] If the moral significance of the noumenal world
seemed to represent a project of man's will, the qualified attempt to discern that significance in history might even more
aptly be designated a project of man's hope. We who now dwell
in the ostensibly penultimate stage must endure the greatest evil,
and for a virtual eternity, since the end of history, or the genuine resolution of the dualism of spiritual motions, is infinitely
distant. At least one must infer this from Kant's warning that
the complete attainment of the political solution is impossible,
that at best we can only approach its idea. When he adds a
few pages later that the goal is "most distant," this would seem
to be a hopeful euphemism for "infinitely far removed." [55] Our
hope must be further qualified by the fact that Kant speaks of
the coming political, *but not moral,* perfection of man within
history. The problem of establishing a legally just state, he remarks in another place, could be solved by a race of intelligent
devils.[56] If attained, it could only be the necessary precondition
for the full development of the capacities of every human being,
and this is not equivalent to the perfecting of his moral nature
or will. Thus, when Kant says that, if our idea of the end of
history is inadmissible, we must look to another world alone for
the satisfaction of man and the justification of providence, it
would seem that this is necessary in either case.[57]

IV.

The first stage in the attempt to resolve the dualism between
nature and Geist has thus failed. Each of the four Kantian projects

54. In addition to the essay cited in the previous note, cf. "Zum
ewigen Frieden," ibid., pp. 125, 139. For a supplementary discussion,
see E. Fackenheim, "Kant's Concept of History," in *Kant-Studien,* Band
48, Heft 3 (1956/1957), 381–98.

55. "Idee," pp. 12, 16.

56. "Zum ewigen Frieden," p. 146.

57. "Idee," pp. 19–20. Fackenheim would seem to be correct on this
point. See his previously cited article, pp. 396- 97.

illustrates this failure from a different perspective. The ends of
reason and those of understanding can be rendered harmonious
only by a series of hypotheses terminating, not in the certitude
of mathematics, but in the highly questionable "fact" of moral
dignity. The disjunction between "faith and knowledge," in
Hegel's famous phrase, is present in the theoretical and practical domains. We cannot know the goodness of reason or ac-
complish its perfection. And the ultimate fact of morality itself
cannot be confirmed or fulfilled within history; witness the disjunction between political and personal morality. By placing the
phenomenal world within time, Kant prepares the "historiciza-
tion" of reason; by placing the highest manifestation of reason
in faith, he prepares the "irrationalism" of historicist ontologies.
We must now turn briefly to the second stage, or Hegel's attempt to reconcile reason and history and thereby to submit
faith to knowledge.

In Rousseau, self-consciousness and reason emerge from
nature; in Kant, they are opposed to nature from the outset.[58]
Hegel formulates his own resolution to this opposition, the
terms of which he takes from Kant:

> The present standpoint of philosophy is that the Idea,
> known in its necessity, makes known the aspects of its
> diremption, nature and Geist, each as exhibition of the
> totality of the Idea, and not only as identical in itself,
> but as producing out of itself this one identity, and this
> therefore as necessary.[59]

What Hegel means by the dualism of nature and Geist can no
more be understood in terms of the contemporary conceptions
of body and mind than the use given those terms in modern Eu-

58. Kant assumes the Christian dichotomy of body and soul, albeit in
a highly sophisticated manner, stemming from the "metaphysical" dualism of Descartes. Rousseau, at least in the *Second Discourse,* derives
the soul from the motions of the body, in a way stemming from Cartesian physics and Hobbesian psychology. Cf. the quotation from Jacobi on Spinoza and Leibniz in n. 36, above.

59. *Vorlesungen über die Geschichte der Philosophie,* Dritter Band,
Sämtliche Werke, ed. H. Glockner, Bd. 19 (Stuttgart, F. Frommann,
1959), p. 684.

ropean philosophy from Descartes onward. Contemporary philosophers are in general irresistibly attracted toward a monistic
interpretation of man and an affiliated bias toward the body,
whether this bias be expressed in terms of behaviorist or phenomenological psychologies. To speak, for example, of "the
lived body" is to take one's bearings by what Hegel would have
called the finite and empirical fact of the unity within life of
body and mind. To describe the empirical behavior of this
unity, whether adequately or not, is to understand neither the
principle of its unity nor the dimensions within that unity. From
a Hegelian perspective (to say nothing of others), there is on
this crucial point no difference between contemporary phenomenology and positivism. Both are dominated by facticity, and
this preoccupation with the factic and the individual are consequences of the revolt against Hegel's full teaching.

Let us consider the expression given by Heidegger to this deviation from Hegel. Heidegger formulates his difference from
Hegel in three points. First, Hegel thinks Being with respect to
the complete or absolute thought of beings (the *Aufhebung* of
the essential thought of the past); hence, thought is for him the
absolute Concept, that is, the one which pervades all beings.
Heidegger, on the contrary, thinks Being with respect to its
difference from beings. "For us, the matter for thinking . . . is
the difference *as* difference." The next two points follow directly
from this. Heidegger is concerned with the historical tradition,
what has been thought about beings, not in order to sublate it
into his own complete teaching, but rather to find what has not
been thought in the tradition, or, in other words, to take a step
backward to the origin of western philosophy, "to the previously by-passed domain out of which the essence (*Wesen*) of
truth first becomes memorable." [60] The tradition of western philosophy, as incorporated in Hegel, conceives Being as logos, or
determinate speech, and hence necessarily by means of speech
about determinations (beings); at the same time, as the speech
of Being (the Absolute), philosophy renders determinations visible only by exhibiting their universality. The particular is both

60. *Identität und Differenz*, pp. 42 ff.

real and rational, to invoke the famous terms, only within, as a manifestation of, the universal. Although the synthesis of the universal and the particular is called by Hegel the individual, the fact remains that Being is thought as the complete thinking of the essential structure of beings and, conversely, that beings are thought, or rather are thinkable, because they are determinations of Being.

Hegel joins thinking and Being in logos; Heidegger joins them, as I believe, in silence. The "difference *as* difference" is the uniqueness of the unique—uniqueness considered independently of its manifestation in unique individuals. So too the source of the essence of truth in the traditional sense is not speech, but silence. Heidegger's "new" thinking is an attempt to bypass western logos and thereby to uncover in some way the *absence* of Being; and so, like the religious attempt to manifest the *Deus Absconditus,* he has recourse to the speech of poetic prophecy. On the other hand, like the traditional philosophers, he attempts to make Being present here and now in the thought of man as the absence of beings. Heidegger's is a speaking silence; this silence is invoked or manifested most directly, not by rational descriptions of things, but by the silent things themselves. Traditional or "logical" speech covers over, or distorts, the way of self-presentation of things. This "way" is the Being that is different from beings, accessible to man in the silent presence of beings, in the *lachrymae rerum,* as one might be tempted to say. The absence of Being is present as the facticity of beings. Let us restate this difficult but crucial conception. In order to think Being, one must think away beings. But one must think them away as determinations of universal or absolute logos, which is itself not Being, but an emanation from, and so a determination of, Being. In thinking away beings as logical projections or constructions, we arrive at the pre-verbal presence of Being in the silent manifestation of beings. So the required "absence" of beings is the same as their required "presence." This is the Heideggerean revision of Husserl's famous imperative, "to the things themselves." Heidegger's "difference *as* difference" is the radicalization of Nietzsche's assertion of the uniqueness of every being. The Being-process, or radicalized differentiation, manifests itself only as difference, i.e. as different things. Therefore, ontological speech in the pure sense is impossible from the beginning, as I argued in the previous chapter. Similarly, the injunction to ignore beings in favor of Being is equally impossible. Heidegger "synthesizes" these two impossibilities in the silent presentation of the emanation-process of beings, the "fourfold" or round-dance of earth, heaven, man, and gods.[61]

In the pre-Hegelian monism of Parmenides and Spinoza, there is no internal articulation between thinking and being, no dualism of motions because no motion, or, in the modern term, no history. When Hegel asserts the necessity of setting the substance of Spinoza into motion, or that Spinoza possessed the "third" [mode], after substance and attribute, but as mere externality, because his substance lacks "the return into itself," we may understand him as follows.[62] Traditional monism identifies Being and the world with eternity; but this is in effect to deny the reality of the visible, heterogeneous, and "moving" world of things.[63] Being does not appear before itself; it does not unfold or develop. Hence it cannot achieve self-consciousness; and therefore logos, or speech as the work of thinking and so as the manifestation of Being's coming to be, is impossible. The absence of motion means an absence of formal development, both in being and in thinking, and so it means the presence of silence. Hegel sublates this silence, thanks to the power of the negative, or renders it articulate by the dialectic of contradictions, whereby pure Being, as Nothing, transforms itself into the history of Becoming. Let us expand this point in

61. Heidegger's *Geviert* is at least in part a poeticized and therefore "silenced" version of the dialectical *Selbstbewegung* of Hegel's Absolute. Cf. *Phänomenologie des Geistes,* ed. J. Hoffmeister (Hamburg, Felix Meiner Verlag, 1952), p. 550; *Wissenschaft der Logik,* ed. G. Lasson (Leipzig, Felix Meiner Verlag, 1951), Bd. I, p. 31; and Heidegger's *Vorträge und Aufsätze,* p. 178.

62. *Logik,* I, pp. 151, 250; II, p. 166; I, p. 337.

63. *Encyclopädie der Philosophischen Wissenschaften,* ed. J. Hoffmeister (Leipzig, Felix Meiner Verlag, 1949), par. 50, p. 76.

terms which do not depend upon a lengthy discussion of Hegel's logic. Hegel conceives of history as the process whereby man's spirit comes to a progressively more complete understanding of itself, through a progressive understanding of the world.[64] The Cartesian project of the mastery of nature is transformed from an enterprise of mathematical physics into an enterprise of speculative thinking (and the middle term is, of course, the thought of Kant). The history of speculative thought is thus identical, when completed and so properly understood, with the identification of subject and object, or Geist and nature.[65] The comprehension of human history is identical with the comprehension of "the whole." [66]

Cartesian mastery, because it is conceived in terms of matter or externality, is for Hegel merely another form of man's servitude or alienation from his spiritual fulfillment and satisfaction. It is not the external control of nature, but the interior comprehension of man's purpose as exteriorized by work, both spiritual and corporeal, that constitutes human freedom. The paradigm of work is not mathematics, in itself a form of silence, nor even the silent corporeal labor of the slave, but logos, or rational speech about the meaning and end of mathematics, corporeal labor, and every other manifestation of absolute Geist. Just as Kant before him, Hegel in a sense takes his bearings by Des-

64. The most profound, and at the same time most accessible, interpretation of this process, in the form of an interpretation of the *PhG*, is A. Kojéve's *Introduction à la lecture de Hegel,* ed. Queneau (Paris, Gallimard, 1947). The defect of Kojève's reading follows from his excessive "secularization" of Hegel, from a Marxism influenced very strongly by the Heidegger of *Sein und Zeit.*

65. This is also the overcoming of the split between theory and practice within history; cf. *Grundlinien der Philosophie des Rechts,* ed. J. Hoffmeister (Hamburg, Felix Meiner Verlag, 1955), par. 28, pp. 342, 346.

66. "Was ich vorläufig gesagt und noch sagen werde, ist nicht bloss— auch in Rücksicht unserer Wissenschaft nicht—als Vorraussetzung, sondern als Übersicht des Ganzen zu nehmen, als das Resultat der von uns anzustellenden Betrachtung—ein Resultat, das mir bekannt ist, weil mir bereits das Ganze bekannt ist." *Die Vernunft in der Geschichte,* ed. J. Hoffmeister (Hamburg Felix Meiner Verlag, 1955).

cartes. He accepts in principle the Cartesian conception of nature, deepens the Cartesian ego cogitans by making it the locus
for the synthesis of pagan *nous* and the Judaeo-Christian soul,
and joins the two in the reason of history by demonstrating the
presence of reason in history. The Kantian philosophy attempted to avoid the silence of monism by preserving the distinct identities of nature and Geist. But the result was the alienation of nature from Geist, and so of man from himself: a *Jenseits,* unachievable by speculative reason, in which reason and
the good remain forever as subjective ideals. Hegel overcomes
this alienation, or claims to do so, in the form of a completely
rational speech, itself made possible by the union of the pagan
and Christian traditions, or the motions of reason and virtue;
and this in turn is brought about through the "mastery" of nature, not by mathematics, but as human history. History is the
developing manifestation of nature as appropriated internally
by human self-consciousness and expressed externally in rationally determined work. But it is also the discovery that the manifestation of nature cannot take place except because of a fundamental unity between nature and self-consciousness. The
development of nature is intelligible because it is rational: nature and Geist are the exterior and interior of the Absolute. The
complete manifestation of the Absolute is then not a reduction
of the one to the other, but the fulfillment of both in their unity.
Man achieves consciousness of the essential structure of the
Absolute, which is at the same time self-consciousness: the activity of achieving self-consciousness is the *Selbstbewegung* of
the Absolute. Hegel reconciles the two motions of reason and
nature in history; he reconciles motion and eternity by conceiving the eternal as circular, hence as complete, and, in a Kantian
sense, as autonomous motion.[67] This eternal, complete, circular motion of the Absolute is logos or dialectic:

> the Idea is itself dialectic [i.e. it differentiates its various
> moments but also reconstitutes them into a unity].

67. *Encyclopädie,* par. 213–15, pp. 187 ff.; *Die Vernunft in der Geschichte,* pp. 180–81.

. . . Insofar as this doubled movement is not temporal, nor in a certain way divided and differentiated—otherwise it would again be merely abstract understanding—it is the eternal viewing of itself in the other; the Concept which has completed itself in its objectivity; the object which in its fitness is essential subjectivity.[68]

Post-Hegelian monism rejects the eternal altogether in favor of pure Selbstbewegung, as differentiation without a principle of reconstitution (Heidegger's "difference as difference"). That is, it accepts Hegel's reconciliation of reason and nature in history but repudiates his reconciliation of history and eternity.[69] The result is in a way a step backward to the Kantian dualism of knowledge and belief. To mention only the most famous examples: Kierkegaard demands a return to the "absurdity" of Christian faith; Marx requires a belief in the coming end of history through the revolution of the proletariat; Nietzsche attempts to overcome or complete nihilism by acceptance of the eternal return; and Heidegger awaits the termination of this "parlous time" by a subsequent revelation from the silent voice of Being. Implicit in post-Hegelian criticism of the western philosophical tradition as the source of dualism, alienation, and despair is a new form of what Hegel might have called the bad infinity: completely discontinuous motion, in which each moment is alienated from the past by the absence of any rational terminus.[70] Hegel himself is frequently blamed for this situation, as one who discredited reason by claiming too much on its behalf. Certainly the historical situation leaves no doubt that, after Hegel, there is a steadily growing disaffection for rational speech in the traditional sense, a disaffection for philosophy that is most dramatically evident in the redefinition of wisdom as the silence of either mathematics or factic existence. Hegel's successors retain his conception of man as radically temporal and his-

68. *Encyclopädie*, par. 214, p. 189.
69. For representative statements by Hegel of the connection between Being and time or motion, *see Phänomenologie*, p. 476; *Encyclopädie*, par. 258, 577.
70. Cf. *Logik*, I, pp. 125 ff.; *Phänomenologie*, p. 535.

torical; they reject his conception of the completeness of time in eternity and history in wisdom.[71] The second stage of the attempted resolution of the duality of nature and Geist fails because it was successful in a way that human beings find unbearable.[72] Hegel claimed to have carried through to completion the Cartesian project to make men gods, but by defining divinity as speculative wisdom rather than as virtue, technics, or merely external work, he made it the genuine possession of the few and therefore unpalatable to the many. This fact has frequently been obscured in our own time by the effort of democratic sympathizers to transform Hegel into John Dewey. Similarly, it has been distorted by those who see him as the father of fascism and a hopeless "reactionary." Suffice it to say here that the many have always disliked philosophy; the new historical phenomenon after Hegel is the acceptance of the tastes of the many by the few, in however esoteric a manner this acceptance might be phrased.

If only the completely rational man can achieve divinity through reason (rather than the inferior status of participating in divinity through the medium of the rational laws and customs of the state), it is easy to understand that the less than completely reasonable man will repudiate reason in favor of some more universally accessible mode of salvation. Hegel's rationalism is incompatible with the moral and political forces of the Enlightenment from which it sprang. The great opposition to Hegel, led by men of genius, is fundamentally moral in its motivation. In Kierkegaard, the moral force has reactionary secular

71. *Phänomenologie*, pp. 527, 531 ff., 546; *Encyclopädie*, par. 566–571; *Logik*, II, p. 484. Perhaps it should be noted that the essential completeness of history as wisdom has nothing to do with the empirical completeness of history. Also, whereas Hegel states his wisdom and so demonstrates the "end" of history, Marx prophesys it. The non-rational character of this prophecy has led to many amusing quarrels among Marxists about the necessity of the triumph of communism.

72. Not even Marx and Kierkegaard, in my opinion, may be said to have refuted Hegel in a systematic and thoroughgoing manner; their rejection is based upon either distaste or misunderstanding, and in terms of fragments of Hegel's thought removed from their context.

implications (usually ignored by his contemporary admirers), whereas in Marx, who is much closer to Hegel, the moral is made progressive by being defined in secular political terms. It is not difficult to see how Kierkegaard's faith comes to be united with Marx's reason, in forms varying from so-called Marxist existentialism to scientific humanism. For Kierkegaard and Marx, in their different ways, are both products of the Judaeo-Christian tradition. The relative triumph of Marx in the contemporary synthesis of the two is a heritage of the Enlightenment, but the synthesis itself is a clear sign of the failure of the Enlightenment. The progressive component in the motion of history seems necessarily to triumph over the rational component. And the necessary step in this triumph is the subordination of reason, now understood as ratio, to the will and imagination. This step is decisively completed in the thought of Nietzsche, the famous anti-Christ and immoralist, who disguises morality as creativity. Having exhausted the spiritual capacities of reason, he believes, man once more girds his loins and attempts to become master and possessor of nature, not by ordering and measuring or by speculatively appropriating it, but by projecting or creating it *ex nihilo*. The happy reveries of the solitary promenader are transformed by the exhausting labors of world history into the painful agonies of the creative genius.

Chapter 4

Historicity and Political Nihilism

I.

It has been suggested in the previous chapters of this study that contemporary philosophy terminates in an obsession with difference qua difference. The two examples which I have given in some detail are Wittgenstein (the grammatical difference) and Heidegger (the ontological difference). The purpose of the third chapter was to give a sketch of the dialectical development of the antecedents common to the characteristic life-forms of contemporary historicism. The culminating figure in the pre-history of contemporary nihilism is Nietzsche, and to this extent one may agree with Heidegger. But Heidegger is mistaken if he believes that his own thought has revealed a radically new stage in the "history" of Being. On the contrary, difference qua difference—in Wittgenstein no less than in Heidegger—manifests itself to the grammarian and to the shepherd of Being as the factic uniqueness of the momentaneity of time. This is precisely the ontological significance of Nietzsche's philosophy, as may perhaps be best seen in his conception of the *Augenblick*.[1] In each instant of the eternal return is contained all of the past and the future. Each instant is thus both same and other, but, as unique, dominated by otherness or difference. How can we see the unique? Is not a unique perspective of a unique moment itself momentary?

This problem might be developed in several different ways. For example, Heidegger himself, in his interpretation of Nietzsche, speaks of overcoming the limitations of perspectivism by

1. Compare Heidegger's own emphasis upon, and interpretation of, the *Augenblick* in his *Nietzsche, 1,* e.g. 431 ff.: *"Die ewige Wiederkehr des Gleichen wird nur gedacht, wenn sie nihilistisch und augenblicklich gedacht wird"* (p. 447); and esp. 465. For the "difference," cf. *Nietzsche, 2,* 207 ff., and *Identität und Differenz,* pp. 42 ff.

the mastery, through a kind of "leap" or revelation, of an essential perspective; namely, one in which man settles into or becomes exemplificative of the Being-process of the eternal return.[2] But this essential perspective, or the articulating of chaos by progressively self-transcending creative transfiguration, is, albeit in human form, the exhibition of chaos, or the fulfillment of nihilism. Not simply is each instant a negation of the "weight" or significance of moments reduced to sameness by virtue of their eternal return, but the instant itself must be negated or rendered invisible. As the sum of all moments, the instant is itself not a moment, not a finite, determinate pattern of finite, determinate events; it is not a perspective or horizon, making vision possible, but the in itself invisible horizonality of horizons. This horizonality of horizons manifests itself uniquely in the uniqueness of each moment of time. Since it is not itself a moment, however, it must be understood as the instant of eternity. The eternal presents itself in and through time, though not as temporal itself. Nietzsche's teaching of the eternal return, designed to overcome the ostensible nihilism of the doctrine of two worlds, in fact asserts that doctrine. To be thinkable or speakable, it cannot manifest a momentary or unique event. On the other hand, its ostensibly thinkable or speakable content is the unthinkably and unspeakably unique, or difference qua difference.

Nietzsche's teaching, precisely as interpreted by Heidegger, is a dualistic revision or disintegration of Hegel's attempt to identify Being as the completely articulated, self-actualized form of Time (which I capitalize to show its identity with Being, what one might call "transcendental time"). Man as creator comes to be identical with the form of Time, and so with eternity; but the form (or eternity), understood as the horizonality of horizons, has no articulation and therefore silences articulateness. This is the ontological consequence of the all too human desire to turn from the excessively arduous pursuit of coherent speech to the immediate security of things or events. In Heidegger, with all his genius, the journey from the beginning of facticity to the end

2. *Nietzsche 1*, 380 ff., 650, and passim.

of the sense of Being as factically manifested is a voyage of nihilism, or much ado about nothing:

> The highest thinking saying rests in this, not simply to
> conceal [*verschweigen:* keep silent] what is authenti-
> cally to be said in that saying, but to say it in such a
> way that it is named in the Not-speaking (*Nichtsagen*):
> the saying of thinking is a silencing (*ein Erschweigen*).
> This saying corresponds likewise to the deepest essence
> of speech, which has its origin in silence.[3]

In short, Nietzsche, like Heidegger (and the less interesting
Wittgenstein), attempts to see not just a unique event or moment, but *uniqueness itself.* According to Heidegger, however,
Nietzsche still suffers from the fatal defect of Platonism, because he attempts to make man correspond to uniqueness itself
(Being understood as chaos), and to articulate it by means of
preexistent categories of the intelligence (a relic of Platonic
Ideas mediated by Kantianism).[4] Nietzsche, therefore, still
reifies or subjectifies Being; in our own terms, he still has something to say about the concrete manifestation of Being in man
and the things of the world. Heidegger, however, aspires to
manifestation without concreteness; he repudiates the "Platonic" apparatus of Ideas, categories, and correspondences by
which beings are projectively viewed in place of Being. The
determinateness or thinghood of the thing is for Heidegger a
product or project of Platonic, subjectivist logos; the presence
of Being in the thing is manifested by its facticity, by its *that*
($\delta\tau\iota$) rather than its *what* ($\tau\iota\ \dot{\epsilon}\sigma\tau\iota\nu$).[5]

The priority of the *that* to the *what* is present in Nietzsche in
an obvious and in a subtle sense. The obvious sense is his rejection of a supersensible or ideal world in favor of a return to the
"earth" or body. The subtle sense is contained in his thesis of

3. Ibid., p. 471. The passage goes on significantly to relate the thinker
to the poet (and also to distinguish them). Cf. *Nietzsche, 2,* 484.
4. *Nietzsche, 1,* 529 ff., 636 ff. Cf. also pp. 575-76, where "Horizont-
bildung" is interpreted as a consequence of Kant's understanding of
Vernunft as essentially practical.
5. Cf. *Nietzsche, 2,* 14 ff. and esp. 403 ff.

the will to power. Traditionally, as for example in Plato and Aristotle, power is defined in terms of an actuality—an activity, goal, or end. According to Nietzsche, these are values, or themselves manifestations of the will to power. The world (represented by the earth or body) is altogether the will to power; as a consequence, power cannot be said to manifest itself *for* an end outside of itself. The temporary and perspectival nature of values reduces them to the status of facts, with respect to the world-process as a whole. The values are devalued; the world is what it is—purposeless play. More accurately, it is not *what* it is (since to say what the world is would entail being outside or beyond the world), but *that* it is; even the metaphor of the world as play or an art work must be understood as a poetic attempt to give voice to the radically unspeakable. Nietzsche and Heidegger agree, then, that the world is more radically possibility than actuality, and so that it is radically temporal, or a continuous presentation of the future within a present empty of its own stable content. They also agree, although less clearly so, on the essential meaning of the will to power. In principle, what Nietzsche means by "will" is what Heidegger means by such terms as "gift," "fate," and "order": the self-presentation of the world as a (temporal) process of possibilities. Perhaps the most obvious difference between the two is over the eternal return, Nietzsche's decayed version of Hegel's conception of the circularity of Being as transcendental Time. On this point, Heidegger seems to be more consistent; if possibility is prior to actuality, then the epochs of history not merely are discontinuous but *need not recur*. Because he recognizes this, namely, that only a ground external to possibility, and hence a stable actuality, could necessitate the actualization of possibility, Heidegger is a much more thoroughgoing nihilist than Nietzsche.

The absence of eternity in any form whatsoever makes the presence of Heidegger's Being a pure possibility.[6] It is therefore represented or symbolized by primordial silence and requires a

6. A similar difficulty, based upon a preference for possibility, seems to be present in Husserl. Cf. the passage from *Ideen* I (p. 194), cited in A. Diemer, *Edmund Husserl* (2d ed. Meisenheim am Glan, Verlag Anton Hain, 1965), p. 108.

correspondingly silent (i.e. nondistorting) saying, as opposed to the correspondence-speech of Platonic metaphysics. Heidegger's more fundamental comprehension of the inner consequences of Nietzsche's thought has thus led him to the effort, not merely of saying the unsayable, but of letting it say itself.[7] Some of Heidegger's most acute critics (especially Karl Löwith) have pointed to the emptiness of his ostensibly positive formulations. We must, however, be careful to observe that this "emptiness" is an intrinsic element in Heidegger's teaching, not an element peculiar to his later writings. In his effort to bring the unsayable to speech, Heidegger devoted himself in a consistent if evolving way to the project of emptying language of its traditional, thing-oriented content, or to the "destruction of western metaphysics." He attempted to redefine the western conception of Being as "presence" in such a way as to turn attention from speech corresponding to presence, to presence itself. Since this presence is possibility, its significance is located in the future. The presented present has, as it were, no stable presence, nothing which speech could attribute or disclose. Instead, the attempt to attribute ($\kappa\alpha\tau\eta\gamma\rho\rho\epsilon\hat{\iota}\nu$) stable properties to *what* is presented serves to conceal or distort it, to replace the possibility of being present by an ontic actuality.[8] The actuality of a thing (*res*), its reality (thinghood), is traditionally identified with its form—its "look," or, as Heidegger interprets this, how it looks to man. Since the *what* is subjective and ontic, because formal or actual, the *that* or facticity is ontologically prior and higher: hence the link between the priority of facticity and the more exalted status of possibility.

Possibility is higher than actuality in the same sense that silence is the source of speech. The Being-process, or pure differ-

7. "Since ever-questioning Dasein only encounters the silence of the gods, since the world only reflects the questioner's vacant stare, since Being gives no answers but only is, i.e. endures and abides, man too has to endure in the face of such ultimate, un-grounded silence." L. Versényi, *Heidegger, Being, and Truth* (New Haven, Yale University Press, 1966), pp. 154–55.

8. Among the many passages that might be cited, I limit myself to these: *Nietzsche, 1,* 344, 393, 410, 640; *2,* 72 ff., 486, and passim.

entiation, is higher (more powerful) than any of the elements of that process of differentiation. So too Heidegger's exaltation of creativity, or rather the creative power, as higher than the products of that power: the creative process is the human exemplification of the Being-process.[9] The link with Nietzsche here is the will to power, which manifests itself in man as the projective creation of a world-horizon or, in Heidegger's terms, as the disclosure of truth, as the power of opening—as the founding of horizonality. And the *that* of disclosure is higher than *what* is disclosed. Here we may perceive Heidegger's characteristic modernity or directedness toward human work, creativity, and hence the future. Heidegger, however, maintains that the activity of creation or disclosure, man's work or being-at-work (ἐνέργεια), is not actuality but possibility. Like Aristotle, Heidegger holds that Being is "working" but, unlike Aristotle, that "working" does not achieve fulfillment (ἐντελέχεια) in a determinate form. Every determinate formation of man's psyche or creativity is a deformation of his existence in the deepest sense—a limitation, and hence an obscuring, of the Being-process by one of its emanations.[10] This is the ontological significance of Nietzsche's remark that the world is an art work continuously giving birth to itself, as well as of his emphasis upon play.[11] Whether in Aristotle or in Hegel, man's work is directed toward, and fulfilled in, an end. In Nietzsche and Heidegger, work is its own end, and therefore endless (in the classical sense, formless), or a kind of hyperserious playing—in Nietzsche's phrase, *incipit tragoedia.*

The eminence of possibility, creation, or play-work as the exemplification of the Being-process has two consequences, or rather one consequence taking two forms, which generally correspond to the early and late teaching of Heidegger. The first is the conception of authentic existence, in which Dasein, reso-

---

9. In addition to the discussion in the *Nietzsche* volumes, see *Der Ursprung des Kunstwerkes,* intro. by H. G. Gadamer (Stuttgart, Reclam, 1960) and *Vorträge und Aufsätze.*

10. Cf. *Nietzsche, 2,* 117.

11. *Der Wille zur Macht,* par. 794 ff.

lutely accepting its own death, silently faces up to the silent call of conscience by choosing or founding a project, expressive of its own integrity, from among the possibilities of its situation. This act of founding is not an actualizing, but a self-definition in terms of a horizon of openness. That is, the "form" of life is not a positive, formal determination, but the ultimate negation of death. Further, death may come at any time; it is a permanent possibility of the human situation, which accordingly changes from time to time, indeed, from moment to moment. In order to be free for authentic choice, man must be free from formal determinations, which prevent him from "realizing his possibilities," as we often say. These possibilities are never fully "realized" until death; so long as we live, we are in the process of disclosing not what we are, but what we will be, or after our death, what we were. In life, it is not the present, but the future, the source of possibility, that predominates.[12] For these reasons it would be a contradiction in terms if Heidegger were to give a positive, "doctrinal" content to his analysis of the existential process of authenticity.[13] Heidegger's silence in this repect is consistent, but it also reveals the necessarily nihilistic implications of his thought. Put bluntly, no one can say anything to anyone about what constitutes genuine choice in a specific situation. It therefore becomes impossible to prevent total suspension of judgment. The Christian may say, "judge not, lest ye be judged," because of the eternal presence of an eternal judge. But the Heideggerian becomes indistinguishable from the nihilist, who says that "everything is allowed," because part of the Christian doctrine has been wedded to a resolute self-reliance in the absence of all gods. Heidegger radicalizes the absence of all gods into a denial of the presence of the eternal; as a result, the

12. Cf. Hans Jonas, "Gnosticism, Existentialism, and Nihilism," in *The Phenomenon of Life* (New York, Harper and Row, 1966), pp. 230 ff.: "the same cause which is at the root of nihilism is also at the root of the radical temporality of Heidegger's scheme of existence, in which the present is nothing but the moment of crisis between past and future."

13. Cf. Heidegger's remarks as to why Nietzsche could not define the *Übermensch* more fully: *Nietzsche, 2,* 125–26.

present has no enduring status in his thoroughly temporalized Being-process.

The second form of the consequence referred to above is the search for an ontologically adequate speech, one which avoids ontic de-formation in fidelity to the silence of Being, whether understood as absent or present. This consequence is unusually difficult to express; it is equivalent to the extraordinary difficulty of Heidegger's most "authentic" later writings. Once again put bluntly, in the deepest sense, Heidegger has no doctrine, no philosophical position, no positive teaching. As he himself always emphasized, and as the title of his last book explicitly asserts, his thought has been from the beginning "on the way toward speech." There is no need to repeat the argument of Chapter 2: the way toward speech, although tangentially illuminating, has led to, and in a sense always been within, the heart of darkness. In more concrete terms, Heidegger began his journey as a student of Christian theology and Aristotle's metaphysics.[14] His response to the nihilism of post-Nietzschean Europe, and specifically to the political situation following the First World War, led him to a reinterpretation of Nietzsche. Heidegger radicalized the significance of Zarathustra's revelation that "God is dead," making use of elements from Christianity, Greek philosophy, German thought, and the spiritual despair of the decades culminating in the Nazi rise to power. His intention was to overcome European nihilism by setting the stage for a new understanding of "the question of Being." In my opinion, it is clear that the development of an ontology of historicity was conditioned by Heidegger's response to the political and social events of 1919 and thereafter. What began as the attempt to overcome nihilism was transformed into a profound

14. The best study of Heidegger's development known to me is Otto Pöggeler's *Heidegger* (Pfullingen, G. Neske Verlag, 1963). For the influence of Christianity on Heidegger, the writings of Löwith and Jonas are essential. See also W. J. Richardson, S.J., "Heidegger and God —and Professor Jonas," in *Thought* (Spring 1965), 13–40, and Karl Lehmann, "Christliche Geschichtserfahrung und ontologische Frage beim jungen Heidegger," in *Philosophisches Jahrbuch,* 74. Jahrgang, 1, Halbband (Munich, 1966), 126–53.

resignation in the face of nihilism. Our task in this chapter is to understand the essence of that attempt and its inevitable failure. This means that the results of Chapter 2 must be dialectically combined with the results of Chapter 3.

II.

In the previous chapter, I discussed the development of the modern world in terms of two key conceptions—mathematics and history. Speaking very generally, the first corresponds to the early modern revision of pagan philosophy, and the second to the revision of the Judaeo-Christian religion. But this general correspondence is immediately subject to a crucial qualification. The revisions in question, although they begin from the distinction between nature and spirit, understood in the light of the distinction between body and soul, in effect place both dimensions within the power of man. As an example, one may recall the difference between the Averroistic tradition of religious skepticism in the pre-modern period and the development of modern scriptural hermeneutics and critique of religion during the Enlightenment.[15] The modern criticism of revealed religion is grounded not simply in the new mathematical physics, but in the growth of the empirical study of man and his history. Both nature and spirit are subject to human reason and therefore to human will. As a consequence, the religious reformation of the sixteenth and seventeenth centuries is inseparable from a political reformation. Regardless of the necessary accommodations to Christian authorities that continue to be made during this period, it is obvious that spirit has been brought within the domain of nature. At the same time, however, thanks to the emphasis upon practice, experience, or human power in the continuing revision of the classical conception of reason, one must also say that nature has been brought into the domain of spirit. This union of nature and spirit culminates in the German philosophies of history. The religio-political reformation of the

15. See Leo Strauss, *Spinoza's Critique of Religion* (New York, Schocken, 1965).

preceding centuries, understood as a project of secular human reason and will, is now assimilated into the revelation of divine reason in the unfolding of natural and spiritual history.

German philosophy from Kant to Hegel may be characterized as the attempt to combine Greek thought and Christian practice in the form of the philosophy of history. The same general formula accurately describes the teaching of Feuerbach and Marx, provided we remember that the elements of the formula receive a somewhat different definition than in the previous instance. Specifically, the atheistic implications of the earlier teachings are now made explicit and central; man is no longer defined as subject to a transcendental moral law, nor as absolute ego or Geist. Instead, he is understood as the creator of God and the potentially free master of nature and history through creative work in accordance with the laws of nature and history. If we combine these essential philosophic principles of Marx and Feuerbach and conceive of the laws of nature and history as human creations or projects, the result is surprisingly Nietzschean. The articulation of these principles takes Feuerbach and Marx in a different direction than Nietzsche, to say nothing of the differences between themselves. But it is important to emphasize the inner harmony in the great diversity of nineteenth-century post-Hegelian philosophy: the harmony derived from acceptance of Hegel's analysis of man as radically historical and rejection of Hegel's doctrine of transcendental Time or History.[16] Post-Hegelian philosophy from Kierkegaard, Feuerbach, and Marx to Nietzsche and Heidegger is for the most part the story of the development of an ontology of radical and immanent historicity.[17] With Nietzsche, however,

16. The best discussion of this is contained in Karl Löwith, *Von Hegel zu Nietzsche,* now available in English: *From Hegel to Nietzsche,* tr. David E. Green (New York, Doubleday, 1964).

17. Even in the case of Husserl, one sees a steadily increasing emphasis upon temporality and historicity, present from the first in his doctrine of subjectivity and culminating in his conception of the *Lebenswelt.* Thus, speaking of "The Last Work of Edmund Husserl" (*Philosophy and Phenomenological Research, 16* [1955], 380–99), Aron Gurwitsch refers to "the essential *inner historicity* of the philosopher" (p.

the aforementioned combination of Greek thought and Christian practice needs to be restated; one could almost say that it is replaced by a combination of Greek practice and Christian thought.

Despite his admiration for Heraclitus, Nietzsche's debt to the Greeks is less theoretical than practical. What he praises among the ancients are their aristocratic "values": the intoxication of Dionysus united to the sobriety of Thucydides.[18] As we have already seen, the fundamental characteristic of Nietzsche's theoretical teaching is his transformation of the primacy of will and imagination into onto-poetic historicism. Among other things, this means that, whereas for his predecessors at least as far back as Kant, politics is subordinated to history, for Nietzsche, politics is subordinated to art. In the deepest and most comprehensive possible sense, Nietzsche agrees that poets are the legislators of society. He begins, we recall, from the premise that order is a human creation. The series of fundamental creations, or the projections of fundamental world views, is history. Differently stated, the historical cycle of man-made, world-defining perspectives is the human expression of the essential nature of the Being-process (Becoming)—the will to power. When a given world-perspective loses its capacity for self-concentration and self-transcendence, or what Nietzsche calls "life-enhancement," when its creative force is spent, the result is decadence. In the nineteenth century, European civilization is engaged in the death throes of a decadence characterized spe-

---

384). Cf. Tran Duc Thao, *Phénoménologie et matérialisme dialectique* (Paris, Éditions Minh-Tan, 1951), pp. 7, 96–97, 106 and passim. Hans Wagner, "Kritische Betrachtungen zu Husserls Nachlass," in *Philosophische Rundschau* (1953/54, Heft 2/3), 96. L. Landgrebe, "Husserls Abschied vom Cartesianismus," in *Philosophische Rundschau* (Jan. 1962), 155–57.

18. "Was Ich den Alten Verdanken," *Götzen-Dämmerung,* par. 2–4. Nietzsche points out that he owes more to the Romans than to the Greeks, no doubt for essentially the same reason that he preferred the biblical Jews (war plus poetry) to the Christians. Nietzsche's attitude toward the Greeks is not dissimilar from that of Machiavelli, whom he also mentions with approval.

cifically by the sickness of historicism. Modern Europeans have realized that world-perspectives are man-made, or transient and subjective. They have tried to overcome this realization either by the narcotic of belief in progress or through the effort to achieve a neutral, universal, scientific perspective in which all historical world views are contemplated and submitted to comparative, objective study. Both remedies, however, are equally sterile; both lead away from creativity, intensified personal experience, and the aristocratic respect for the noble or exalted. In principle, the democratic and socialistic tendencies of modern bourgeois society lead to precisely the same destruction of rank, hence to the depreciation of creativity or power, as does the objective rationalism of modern science and the cultivation of a learned historical relativism. Modern Europeans have lost or are losing their physiological instinct for life, their belief in the meaningfulness of life: they have betrayed the creative and vital origins, the earth and the body. Where everything is equal (as happens when mathematical physics is the paradigm for physiology), or when all perspectives are objective and "value-free," then everything is of equal worth; more accurately, nothing has any worth. In the famous formula, everything is permitted, and the result is nihilism.

Nietzsche's response to this situation is not to seek narcotics in a return to the past or a flight to the supersensible, but instead to assert, and in a deeper form to accept, even to accelerate, the approach of nihilism on a European, if not global, scale. A rejuvenation of the human spirit is possible only through a complete destruction of the decadent present, which in turn is merely the last moment of western history since Plato and Christ. Nietzsche's road to health lies through an intensification of the European malady of historicism. The destruction of Europe is thus simultaneously an effort to hasten the convalescence of the European spirit.[19] More explicitly than Des-

19. This attitude is also characteristic of the nineteenth-century socialist thinkers. For a formulation from the socialist camp which comes unusually close to Nietzsche, see Alexander Herzen, *From the Other Shore* (Cleveland, World, 1963), e.g. pp. 3, 10, 54, 58–59, 128.

cartes, Nietzsche advocates that we tear down the dwellings which constrict and distort man's spirit; but whereas for Descartes the instrument of liberation is physics, for Nietzsche it is poetry or creativity. Physics and history make awkward partners in the struggle for human self-transcendence and superhuman mastery; the language of physics tends to stifle the language of history, and so to de- or subhumanize man. Once physics is recognized as a dialect of poetry, the proper language of man the historical animal, the situation seems to change decisively. Whereas the physicist, as his name reminds us, is bound by the properties and "laws" of nature, the poet is free to create his own laws, or to transform nature into history. As is most evident in the etymologizing of Heidegger, nature is transformed into a poem.[20]

Nietzsche's historicist ontology therefore takes practical shape as poeticist politics. The facticity or fatality of the eternal return is ignored on behalf of an injunction to destroy as the necessary prelude to creation. Like very few before him, Nietzsche sees the necessary link between radical creativity, on the one hand, and war, courage, and brutality, on the other.[21] The great creators abominate everything that interferes with the full expression of their will to power; they are not egalitarians, democrats, or refined and tolerant appreciators of the poems of their competitors. Nietzsche's transition from praise for societies which combine martial and creative vigor to an invocation of the blonde beast and continent-wide bloodletting is a terrifyingly lucid expression of his poeticist politics. The bestiality of the blonde beast may be understood not simply as an expression of the need to destroy in order to create, but as a consequence

20. I refer to Heidegger's etymologies of $\tau\epsilon\chi\nu\eta$ and $\pi o i\eta\sigma\iota s$ as originally the same as $\phi\upsilon\sigma\iota s$ and $\dot{\alpha}\lambda\dot{\eta}\theta\epsilon\iota\alpha$.

21. For a discussion of this theme in Plato, see my *Plato's Symposium* (New Haven, Yale University Press, 1968), especially Chapter 6. Julien Benda sees very clearly the new exalted rank given to courage by Nietzsche and his successors, as well as the connection between the praise of art and the preference of action to contemplation: *The Betrayal of the Intellectuals* (*La Trahison des clercs*), tr. R. Aldington (Boston, Beacon Press, 1955), pp. 107, 119.

of Nietzsche's fundamental identification of Being and history. This identification makes possible the exalted status given by Nietzsche to art or creativity. History is the dissolution of Being into chaos, as reorganized by the shifting perspectives of man, the highest incarnation of the will to power. Creation or perspectival projection, however, is dependent upon freedom from servitude to previous historical manifestations of the will to power. The cruelty of pre-creative destruction and of creative sustaining vigor is the human form taken by what one may call the necessary ontological forgetfulness of radically historical beings.

This point is identical with Nietzsche's definition of the positive and negative aspects of nihilism in terms of man's attitude toward history. The perception of historicity is the necessary condition for liberation from static Being in the Greek and Christian sense, for freedom from the will of God and the restrictive rational order of supersensible form. On the other hand, this perception may also lead to world-weariness, relativism, or sterility, to say nothing of dread and nausea, and not to creative exhilaration. If all civilizations are historical creatures, and history is just the perpetual recurrence of similars, a cosmic play with no author and no audience; if worth stems from man, who in turn stems from genesis and decay; if the world, even though it endure forever in time, is surrounded by and grounded in nothingness, then knowledge of historicity must lead inevitably to a sapping of strength, a loss of faith in the superhuman status of the superman. Enlightenment, or what Nietzsche calls *amor fati,* would seem to be tantamount to the greatest obscuration. If civilizations are great and creative only through complete self-absorption and self-confidence, whereas historical enlightenment brings superficial "objectivity" toward one's own, or excessive tolerance toward all other, civilizations and ages; if knowledge is knowledge of history, whereas creativity is not knowledge but spontaneous passion, desire, and intoxication, should we not prefer ignorance to enlightenment?

What Nietzsche means by "the death of God" is then not merely the decadence of western Christian civilization, but the opening of an abyss: the self-presentation of chaos as a disjunction in history, within which man is given the opportunity to renew his creative strength by a rebirth which is also a destruction of his past. To be reborn means to recur to the level of the beasts through *the loss of one's memory*. There is, of course, an ambiguity here; one might be inclined to say that, in being reborn, man becomes an infant rather than a beast. In neither case, however, is he a superman; at best, he is condemned to relive the past rather than to transcend it. At worst, he may be said to have escaped history for the despiritualized eternity of a perpetual present. To become a superman, man must remember the lesson of the enslaving character of the past, which is to say that he must will both to remember and to forget it. The defect of a doctrine of radically historicist creation is that, in the absence of a creator God, creation ex nihilo is unintelligible. In the language of the previous section of this chapter, there is no reason for pure possibility to become actual. The line of distinction between the infant and the beast is drawn by the memory, which overcomes temporality and is not explicable in purely temporal terms. This is the only way in which one can render intelligible Nietzsche's image of man as paradox, a tightrope walker who is also the rope upon which he crosses the abyss. The same point may be put in another way. For Nietzsche, history is both the cause and the cure of nihilism. The past may be dissolved because it *is* dissolving; the future may be created because dissolution leaves room for reformation. We may run the risk of lethargy from the recognition that our future creations are also doomed to dissolution. But this lethargy, according to Nietzsche, will evaporate if we immerse ourselves in the intoxication of creativity and the supreme sobriety of the recognition of the eternal return. However, there is a synthesis of opposites here that takes us beyond Nietzsche's own formulation of his teaching. Godhood entails both creativity and eternity, but these two characteristics depend upon separate attributes. The exhortation to intoxication and sobriety is identical with an exhortation to forget and to remember.

Simply to remember would lead to perpetual old age and

sterility; simply to forget would lead to perpetual infancy or bestiality. Nietzsche's ontological historicism makes nonsense of his onto-poeticism. Remembering and forgetting can be for him only the tokens of coming to be and passing away. Nietzsche's man, like his cosmos, is a continuous discontinuity, unthinkable and unspeakable. The eternal return is not a complete speech or completely rational account, but a cycle of poems, each of which is ultimately silent about itself. Hence speech about the eternal return is itself a poem, or a kind of silence, which does not express or preserve the contradiction between the exemplification and the transcendence of nihilism but is annihilated by it. The practical consequence of an invocation to creative destruction, which is, for all its praise of nobility and beauty, silent on the basis for distinguishing between truth and error, is bestial violence. Historicity, or pure possibility, is nothingness. It is therefore less than impotent in the face of the dualism of history, which is sterility as well as creativity. On the basis of Nietzsche's ontology, history lacks any capacity to prevent universal application of the novelties it generates; and this, as Nietzsche himself warned, leads to their trivialization. Again, history is remembering and forgetting, but with no control over what is remembered and what forgotten, unless we agree that the vulgar is more likely to be remembered than the noble, and the noble more likely to be debased than the base ennobled.

III.

The modern age begins with the definition of knowledge as power; it terminates with Nietzsche's conception of the will to power. Knowledge is replaced by, or reinterpreted as a species of, poetry. The political meaning of this evolution from the sovereignty of reason to that of the will and imagination is evident from a comparison of the political philosophies of the seventeenth century and the poeticist politics of Nietzsche. One lesson we must draw from such a comparison is the degree to which Nietzsche's fundamental principles are already present in philosophers like Machiavelli, Descartes, Bacon, and Hobbes.

The crux of the matter is not one's attitude toward science and technology, and certainly not whether one is a "liberal" or "conservative" in the debased and largely mindless sense in which these terms are used today. Instead, it is our conception of reason, and specifically of the connection between reason and the good. Those who define the good as the powerful, whether they be positivists or existentialists, at once deprive themselves of the capacity to distinguish between good and evil, and so they cannot speak rationally of the goodness of reason. On this absolutely fundamental point, it is irrelevant whether one employs the language of mathematics or of history. Logical calculi and linguistic frameworks, as projects of a reason instrumental to man's "creativity," are simply unedifying poems. The net result of a reliance upon unedifying poetry, however, is to accelerate the turn to edifying poetry. The stolidity of epistemologists is easily transformed into the resoluteness of authentic individuals.

When the pride of the scientific revolutionary is diluted by time, the result is sadness and, finally, anxiety and nausea. These are the last emotions of a decadent enlightenment. This was already evident to Pascal, who described the natural life, lost between the infinities of outer space and inner divisibility, as "an eternal despair" and anticipated contemporary existence in his famous lament, "the eternal silence of these infinite spaces frightens me." [22] Pascal's conception of the natural life, of course, is that of the Christian; he refers by that phrase to the life of reason as distinct from the life of grace, and by "reason" he understands essentially the mathematical ratio of Descartes. This union of mathematics and Christianity leads to a conventionalist understanding of human nature, that is, as a creation of God or history:

> What are our natural principles, if not principles to which we have been accustomed? . . . Custom is a second nature, which destroys the first. But what is na-

22. *Pensées,* "La Place de l'Homme dans la Nature," nos. 84, 91, in *Oeuvres complètes,* ed. J. Chevalier (Paris, NRF, 1954), pp. 1107, 1113.

ture? Why is custom not natural? I am greatly afraid
that this nature may itself be nothing but a first custom,
as custom is a second nature.[23]

Pascal offers the joy of grace as a more secure alternative to the
pride of the philosopher (and scientist), which he rightly
anticipates will not endure. By the nineteenth century, the
possibility of happiness for Christian and pagan alike seems
to have evaporated into the silence of infinity. Of course, we
continue to find predictions of a happy future, but at the end of
history, whether in heaven or on earth. Schelling's account of
the sadness of finite existence, reminiscent of Pascal, may be
cited as a fair example of the pervasive mood of the time:
"hence the veil of melancholy that is stretched out over all of
nature, the deep, indestructible melancholy of all life." [24] From
the melancholia of Schelling and the boredom of Leopardi, it is
a short road to Kierkegaard, who characterizes finite existence,
both in its innocent and sinning stages, as attuned by dread.[25]

Let these examples suffice. From Pascal to Kierkegaard, one
finds a more or less Christian insistence upon the sadness of natural life, in which the normal Christian motives are stimulated
by the extraordinary threat of modern scientific rationalism. Unlike the rationalism of pagan philosophy, the modern version
implicitly rejects popular religion as a political force and aspires
to godhood or mastery of nature for man. At the same time,
however, this aspiration to godhood entails a revised conception
of nature which, entirely apart from its technical attributes, is
theoretically close to the Christian conception. The dialectical
interaction of these two conceptions, as we have seen, results in

23. Ibid., "Misère de l'homme," nos. 119–20, p. 1121.
24. "Philosophische Untersuchungen über das Wesen der menschlichen
Freiheit" (1809), in *Werke,* ed. M. Schröter, *Vierter Hauptband* (Munich, C. H. Beck and R. Oldenbourg, 1927), p. 291. "Die Angst des
Lebens" drives man out of union with God into finite existence, where
sin and death destroy his individuality and return him to union with the
Absolute (p. 273). It is interesting to note that Heidegger praises this
essay on several occasions (e.g. in *Nietzsche, 1*).
25. *The Concept of Dread* (Princeton, Princeton University Press,
1944), pp. 49, 51.

the philosophy of history. It also accounts for the Christian atmosphere of Marxism, of Nietzsche's attack on Christianity, and of
Heidegger's philosophy of radical finitude. In the nineteenth
century, one sees with great clarity the degree to which Christianity and scientific rationalism, whether as opponents or as
allies, have destroyed each other's vigor and purity.[26] This is of
course not to deny their continuing dominance over European
man, but to try to understand why that influence has taken on
the forms of nihilism. The spiritual power of Christianity is
brutalized by its transformation into secular terms; the dynamo
(to use Henry Adams' image) replaces God as the expression
of human transcendence. But this same transference of psychic
energy, the culmination of processes begun two or three centuries earlier, gives a spiritual, even religious, aura to the secular power of history, the state, and the interactions of political
and technological flux.

It would be superfluous to give a résumé here of the extraordinary combination of spirit and bestiality which brought about
the final transition from nineteenth- to twentieth-century Europe. I shall merely refer to an essay by Paul Valéry, written in
1919, in which he discusses the contemporary situation as a
"Crisis of Spirit" and shows how the virtues of Europe have led
to her present debasement:

> the active avidity, ardent and disinterested curiosity, a
> fortunate mixture of the imagination and logical rigor, a

26. "I have no desire to speak in strong terms about this age as a
whole, but he who has observed the contemporary generation will surely
not deny that the incongruity in it and the reason for its dread and rest-
lessness is this, that in one direction truth increases in extent, in mass,
partly also in abstract clarity, whereas certitude steadily decreases"
(Kierkegaard, ibid., p. 124). With this, compare the following passage
from Max Stirner: "The web of the hypocrisy of today hangs on the
frontiers of two domains, between which our time swings back and forth,
attaching its fine threads of deception and self-deception. No longer vig-
orous enough to serve *morality* without doubt or weakening, not yet
reckless enough to live wholly to egoism, it trembles now toward the one
and now toward the other in the spider-web of hypocrisy, and, crippled
by the curse of *halfness,* catches only miserable, stupid flies" (*The Ego
and His Own,* tr. S. Byington [New York, Modern library, 1963], p. 55).

certain non-pessimistic skepticism, an unresigned mysticism . . . are the most specifically active characteristics of the European psyche.[27]

Valéry symbolizes the consequences by personifying the European intellect as Hamlet, whom one may describe in turn as a kind of Parisian Nietzsche, contemplating the skulls of Leonardo, Leibniz, Kant, *"who generated Hegel, who generated Marx, who generated . . ."* [28] Neither Valéry nor his Hamlet speak of Christianity; the sadness of existence is now taken for granted as the dialectical result of man's historical energy:

> and from what was this disorder of our intellectual Europe produced?—From the free coexistence in all cultivated spirits of the most dissimilar ideas, of the most opposed principles of life and knowledge. It is this that characterizes a *modern* epoch.[29]

And finally:

> the phenomenon of the subjection of the planet to exploitation, the phenomenon of the equalization of techniques and the democratic phenomenon, which make us foresee a *deminutio capitis* of Europe: must they be taken as absolute decisions of destiny? Or have we some freedom against this menacing conspiracy of things? [30]

Valéry, despite—or rather because of—his manifest pessimism with respect to these questions, continued to speak as a culti-

27. "La Crise de l'esprit," in *Oeuvres,* ed. Jean Hytier (Paris, NRF, 1957), *1,* 996.

28. Ibid., p. 993. Valéry's "Nietzscheanism" is evident from his admission that the intellect is an idol (in the Baconian sense) but the best one he has found (p. 994), and that the point of view of intelligence is false in its separation from other human activities, but that "tout point de vue est faux" (p. 995).

29. Ibid., pp. 991–92; this thought too is quite Nietzschean. Cf. pp. 997 ff., where he illustrates the dialectical transformation of man's progress into decadence in terms of the transformation of geometry from a pure "activité artistique" into a scientific and materialistic force.

30. Ibid., p. 1000.

vated European of aristocratic spiritual tastes. But the spiritual enervation of the cultivated European is obvious from his own formulations. In thirteen years, Valéry's Hamlet is himself a skull, replaced as a symbol of the past by "the worker," Ernst Jünger's symbol of the rapidly approaching future.

Jünger provides us with an illuminating transition from the Nietzschean heritage of Valéry to that of Heidegger. Although *The Worker* was published five years after *Being and Time,* it embodies a more immediate and more universal portrait of the anti-rationalism of post-Nietzschean Europe. Heidegger's "authentic individual" is at bottom very close to Rousseau's "solitary promenader," reconstituted in terms borrowed equally from Kierkegaard and contemporary intellectual despair, not to say self-laceration against the works of intelligence. His existential rebellion against contemporary European decadence, although emphasizing action over contemplation, dynamism over action, and the resoluteness of choice over the content or goal chosen, is still meant to exhibit an affirmation of the genuine European tradition of the concern for Being. Although the manner of this affirmation had the deeper significance of a negation of European "intelligence," the Heidegger of *Being and Time* is nevertheless closer to the intellectual Valéry than is the author of *The Worker.* Heidegger's descent from Nietzsche was mediated by the study of Aristotle and Christian theology; Jünger's immediate impetus was his experience as a soldier and the study of Sorel and Spengler.[31] The "worker," as a Gestalt of the contemporary spirit, is an explicit affirmation not of anguished and solitary resolution, but of war, technics, and "total mobilization." Jünger seeks an authentically German conception of freedom not in the principles of the Enlightenment, but in "German" responsibility and "German" order.[32] The dynamo of Henry Adams [33] is linked to the political disintegration of

31. Hans-Peter Schwarz, *Der konservative Anarchist: Politik und Zeitkritik Ernst Jüngers* (Freiburg, Rombach, 1962), pp. 41, 69, 91 ff.

32. *Der Arbeiter,* in *Werke* (Stuttgart, Ernst Klett; orig. pub. 1932), Band VI, pp. 19–23.

33. Cf. ibid., p. 42: the heroic realism of our age is symbolized by the motor; p. 232: "Die Aufgabe der totalen Mobilmachung ist die Ver-

postwar European politics, and its vibrations assume a Teutonic hum of metaphysics, historicism, nationalism, and a love of violence.

Jünger attacks the bourgeois order, the civilian, the spiritual values of the Enlightenment, all of which lead to romanticism and nihilism because they are rooted in the Ideas, concepts, and appearances of reason (*Vernunft*) and sensibility (*Empfindsamkeit*), and not in the form of the age.[34] This Gestalt is the expression of "fundamental forces," of the deepest German force, symbolized by the best Germans, the soldiers of the trenches in World War I. It is the knowledge not of rationalism and its concomitant bourgeois desire for security, but of how to fight and die.[35] Unlike the romantic nihilism of European utopian rationalism, the genuine demand of the elemental form of the age is for the here and now, for transition from protest to action, from security to danger, from reason to the will to power: "In the great vicinity of death, blood and earth, the spirit assumes harder features and deeper colors." Hence one must experience that point within destruction at which freedom becomes perceptible. To do this, one must share in the deepest seeds of the time—fate and freedom. One must be the bearer of historical might and grasp one's responsibility by a union in the elemental violence of the here and now: "Here anarchy is the touchstone of the indestructible, that tests itself with pleasure against annihilation." [36] One must be a worker; that is, not a member of a given class, and not an economic factor, but an instance of a new, ruling, and total historical form, possessor of every great contemporary manifestation of the will to power.[37]

A historical Gestalt in Jünger's sense is presented within human existence at once and as a whole; it is not the sum of a process, and historical development "is not the history of the

---

wandlung des Lebens in Energie, wie sie sich in Wirtschaft, Technik, und Verkehr im Schwirren der Räder oder auf dem Schlachtfelde als Feuer und Bewegung offenbart."

34. Ibid., pp. 39, 43, 51–52, 62, and passim.
35. Ibid., pp. 43, 45, 53–54, 56.
36. Ibid., pp. 62–66.
37. Ibid., pp. 74, 79.

form, but at best its dynamic commentary." [38] One may perhaps call this a mystical, vitalized revision of a Platonic Idea,
transformed from the domain of reason to that of the will, from
"heaven" to the "earth" (if not to hell). As such, it is beyond
the reach even of the rationalism of philosophies of history; and
further, it is "beyond values; it possesses no quality." [39] This
dynamic emptiness, so similar to the ontological identification
of empty temporal flow as Being, permits Jünger to unite his
conception of form with his desire to annihilate the rationalist,
bourgeois, romanticist content of modern European civilization:

> one must here pass beyond a point to where nothingness
> (*das Nichts*) looks more desirable than anything in
> which the least possibility of doubt dwells. Here one
> knocks up against a community of more primitive souls,
> an ur-race, which has not yet emerged as the subject of
> a historical task, and is thus free for new mandates.[40]

In his return to the ur-race, which dwells in death, blood, and
the earth, the worker purifies himself of the thing-oriented civilization of reason and sensibility, of its values, its impotent longings for future justice, and so too of the sadness of the aristocratic aesthete and intellectual. The unhappy consciousness of
the Enlightenment, still audible in Valéry's detached and ele-
gant cadences, has been transformed into the clangor of the
"storm of steel." Resolution, mastery, command, obedience,
order; will, blood, death, annihilation: these are the modalities
of total mobilization, of the global unification of every type of
power, technical, social, metaphysical—and for what? [41]

Jünger's nationalism, his enthusiasm for the German folk and
race, his imperialism, must not be confused with a specific and
articulate political program. Fundamental to his conception of
the worker is a Nietzschean dedication to the purification of

38. Ibid., p. 89.
39. Ibid., p. 90.
40. Ibid., p. 91.
41. Ibid., p. 233.

reason by will, of spirit by blood, in the service not of ends, but of the process of "life-enhancing" self-transcendence. This process is described as "form" rather than as determinate content, and as "completeness" rather than as change. But the complete form is one of pure possibility, in short, of the will to power understood as the will to will, to borrow a phrase from Heidegger. It is a product of a soldier–aesthete's hatred for the weakness, inconclusiveness, and self-negating divisiveness of discursive speech, but also of a verbally oriented hatred for the distance between words and sensuous, passionate reality. *The Worker* is the expression by an intellectual of a set of moods which is given philosophical expression by Heidegger in *Being and Time*. It is a cruder, more brutal, and hence more easily visible expression of the anti-rational passion of the period between the two world wars. For this reason, it is of special interest in showing us the subterranean connection between the doctrines of *Being and Time* and the contemporary forces that culminated in the rise to power of national socialism.[42] Jünger purges sadness and anxiety in the frozen hysteria of spiritual violence. The worker identifies with the annihilation of western civilization; he does not mask his nihilism beneath the quasi-Christian romanticism of the solitary authentic individual or the ontological investigations of the learned German professor of philosophy. And finally, Jünger is of interest because his career provides us with a series of steps similar to those traversed by

42. Schwarz (*Der konservative Anarchist*) discusses the contribution made by Jünger to the progress of national socialism, as well as his personal attitude toward the party. He calls Jünger's influence "symptomatisch, gewiss, doch nicht entscheidend" (p. 126). Even if we assume this to be true, such a judgment fails to bring out the peculiar responsibility of a thinker, poet, and (initially) political publicist who articulates in a powerful and persuasive way ideas "symptomatic" of nihilism and fascism. It is instructive to compare the details of *Der Arbeiter* with Herman Rauschning's description of the doctrineless philosophy of nihilistic dynamism employed by the Nazis. See *The Revolution of Nihilism* (New York, Alliance Book Corporation, 1940), pp. 12, 23 ff., 55–58, and passim. For reference to Jünger as the spokesman for revolutionary youth, see esp. pp. 63, 71, and passim.

Heidegger: at first, an active encouragement of contemporary
nihilist motives; then, disillusion with the political mobilization
of what was supposed to be a spiritual purification; last, total
detachment from merely human activity in a mystical *Gelassenheit,* or waiting for new, anti-nihilistic revelations of Being. I
mention only the large similarities; there are, of course, considerable differences between the two. The main point here is that
both show the radical dangers of a metaphysics of dynamism:
first, a strengthening of political nihilism, for however "exalted"
a motive; and then, an incapacity to accept responsibility for the
consequences of their call to responsibility. The same impotence
for which both castigated European rationalism once more re-
appears, only now concealed by theological and transcendental
posturing before the gifts of fate.

In an essay on nihilism dating from 1950, Jünger summarizes
the two great contemporary anxieties: the fear of inner emptiness which drives man to external action at any price, and the
assault from outside of a daimonic and immense, automatized
world.[43] One may recognize in these words a tacit criticism of
the forces which were previously described affirmatively as
underlying the form of the worker. Instead of total mobilization,
Jünger now identifies the "wilderness" as the ur-ground of
human existence and the source of freedom.[44] Like Rousseau,
Jünger sought purification from the corruption of politics in
botanizing; unlike Rousseau, his solitary promenader seeks
freedom from temporal existence in the creation of new orders
by Being. Heidegger, in his contribution to the Jünger Fest-
schrift of 1955, in effect condemns the later teaching of Jünger
as leading to nihilism.[45] Metaphysical transcendence, according
to Heidegger, is the last stage of the will to will, an effort by
man to ignore the absence of Being, hence to prevent the possible overcoming of this absence. Instead of rationalist activism,
man must understand himself as "the place-holder of nothing-

43. *Über die Linie* (Frankfort, Vittorio Klostermann, 1950), p. 35.
44. Ibid., p. 39.
45. Published separately in 1956 as *Zur Seinsfrage* (Frankfort, Vittorio
Klostermann), pp. 32 ff.

ness." That is, "man holds open in what is altogether other than beings the place so that, in this openness, such a presence (Being) can occur." [46] Our last task in this chapter will be to trace the main steps in Heidegger's historicist ontology in terms of its contribution and surrender to political nihilism.

IV.

I have given a brief summary of some aspects of Jünger's teaching as a prelude to the discussion of the connection between historicity and political nihilism in Heidegger. It is interesting to observe that Jünger, the soldier, war hero, and political journalist, however he may have assisted indirectly the Nazi rise to power, never became a member of the party and from a rather early period (1930) began a process of increasing criticism, both direct and in the form of literary parables.[47] The same cannot be said of Heidegger, the only thinker of the first rank to join the Nazi Party and to speak out, albeit for a brief period, regularly and with great force on its and the Führer's behalf. The attitude of Heidegger toward the Nazis, in the years following his resignation as rector of Freiburg in 1934, is not as easy to determine as he and his followers suggest.[48] There

46. Ibid., p. 38: "der Mensch hält dem ganz Anderen zum Seienden den Ort frei, sodass es in dessen Offenheit dergleichen wie An-wesen (Sein) geben kann."

47. Cf. Schwarz, p. 112. Jünger's first criticism of the Nazis, however, blames them for being insufficiently radical, for trying to retain a semblance of legality and adapting to bourgeois jurisprudence.

48. For Heidegger's only (to my knowledge) long (six pages) defense of his political activities, one must consult his statement to the Allied occupational authorities, dated November 4, 1945 (for my copy of which I am indebted to Dr. Al Lingis). The main points are these: Heidegger assumed the position of rector upon the urgings of the faculty and in order to defend the spiritual life of the university. He joined the Nazi party for similar reasons but never took any part in its activities. His own thought was constantly subject to criticism by ideological spokesmen for the Nazis. He was never guilty of anti-Semitic feelings or activities and did all that he could to assist the careers of his emigrating Jewish students. His lectures from 1934–44 to thousands of students opened

are ambiguous remarks on the Nazi period in *Introduction to Metaphysics,* a lecture course dating from 1935 and republished in 1953 *"without change of content."* [49] The claims made on his behalf, usually not in print, may be balanced by a conflicting oral tradition stemming from former students and auditors of various backgrounds. The best policy, so far as we are concerned, would seem to be a complete reliance on the printed word of Heidegger; each reader may decide for himself which of the oral traditions concerning Heidegger's behavior and character is valid. There can be no doubt, however, of the need to consider the connection between the speeches and deeds of Heidegger. One would have to be unusually naïve not to be interested in the political activities of the greatest "thinker" of the epoch, and especially of a thinker who teaches (or taught) the need for authentic choice and existence. One point, however, which I feel must be stated frankly is that Heidegger's influence leads precisely to this sort of naïveté. And whatever the claims of Heidegger and his students about the nature of philosophy, our concern is with the nihilistic consequences of those

---

their eyes to the metaphysical foundations of the age. I add the following quotation: "Ich stand schon 1933–34 in derselben Opposition gegen die n.s. Weltanschauungslehre, war damals aber des Glaubens, dass die Bewegung geistig in andere Bahnen gelenkt werden könne und hielt diesen Versuch vereinbar mit den sozialen und allgemein politischen Tendenzen der Bewegung. Ich glaubte, Hitler werde, nachdem er 1933 in der Verantwortung für das *ganze* Volk stand, über die Partei u. ihre Doktrin hinauswachsen u. alles würde sich auf den Boden einer Erneuerung u. Sammlung zu einer abendländischen Verantwortung zusammenfinden. Dieser Glaube war ein Irrtum, den ich aus den Vorgängen des 30. Juni 1934 erkannte. Er hatte mich aber im Jahre 1933 in die Zwischenstellung gebracht, dass ich das Soziale u. Nationale (nicht Nationalistische) bejahte u. die geistige u. metaphysische Grundlegung durch den Biologismus der Parteidoktrin verneinte, weil das Soziale u. Nationale, wie ich es sah, nicht wesensmässig an die biologisch-rassische Weltanschauungslehre geknüpft war." Heidegger also explains his absence from Husserl's funeral as due to illness.

49. The quotation is from the *Vorbemerkung* to *Einführung in die Metaphysik* (Tübingen, 1953), where Heidegger also says that "errors have been removed." For the remarks in question, cf. pp. 36, 152.

claims. The issue is not one of "vengeance" (in Nietzsche's sense) but of truth.

During Heidegger's brief tenure as rector of Freiburg University, he delivered a number of speeches and official pronouncements which may fairly be described as an effort to justify national socialism by assimilating the terms of his own philosophy to those of the popular Nazi vocabulary.[50] One of the most useful attempts by a student of the period, J-P. Faye, to demonstrate this point seems to be virtually unnoticed by English writers. In his analysis of Heidegger's language, Faye shows, for example, how Heidegger accommodated to the rhetoric of the vulgar and to that of the academic community depending upon the occasion, and how his own rhetoric permitted him to introduce revolutionary and demagogic political idiom into theoretical speeches.[51] The least one can say is that the ease with which Heidegger succeeded in accommodating the teaching of *Being and Time* to the resolute choice of Hitler and the Nazi party provides us with an

50. *Die Selbstbehauptung der deutschen Universität* (Breslau, G. Korn, 1934); Nachlese zu Heidegger, ed. G. Schneeberger (Bern, published by editor, 1962). The only serious studies of the philosophical significance of these speeches, so far as I know, are by Europeans. See esp. K. Löwith, *Heidegger: Denker in dürftiger Zeit* (Göttingen, Vandenhoeck & Ruprecht, 1960) and *Gesammelte Abhandlungen* (Stuttgart, Kohlhammer, 1960), as well as his article, "Les Implications politiques de la philosophie de l'existence chez Heidegger," in *Les Temps Modernes* (Paris, Nov. 1946). More recently, A. Schwan has published a very valuable study, *Politische Philosophie im Denken Heideggers* (Köln und Opladen, Westdeutscher Verlag, 1965), which has been of great assistance to me in writing parts of the present chapter.

51. J-P. Faye, "Heidegger et la 'révolution,' " and "Attaques Nazies contre Heidegger," in *Médiations* (Autumn 1961, pp. 151–59 and Summer 1962, pp. 137–54). I am again indebted to Al Lingis for bringing these essays to my attention. See esp. the second article, pp. 138 ff. Faye is very illuminating on Heidegger's use of the terms *"Volk," "völkisch,"* and *"volklich,"* on the conservative–revolutionary breakthrough and reversal, i.e. disruption of traditional values in a return to the *Ursprung,* and on Heidegger's translation, in his *Rektoratsrede,* of ἐπισφαλῆ (quoted from Plato's *Republic* 479d9) as *Sturm:* "en 1933 la *Sturm Abteilung* tient la rue en Allemagne" (p. 142).

essential clue to the political philosophy implicit in his ontological analysis of human existence.[52] Let me state in advance the
general difficulty of the political implications of Heidegger's
thought. On the one hand, Heidegger places man in the position
of having necessarily to choose, and to translate into action, the
historical manifestation of Being. On the other, he forewarns
man against the possibility of making a correct choice and even
maintains that to choose at all, in the terms of acting for or
against what is humanly desirable or undesirable, is to contribute to nihilism. To some degree, the apparent contradiction
in this advice may be explained by a change in Heidegger's
thought, but, in harmony with his own interpretation of this
"change," such an explanation is inadequate. It can be shown
that the contradiction is inherent in Heidegger's teaching from
beginning to end. Heidegger regards his thinking as "neither
theoretical nor practical." As a remembering of Being, "such
thought has no result. It has no effect. Its essence is fulfilled in
that it is." [53] Unfortunately, the divine status attributed to this
thinking overlooks two facts. First, God's thinking did have a
consequence or result—the world and man. But second, for a
philosophy to assert that it has no results (as does the mathe-
maticized epistemology so disliked by Heidegger) is thereby to
define the nature of the connection between philosophy—or
thinking—and political existence. This is itself a result, and an
altogether crucial, even disastrous result.

At least in the early period of Heidegger's thought, the process by which Being reveals itself in history (as historicity) was
regarded as a consequence of human activity.[54] Therefore, the

52. Cf. Löwith, "Les Implications politiques," p. 358: "La possibilité
de la politique philosophique de Heidegger n'est pas née à un 'déraille-
ment' qu'on pourrait regretter, mais du principe même de sa conception
de l'existence qui combat à la fois et assume 'l'esprit du temps.'" For the
detailed documentation, cf. the by no means hostile work of Schwan,
cited previously.

53. "Über den 'Humanismus,'" in *Platons Lehre von der Wahrheit*
(Bern, Francke Verlag, 1954), p. 111. Cf. pp. 99, 105–06.

54. Cf. *Sein und Zeit,* pp. 212 ("Nur solange Dasein ist . . . gibt es
Sein"), 226 ("Wahrheit 'gibt es' nur, sofern und solange Dasein ist");

process could be modified by man's will or choice, and indeed would have to be so modified in order to continue to occur.[55] The fate of Being in the west was said to be dependent upon the authentic and profound resolution with which Germany responded to its historical situation.[56] In a rather Hegelian sense, Hitler was described as the leader not simply of the state or people, but of the next epoch of world history. In a sense peculiar to Heidegger, German students were told by him that "the Führer himself and alone *is* the present and future German reality and its law." [57] The will of the Führer as the expression of the historical destiny of the German people thus replaces Ideas, science, and the specious freedom, academic or otherwise, by which an objective rationalism duped the west.[58] These practical translations of Heidegger's teaching, which remind us of the

---

Nachlese, pp. 12, 149 ("Wahrheit ist die Offenbarheit dessen, was ein Volk in seinem Handlen und Wissen sicher, hell und stark macht"), 212, 214; *Die Selbstbehauptung,* pp. 9–10 (Theory is "selbst als die höchste Verwirklichung echter Praxis zu verstehen": an assertion that should be compared with the later "resigned" passage quoted in the text from the *Humanismusbrief*), 20 ("Alle willentlich und denkerischen Vermögen, alle Kräfte des Herzens und alle Fähigkeiten des Leibes müssen durch Kampf entfalten, im Kampf gesteigert und als Kampf bewahrt bleiben." Heidegger then goes on to quote Clausewitz' saying that one must not hope for salvation through chance).

55. Cf. *Sein und Zeit,* pp. 386 (the *Geschichtlichkeit* of *Dasein* is grounded in its *Sein zum Tode,* which in turn is a consequence of resolution, etc.), 391 (in unauthentic Geschichtlichkeit, Dasein avoids making a choice); *Die Selbstbehauptung,* p. 22 (the spiritual strength of western culture will fail unless "wir als geschichtlich-geistiges Volk uns selbst noch und wieder wollen"); *Nachlese,* pp. 42 (German responsibility to history), 145 (there is an *Urforderung* for every Dasein to maintain its own *Wesen*), and passim.

56. *Die Selbstbehauptung,* p. 22; *Nachlese,* p. 258 (the historical mission of the German people is the deliverance of the west); *Einführung in die Metaphysik,* pp. 28–29 (Germany, the metaphysical folk, lying in the pincers between the metaphysically identical Russia and America, can effectuate the fate of Being only by finding a response to that fate in itself, by a creative comprehension of its tradition).

57. *Nachlese,* pp. 135–36.

58. *Die Selbstbehauptung,* pp. 5, 15–16; *Nachlese,* pp. 45, 74, 92, 201, and passim.

previously studied assertions of Jünger and scarcely conform with Heidegger's own account of his professional activities under the Nazi regime, have never been repudiated by him, nor were they altogether superseded by later developments in his thought. They follow from Heidegger's peculiar identification of Being with Time (which I capitalize to indicate its ontological sense) or Historicity, in the first as well as the last stages of his thought.[59] Our previous analysis of historicist ontologies must now be retraced, even at the risk of some repetition, in order to make explicit the political dimension.

As we have seen, by "Being," Heidegger does not refer to a thing, substance, or logical category, nor to the sum or essence (in the static sense of the term) of the sum of things, but to the whole process of illumination, unveiling, or clearing, together with the inseparable function of concealment or disappearance, which give rise to the world in its dual character of presence and absence.[60] Being, to repeat, is a process, and a total process, rather than a static entity, substratum, substance, or principle. In what are perhaps the most obscure passages in Heidegger's published writings, he refers occasionally to the unknown and unthought "source" of the Being-process.[61] But that this "source" cannot be understood as a transcendental ground of Being is clear from Heidegger's interpretation of Being as "groundless" or an *Abgrund,* in the sense that it *is* as that-which-grounds, or *is* the same as its ground.[62] In any case, as the following statement by Heidegger makes clear, there is no doubt that Being as process, and so as the opening within which this process unfolds, is Time:

59. *Sein und Zeit,* pp. 17, 183, 212, 386; *Vom Wesen des Grundes* (Frankfurt, Vittorio Klostermann, 1955), pp. 45–46; *Einführung,* p. 64; *Der Ursprung des Kunstwerkes,* p. 58; *Unterwegs zur Sprache* are representative texts.

60. The *Humanismusbrief* contains perhaps the clearest statement of Heidegger's "mature" conception of Being.

61. E.g. *Identität und Differenz,* p. 44; *Nietzsche, 1,* 471; *2,* 484; *Unterwegs,* p. 31.

62. *Der Satz vom Grund* (Pfullingen, G. Neske Verlag, 1957), pp. 184–85.

if we replace "Time" by: the lighting of the self-hiding of *Anwesen* (presence as holding itself together and before), then Being defines itself out of the projective scope of Time. But this results only in so far as the lighting of self-hiding puts to its use a thinking that corresponds to it. *Anwesen* (Being) belongs to the lighting of self-hiding (Time). Lighting of self-hiding (Time) produces *Anwesen* (Being).[63]

That is, Being belongs to Time as that which hides itself within it: as so hiding it appears (*es gibt Sein,* i.e. presents itself) as the "way" in which Time pro-cedes.

The Being-process, then, has no ground other than its own activity (emittence, occurrence), which is thus involved with nothingness, and in two senses. First, Being as a totality or whole is delimited or finite, and so defined by nothingness.[64] We cannot conceive of Being as a whole except by an encounter with nothingness. But second, we cannot grasp the sense of our life as a whole except by facing up to our death: nothingness is not simply external to Being but occurs within the world of human existence.[65] Since man is a being-in-the-world, he could never encounter nothingness if it did not occur within the world. The world, one might say, is woven together from the threads of Being and nothingness.

Although the importance of nothingness in Heidegger's later thought may perhaps be said to have decreased, the same fundamental theme is enduringly present in the relationship between Being and Time. Time is the horizon within which Being *occurs* or *happens,* but as occurrence or happening, Being is radically temporal. Time not merely reveals or "gives birth,"

63. W. J. Richardson, S.J., *Heidegger* (The Hague, M. Nijhoff, 1963), p. xxi. Cf. my article, "Heidegger's Interpretation of Plato," in the *Journal of Existentialism,* (Summer, 1967), 493 ff.

64. *Was ist Metaphysik?* (Frankfurt, Vittorio Klostermann, 1951), pp. 35–36; cf. also pp. 21, 27–28.

65. *Sein und Zeit,* pp. 184 ff.; *Was ist Metaphysik? p.* 29. The two senses are brought together in the foreword to the 3d ed. of *Vom Wesen des Grundes.*

but also conceals or "destroys." [66] In conformity with Heidegger's own characterization of his thought as a "being under way," Being is itself the ways in which beings come to be and pass away, or the "way of ways": it is not the Greek φύσις, but the Chinese Tao.[67] For these ways, since they are patterns or accumulations of temporality, are themselves coming to be and passing away. They are the ways in which Being is seen as absent, or as masked by beings in temporally directed order (*Geschick*). This temporally directed order, the unity of Being and Time with respect to openness, visibility, and presence, i.e. with respect to thought, and so to man (who, as the placeholder of nothingness, thereby stands in the lighting of Being), is *Ereignis*.[68] Heidegger speaks of Being as event, occurrence, gift, and so forth, because of his intention, constant since *Being and Time,* to eradicate from the domain of philosophy (or recollective thinking) any vestige of eternity. The constant presence of nothingness in Heidegger is identical with the perpetual absence of the eternal.

The Being of Heidegger is a genesis without a generator, or, as Nietzsche said, "a work of art giving birth to itself." [69] In the absence of eternity, a radically temporal, radically immanent world owes its "sense" or "significance" to the way in which it presents itself to man.[70] Differently stated, the world is a presentation only to and because of man, who assists it in its birth throes and who may thus be understood as the midwife of Being

66. "Der Spruch des Anaximander," in *Holzwege* (Frankfurt, Vittorio Klostermann, 1952).

67. Cf. *Sein und Zeit,* p. 304; *Der Satz vom Grund,* p. 154; *Unterwegs zur Sprache,* p. 198.

68. Cf. Richardson, *Heidegger,* pp. 638 ff., on the ambiguity of *Ereignis:* it means (1) some third thing other than εἶναι and νοεῖν, prior to and unifying both; (2) Being itself as *Geschick*.

69. *Der Wille zur Macht,* no. 796. Cf. *Der Satz vom Grund,* p. 188.

70. Heidegger's conception of the "sense" of Being is an obvious development of Husserl's phenomenology, in which the sense of the thing viewed, as constituted within subjectivity, is the same as the being of the thing: in other words, it is not possible in Husserl to distinguish between *noēsis* and *noema,* any more than it is in Heidegger. And the temporality of subjectivity, when thought through, gives rise to the problem of historicism.

and truth.[71] Just as the radical temporality of the Being-process excludes any eternal or "objective" standards by which to distinguish between truth and error, which are even said to be essentially the same, so it subtly erases the distinction between thinking and doing in the sense of making.[72] Man is not merely a midwife but an artist, or that being to whom, and so in terms of which, the world presents itself in its comings and goings.[73] Man "creates" the truth by those fundamental activities which uncover ("let" in the sense of "make" appear) the happenings of Being. Hence the extraordinary importance which Heidegger gives to poetry and "poetic thinking." [74]

Heidegger claims to avoid the problem of perspectivism or subjectivity implicit in western philosophy from Plato to Nietzsche, despite the central role he gives to man in the revelation of Being or truth. Since Being is process, it has no fixed nature in the traditional sense of the term. Instead, it may be described as a process which reveals itself, epoch by epoch, to man and thereby, since man is that aspect of Being through which the revelation occurs, to itself.[75] Beneath the Nietzschean surfaces of Heidegger's thought, we may detect a continuing Hegelian

71. This is expressed in Heidegger's earlier work in the notion of "world" as opened by *Dasein,* and so of "ontology" as an *Entwurf* rather than as *Erkenntnis:* cf. *Kant und das Problem der Metaphysik* (Frankfurt, Vittorio Klostermann, 1951), p. 210. For the later, "revelational" formulation, cf. *Zur Seinsfrage,* p. 38, and *Der Ursprung des Kunstwerkes,* pp. 86, 89.

72. *Der Ursprung des Kunstwerkes,* p. 58; *Vorträge und Aufsätze,* p. 119. In this respect, Heidegger carries through a pervasive theme in modern philosophy, to which he ostensibly objects, but which he gives a "poetic" reformulation in place of the mathematical or epistemological. Relevant here is his explication of the authentic sense of σοφία, ἀλήθεια, and λόγος in pre-Socratic thought. For further discussion, see my article, cited in n. 63, and the next chapter of the present study.

73. *Der Satz vom Grund,* pp. 157–58; *Vorträge und Aufsätze,* pp. 249 ff.; *Gelassenheit* (Pfullingen, G. Neske Verlag, 1959), pp. 64–65; *Was Heisst Denken?* (Tübingen, Max Niemayer Verlag, 1954), pp. 124–25: "letting be" is "gathering together" and so *imprinting as.*

74. For the latest and fullest statement, see *Unterwegs zur Sprache,* e.g. pp. 173 ff., 196 ff.

75. Representative texts: *Der Satz vom Grund,* pp. 158, 176; *Nietzsche, 1,* 173–74; *2,* 257.

resonance. Being is not nature, but History (Historicity). Human history is then the medium through which Being as Historicity presents itself to itself, or *becomes self-conscious.*[76] Man, as we may say, is the self-reflexive dimension of Being. As a consequence, the dominant philosophical interpretation of Being in a given historical epoch is not, Heidegger claims, a merely subjective perspective or Weltanschauung, a mere project or creation of the arbitrary human will, but what Being actually signifies, the way in which it has chosen to reveal itself through and for the given time. At the same time, each revelation is also an obscuration, and in two different senses.

The first sense is in a way analogous to Hegel's understanding of each philosophical teaching prior to his own as a necessary but incomplete element in the final revelation of the whole. Given the identification of Being as Historicity, no speech can manifest the truth of Being as a whole in any way other than to show that the Historicity of Being precludes a final wisdom concerning it. But second, since Being is a process whereby beings occur, the process itself is obscured by the very manner in which it functions. It is possible for man to attain to the understanding that Being as a whole reveals-and-conceals itself as a series of epochs or perspectives. The term "perspective" must then be understood as referring to Being rather than to man. In attaining to this understanding, man *lets Being be* in its own terms, or as it conceals-and-reveals itself in and through the fundamental activities of man. He does not enforce a partial and subjective interpretation *onto* the Being-process, as, for example, the Platonic theory of Ideas or the Aristotelian categories. Such an interpretation erects a static and distorting screen between man and the self-revealing-and-concealing process of which man is himself, so to speak, a sub-process.

The fact that man sees beings rather than Being means that he fails to see the absence of Being. He fails to see that he does not see Being, and that he cannot "see" Being if "to see" means "to reason" in the traditional sense. For "seeing" qua "reason-

76. Consider here Heidegger's qualified praise of Marxism in the *Humanismusbrief* (published together with *Platons Lehre*), p. 87.

ing" or ratio is a seeing of things, a measuring of the forms of beings as they look or appear to us, and not an openness to Being as the process whereby things take shape, whereby beings form (in the active sense of the word). In sum, there are two different senses in which Being is concealed. The first and structurally intrinsic sense is the concealment of Being by its own activity, by the emergence of beings. The second sense is the concealment of Being by philosophical theories or perspectival visions imposed onto Being by the human will. As I noted in the comparison with Hegel, these concealing theories are not simply deplorable mistakes, all-too-human errors which might have been rectified by greater intelligence or closer scrutiny. They are necessary errors, the "errance" of truth, the way in which Being has hitherto chosen to reveal—or rather to conceal—itself.[77] The gift of Being, even though requiring man for its disclosure, seems very much like fate. But what has happened to the resolute choice by which the individual and the people were said in *Being and Time* and the political speeches to determine their future and even save the western world? The attempt to give a coherent account of Heidegger's teaching would seem to founder upon a change in that teaching. And so we must turn again to Heidegger's own history.

The least one can say is that there is a shift in emphasis, following the early writings, on the degree of autonomy and so of freedom enjoyed by man.[78] It is interesting to note that this change takes place in the time just following Heidegger's resignation from his post as rector of Freiburg. A cynic might express the change as follows.[79] Prior to Heidegger's disillusion-

77. A good summary and documentation of this point will be found in Schwan, Ch. 2.

78. *Die Selbstbehauptung*, p. 15: freedom is self-legislation. This corresponds to the notion of *Eigentlichkeit* in *Sein und Zeit*. In the later work, freedom is called "das lichtend Verbergende": *Vorträge und Aufsätze*, p. 33.

79. Löwith, *Denker in dürftiger Zeit*, p. 55; Schwan, pp. 94, 105, 171. For a more sympathetic account of Heidegger's *Kehre* by an intelligent author, cf. W. Schulz, "Über den philosophiegeschichtliche Ort Martin Heideggers," in *Philosophische Rundschau* (1953–54, Heft 2–3, 4), esp. pp. 83 ff.

ment with the Nazis, he emphasized the contingency of Historicity and of man's capacity to ground a true understanding of Being in historical actions. After this disillusionment, he came to insist upon the necessary duality of truth and error and man's incapacity to resist or alter what fate gives us in the shape of each epoch.[80] Heidegger himself has uttered a complex statement concerning this much-debated issue of the "turn" in his thought.[81] He affirms the turn in the admission that the thinking of *Being and Time* was still a prisoner of the metaphysical language it sought to overcome. But he denies it by insisting that he has always remained within the "matter for thought" of *Being and Time*—namely, the "time-character" out of which Being occurs. The "happening" of the turn is then interpreted as a happening of Being, and so the "transition" between the two stages of his thought is a gift of Being, or consequent expression of the light-that-conceals.

The new, recollective thinking that follows Heidegger's turn is decisively defined as a turn away from the primacy of Dasein to a direct meditation upon Being itself. The existential analytic disappears altogether, or at least sinks into the background. So too with the manifest political implications of that analytic. Like Ernst Jünger, Heidegger turns from the will to action toward a will-less will to Gelassenheit. In this vein, his language is no longer phenomenological nor ontological, but that of a prophet. In *Being and Time,* Heidegger, like a son of the Enlightenment, looked to the future. After the turn, he looks back not simply to the historical past, but to the *origin*. The function of foundational, recollective, or "poetic" thinking is to return man to the origin, in a way sufficiently reminiscent of both pagan and Hebrew thought as to lead to the greatest confusion.[82] This kind of thinking is a "caring for," "dwelling in,"

    80. For a relatively straightforward presentation of the "new" position; see *Vorträge und Aufsätze,* p. 25.
    81. In a *Vorwort* to the Richardson volume.
    82. For the new mode of thinking, *Vorträge,* pp. 138 ff.; *Unterwegs,* pp. 30 ff., 180, 200, and passim. "Dichtendes Denken," of course, is not equivalent to poetry: cf. *Was ist Metaphysik?* p. 46; *Was Heisst Denken?* pp. 8, 92 ff., 125 ff.; *Humanismusbrief,* pp. 75, 79, 115, 119.

"naming," and even "silent listening." Heidegger speaks, or rather sings, as a shepherd of Being, as a new Hesiod whose muse is not human experience but Being itself. Heidegger is nevertheless right to insist upon the continuity between the two stages of his thought. In both stages, Being is understood from within the horizon of temporality. And both stages manifest the same fundamental difficulty in his teaching—how to distinguish between man and Being.

I have emphasized that, for Heidegger, Being is a process that "occurs" as a "show" in and through man's Dasein. Not merely is the horizon of man's vision temporal, but, as the opening within which the show of the Being-process transpires, it is identical with, or exemplifies, the Being-process. The openness of *Sein* and the openness of Da-sein are one and the same. For this reason, the dominance of political nihilism in the actions of man is identical with the self-concealing "gift" of Being to and through man. It is a strange consequence of Heidegger's doctrine that the dominant political configuration of the day must be taken as a sign of the character of the revelation of Being in the given epoch. Ostensibly beyond theory and practice, this doctrine gives a special importance to practice. Such is the result of Heidegger's adaptation of Parmenides' dictum that "thinking and Being are the same" to a teaching of radical Historicity. "The same" is for Heidegger the scission within Being between itself and thought; but at the root of this duality is a unity which one may follow Heidegger in calling their need for each other.[83] This need is Heidegger's revision of the Hegelian doctrine of the unity of Being and thought in the Absolute. Hegel's Absolute, however, is an interpretation of the Christian God. Heidegger, as I noted previously, vacillates between Judaeo-Christian and pagan motifs. In this particular case, his inspiration is pagan, as the following crucial illustration suggests. According to Heidegger, to name "man" is to name residence in the fourfold unity of heaven, earth, divine, and mortal; this fourfold unity is also the "structural" framework of a "thing" or "being" and hence is identical with the structure of

83. See *Was Heisst Denken?* pp. 114–26, 146 ff.

Being or the world.[84] The thing chosen as an example of Being is a Greek prayer vessel, or an implement of the *gods;* and the same point could be made by reflecting upon the significance of Heidegger's fondness for Hölderlin. Heidegger's fourfold unity is Hegel's Absolute, only recast into terms derived from pagan poetry. It articulates the structure of the way of ways and so too underlies the capacity of human activity to reveal Being by living in harmony with it. It is a blending of poetry and history.

As is suggested by the unusual importance Heidegger gives to agricultural imagery, Being "grows" from the soil as a harmony of the gift of heaven and the shaping work of man, who thereby shapes himself as well. Since the speech of man is the speech of Being, man both creatively participates in the (self-) revelation of Being and is the passive audience of that revelation.[85] This ambiguity in the relationship between man and Being gives rise to two different temptations when we try to understand the genuine sense of the "gifts" or "happenings" which constitute the Historicity of Being.[86] As we have already noted, the temptation is very great, despite Heidegger's consistent denial of eternity, to understand Being as the gift of a *Deus Absconditus,* a temptation to which contemporary theologians are submitting

84. *Vorträge,* pp. 163 ff.; *Identität und Differenz,* pp. 21 ff. There is also a Christian inspiration for the doctrine that Being needs man. Speaking of Hegel's theological predecessors, N. Lobkowicz remarks: "God fulfills his self-glorification in man. This is the classic *topos* of all (pseudo) mysticism from Eckhardt through Böhme and Angelus Silesius up to R. M. Rilke's *Stundenbuch:* God needs man to reach his ultimate completion, and by uniting with God, man comes to stand so close to the First Cause that he almost becomes a *causa sui"* (in *Theory and Practice* [South Bend, Notre Dame University Press, 1967], p. 173).

85. See *Was Heisst Denken?* pp. 127–28, and *Vorträge,* pp. 208 ff., for a confrontation of the passive and active sides to speech or thinking. The reinterpretation of *Sein und Zeit,* p. 212, given in *Humanismusbrief,* p. 83, is extremely illuminating here. See also *Einführung,* pp. 131 ff. and Richardson, p. 296. In Heidegger's political speeches, the active side is exaggerated to the point of violence—the Nietzschean heritage.

86. Heidegger plays upon the etymological relation between *Geschehen* and *Geschenk* to *Geschichte.*

with steadily increasing momentum.[87] On the other hand, we may feel ourselves tempted to say that, since Being reveals itself to the vision and speech of man, it is really man who gives himself the gift of Being, albeit in such a way as to prevent himself from making full use of it.

These two temptations are strangely similar to the two extreme interpretations that have been given to the teaching of Hegel—namely, either that the world is the unfolding of God, or that it is the self-fulfillment of man. The "orthodox" interpretation of Hegel would presumably maintain that both alternatives are correct; that is, man becomes fulfilled by the unfolding of God, or the final identification between the development of Absolute Geist and human history. Such an interpretation is possible in the case of Hegel because of his claim that both developments have a culmination or completion in his own time, as reflected in the systematic exposition his writings give to wisdom. For Heidegger, of course, there is no wisdom in this sense because there is no transcendence of Time; the Being-process is not circular. Nietzsche once remarked that he who would understand Zarathustra must have one foot beyond life.[88] This expression very well captures the dilemma faced by a thinker who identifies Being with Time. If the identification is true, it can be seen only by one who transcends and so contradicts it. Nietzsche is more consistent than Heidegger, at least in this sense; he recognizes that his teaching gives man the gift of eternity. Heidegger makes no such claim; as a result, his revelation stands unprotected before the winds of Time by anything other than the resoluteness, or finally the submissiveness, of the prophet.[89]

But how are we to distinguish resoluteness from deluded stubbornness, or submissiveness from enslavement? What distin-

87. Cf. Hans Jonas, "Heidegger and Theology," in *The Phenomenon of Life,* and Richardson's reply, "Heidegger and God—and Professor Jonas."
88. *Ecce Homo,* in *Werke,* ed. Schlechta, 2, 1074.
89. Cf. *Was Heisst Denken?* p. 52.

guishes the revelation of God from the cunning of Satan? What
is to prevent the ostensible merits of Heidegger's revelation
from being erased by the next epochal gift of the Historicity of
Being? Heidegger's conception of genuine thinking as the thinking "of" Being bears a superficial resemblance to the teaching of
Parmenides, Spinoza, and Hegel; but the Historicity of Being
deprives him of a standpoint *sub specie aeternitatis*. Despite
Heidegger's claim that the genuine thinker can attach no
"worth" to "what happens," and that to pass judgment on the
justice, dignity, or excellence of the gifts of Being is to succumb
to "moral pharisaism," [90] the result is a surrender to the worth
of what happens as defined by the force of the times. Heidegger
denounces merely ontic interpretations by which subjective or
"objectified" projections of man replace the genuine apprehension of the voice of Being, and which degrade the dignity of
Being to the level of mere utility.[91] Genuine thinking, exactly
like mathematical ontology, is unable to make "value judgments." Heidegger, however, attributes the superhuman status of
numbers to the all-too-human configurations of history. The
authentic or genuine thinker, whether resolute in his acceptance
or resigned in his rejection of political action, understands himself as the manifestation of the Historicity of Being; this refusal
to take politics and morality seriously is transformed at once
into an excessive attribution of significance to politics and
morality. And this is the underlying unity between the contradictory political consequences of the early and the late teaching
of Heidegger. It is the historical situation which determines our
action or passivity.

The prophet–shepherd of Being is in fact a plaything of the
absent gods. He cannot err in the human sense because his
"errance" is not human or ontic, but ontological. Adherence to
the Nazi party in 1933, when interpreted at the ontological or
genuine level insisted upon by Heidegger himself, cannot be
understood as an act of naïveté, as Heidegger's admirers incon-

90. *Sein und Zeit,* p. 291.
91. *Humanismusbrief,* pp. 99, 105–06, 111; Schwan, pp. 142, 157;
Nietzsche, 2, 222 ff.

sistently and (from his viewpoint) superficially maintain. Similarly, his negative attitude toward the party after 1934 cannot be understood as he himself explains it in his statement to the Allied authorities of 1945, that is, merely as the recognition of a political miscalculation while in the service of man's philosophical spirit.[92] It is the gift of Being, and not the ontic judgment of Martin Heidegger, that must assume responsibility, and so too credit if credit is due, for the "new" attitude. As Heidegger expounds its theoretical sense in his philosophical writings, the practical stance of 1934 and thereafter is not a moral condemnation of the Nazis, but an acceptance of their historical inevitability, exactly as was the case in 1933. The obscuring of Being by beings, we are now told, is encouraged by the technical, calculative, or objectifying thinking which seeks to dominate the world instead of achieving a genuine unity with it. But this process of domination cannot itself be dominated or terminated: *it must fulfill itself as a mandate from Being.*

This mandate, despite its parlous and even nihilistic character, with the danger it brings of the destruction of the human race, also reveals the sense of Being as Historicity.[93] It reveals the sense of Being as presence-and-absence, but also as temporal process which, in completing each stage, "clears the stage" for new possibilities for which man, and the exemplary authentic thinker, can only wait. To attempt to accelerate by political action the demise or completion of our present parlous stage would be to surrender to its intrinsic nihilism, for nihilism is the will to will, the will to dominate Being instead of letting it be. Nihilism is both man's forgetting of Being and the gift of Being. Being gives man nihilism, yet man is the agent of nihilism. Hence the strange conclusion that to act against nihilism is to act against Being, and so to perpetuate nihilism. This is the ontological conclusion of the long revolt against Platonism, in the version given its decisive shape by Nietzsche and Heidegger. *In his desire not to do violence to Being, man is violated by*

92. See above, n. 48.
93. Schwan's summary of texts on this point is clear and convincing: Ch. 8, pp. 146 ff.

Being. Having identified action with radical destruction, or a purifying self-laceration, the ontological nihilist retreats into total inaction. Being is for him what Valéry called "un défaut dans la pureté du Non-Être." [94]

V.

It is now appropriate to summarize briefly the course of our analysis thus far. Nihilism as a political and moral problem of our epoch has its roots in the epistemological and ontological teaching of the day. This means not that nihilism is a "theoretical" problem in the sense of being an object for scientific investigation, but rather that the need to investigate it objectively springs from the nature of man. It is false, or certainly inadequate, to say that nihilism is a contingent historical event. The shape of contemporary history is itself a consequence of the same forces which gave rise to contemporary epistemology and ontology. I have implicitly maintained that the principal engine of history is man's conception of the nature of reason, more specifically, of the relation between reason and the good. I have tried to suggest how the transformed conception of this relation, characteristic of the beginnings of the modern revolt against antiquity, underlies the emergence of nihilism in our time. Two comments, one obvious, the other less so, must be made at this point. First, I have not intended to give a history of the origins of modernity. My illustrations have come from philosophy and, to a much smaller degree, from science. The Marxist, for example, would find the absence of detailed discussion concerning the transformation of the feudal into the bourgeois world, or, more generally, the failure to reduce theory to economics, a fatal defect. My answer to this charge (which I am taking as representative of other objections concerning restrictions of subject matter) must be very brief at this point, especially since I plan to return to the issue in a subsequent chapter. The central thesis of the priority of physical labor to speculative reflection,

94. Quoted in F. J. von Rintelen's thoughtful book, *Beyond Existentialism* (London, Allen and Unwin, 1961), p. 43.

that is, of the claim that philosophy is an ideological "rationalization" of the given modes of production, is itself a philosophical thesis and not a matter of empirical fact. Taken as such, and disregarding here the many interesting and valuable theoretical productions which it has generated, it is a debased version of a Hegelian teaching concerning the nature of work. The Hegelian analysis of work, in its turn, is a long reflection upon the history of philosophy, which one could summarize by saying that it amounts to a criticism of Aristotle's understanding of properly human work. The first step in a genuinely Marxian analysis of modern nihilism would therefore be a philosophical critique of modern philosophy, and hence of its classical antecedents. Whether this is understood by apologists for Marx, who in fact have no grasp of his own philosophical significance, is a matter of no interest to philosophers, except as a deplorable political consequence of a hatred for philosophy. The philosophical Marxist, however he may disagree with my judgments, ought to be sympathetic with my general procedure.

This brings me to my second comment. I do not wish to maintain, and have not maintained, that nihilism is a peculiar feature of the modern world, representative of its complete inferiority to classical antiquity. In this essay, I am not taking my stand as an enemy of the Enlightenment, mathematical science and technology, or political liberalism. Such a stand is, in my view, erroneous for two related reasons. First, nihilism has its origins in the nature of man, and not in contingent historical events. In one version or another, it may be found in antiquity at various crucial periods, although not, of course, in the precise form it takes today. Nihilism is a philosophical problem, not merely a historical phenomenon. More fundamentally put, history, which in its modern sense has given rise to the modern form of nihilism, is a philosophical problem. Second, and as a consequence of what I have just said, it would be a form of historicism, or surrender to the very forces which have produced modern nihilism, to look for its solution in one historical epoch rather than in another. To prefer the philosophy of Plato to that of Marx is by no means necessarily to wish for a return to the Greek polis. And even if such a preference were to be accompanied by such a wish, the Platonist knows very well the difference between wishing and practical political action. To come to my own case, I regard the fundamental teaching of Plato as in no sense peculiar to his own time and place. If I am a Platonist in any degree whatever, I have not failed to overhear the advice whispered by Nietzsche to conservatives: there is no political reversion to the past.[95] I understood this advice because I had previously learned from Plato that it is wrong to understand the return to the origins in a historical sense.

My criticism of certain aspects of modern philosophy, then, was not motivated by a distaste for modernity as such. It began from the premise that the Platonic–Aristotelian conception of the relation between reason and the good is superior to the modern, or predominantly modern, conception. As a corollary to this premise, I suggest that the classical conception is entirely relevant to our own situation, that we might learn from and even adopt it, without repudiating our birthright as citizens of a post-classical epoch. In the construction of this book, I began not with an analysis of my premise, but with an effort to convince the contemporary reader that such an analysis is desirable. I have tried to carry through a critique of modern nihilism by showing how, on its own principles, it reduces to silence and slavery. As the previous chapters have made evident, I mean something more by "modern nihilism" than a particular social condition. The phrase refers to the nihilist component in modern philosophy generally, and not just to the ontological nihilism of Nietzsche and Heidegger. The next step is to turn to the Platonic statement of the relation between reason and the good. This step is dictated by the claims of modern philosophers, and especially of Nietzsche and Heidegger, to show the inadequacies of "Platonism." The crux of the matter is this: Heidegger claims that Plato is responsible for nihilism in the western tradition. Regardless of whether we are, or wish to become, Platonists, it is incumbent upon us as students of nihilism to see whether Heidegger's interpretation of Plato is true. This would

95. "Streifzüge eines Unzeitgemässen," *Götzen-Dämmerung,* no. 43.

be so independently of whether the reader accepts my criticism of Heidegger's own teaching. Whether as friends or as enemies, then, but certainly not as vulgar historical partisans, let us try to return to the origins in order to renew our strength to face the present.

Chapter 5

The Good

Nihilism is fundamentally an attempt to overcome or to repudiate the past on behalf of an unknown and unknowable yet hoped-for future. The danger implicit in this attempt is that it seems necessarily to entail a negation of the present, or to remove the ground upon which man must stand in order to carry out or even merely to witness the process of historical transformation. The mood of boredom or hopelessness that is the most visible negative manifestation of nihilism testifies to the incoherence of the hidden essence of nihilism. The attempt to overcome the past is necessarily rooted in a judgment upon the past; the nihilist inevitably and rather inconsistently asserts that, at the present moment, the past is worth less than the future. Because of the complex character of the instructions for overcoming the past, whether by political revolution, creative will, or ontological Gelassenheit, we often fail to recognize the undefined character of the hoped-for future. The nihilist invokes us to destroy the past on behalf of a wish which he cannot articulate, let alone guarantee fulfillment. The classless society, the superman, the next epoch of *Seinsgeschichte,* so far as we in the present are concerned, are extreme revisions of the kind of wish described by Socrates in the *Republic.* Not even Plato's modern enemies have pointed out with sufficient emphasis that the just city, the city for which just men wish, depends for its actualization upon the destruction of the past. This is obvious from the need to expel everyone (with the unstated exception of the founding fathers) above the age of ten from the new city; it is also obvious from Socrates' criticism of the poets, especially of Homer. One cannot understand the *Republic* by means of popular political categories like "conservative" and "reactionary." Plato, like every philosopher, whatever his politics, is a revolu-

tionary: he wishes to "turn men around" (the famous
περιαγωγή), to make them face in a direction different from that
of tradition.

The difference between Plato and the nihilists, however, is
this: whereas nihilism points us toward the historical future,
Plato turns us neither backward nor forward in a historical
sense. The Platonic περιαγωγή is directed *upward*. Plato wishes
us to take our bearings in time by a vision that remains free
of the transience of temporality. If such a vision is possible,
then and only then has one acquired a "steadfast" or secure
ground for the present. Only then may one overcome not merely
the past, but the dangers inherent in the undefinable character
of the future. The nihilist's future is a creation ex nihilo; the instructions for the overcoming of the past do not serve as the
"matter" in which the new possibility is to be actualized. Differently stated, since temporality is the only substratum common
to past and future, the one steadfast characteristic that may be
attributed to the future is transience, negativity, or imminent
worthlessness. The wished-for creation of new value, even as a
wish, is on the way toward becoming a valueless past. What
seems like the positive aspect of the nihilistic repudiation of the
past arises not from a vision of the future, but from an illusion
about the present. This illusion concerns the mode of presentation of the present, that is, of present instructions for replacing
the past by the future. For given the nonexistence of the future
and the valuelessness of the past, how can a radically temporal
present stand on its own, or signify in its own terms? What
terms can the discontinuous temporal moment of the present
call its own?

The present as the moment of nihilistic decision is a transient
version of the nonarticulated monad of Eleatic ontology. Hence
the speech in which nihilism is formulated as a positive doctrine
is in fact silence. The distinction between the positive and negative versions of nihilism cannot properly be expressed as a
difference between two speeches or accounts; instead, the
account must be one of the difference between two moods. For
the positive nihilist, the genuine response to a transient, worth-

less, and silent world is courage or resolution; for the negative nihilist, it is dread or nausea. Since courage or resolution is itself rooted in dread or nausea, it is easy to see that the mediating term is not reason, but hope. The nihilist perseveres in the face of despair not because he has a reason for so doing, but because his ostensible comprehension of the worthlessness of all reasons is understood by him as freedom. The nihilist is freed by the instability of the world to find stability in his own despair. Like the arguments of modern mathematical epistemology, the nihilist is *value-free*. He is a fact. In one decisive respect, however, the nihilist is much more acute than the epistemologist. If "the world is everything that is the case," or the value-free fact of all facts, then the facticity of those facts has itself no value. Facticity is merely a synonym for transience. The significance of "what is the case" depends not on the fact that it is the case, but upon the peculiar fact of human consciousness, that is, of the (nihilistic) consciousness which grasps the intrinsic valuelessness of the factic. It is not the facts that count, but their significance; and their significance has nothing to do with their facticity. This is the paradoxical inference from the primacy of facticity: to persevere in the face of the value-free is to become free for the projection of value.

According to Hegel, modern philosophy is decisively characterized by giving primacy to the freedom of subjectivity. Nihilism in its full or positive version shares that characteristic and may perhaps be its last necessary consequence: *despero ergo sum,* or even *spero quia absurdum est.* Again, the nihilist despairs because he is fully enlightened (the ultimate consequence of the Enlightenment) or free from all illusions. His despair is the sign of his enlightenment or freedom, the seal of his integrity. One is tempted to say that the nihilist hopes for despair in order to be free for the possibility of hope. Value and significance, if they are the ground of facticity, restrict man's freedom by the chains of objectivity. The nihilist dissolves these chains by the acid of despair and re-solves himself in the hope of hopelessness. This is the existential manifestation of his essential incoherence. In terms of an older vocabulary, nihilism is doomed to shipwreck because it sunders courage from wisdom, justice, and moderation.[1] As we have seen, a reliance upon courage led Nietzsche to invoke the unleashing of the blonde beasts and wars of universal destruction as the negative prelude to the advent of positive nihilism. Similarly, Heidegger was led to mistake madness for courage in 1933 and to identify the destiny of the Third Reich with that of Being. This mistake would seem to be consequent upon the elimination of the divine, and hence of divine madness. The least one may say is that the courageous turn to Being, when unaccompanied by justice or moderation, raises political dangers of so great a magnitude as to cast a shadow on the wisdom of unmitigated hybris.

One sees already in Hegel the notion that freedom depends upon the assumption of a position beyond good and evil. Whereas philosophers had always understood the difference between truth and opinion, the view that opinion must be replaced by truth, thanks to the historical "cunning of reason," is relatively recent. The point here is not simply the advisability of accommodation to the political need for noble lies. It turns rather upon comprehension of the ontological status of the domain of opinion, of what is today called the *Lebenswelt*. An indifference to the merely human, whether inspired by Historicity or mathematics, does not prevent us from choosing the bestial in place of the divine. That this problem is not peculiar to modern historicism is implicit in the demands of the ontological nihilists for a return to the world of the pre-Socratics, in order to gain a hint of the truth of the future. This demand is an essential ingredient in a critique of Socrates for having "humanized" philosophy, for having brought it down from the heavens to the cities of man. Socrates is accused of having veiled the self-manifestation of Being with a representation of how Being looks to man. In Heidegger's version of this accusation, the

1. Consider Nietzsche, *Also Sprach Zarathustra*, Vorrede, par. 4 (ed. Schlechta), p. 282: "Ich liebe den, welcher aus seiner Tugend seinen Hang und sein Verhängnis macht . . . . Ich liebe den, welcher nicht zu viele Tugenden haben will. Eine Tugend ist mehr Tugend als zwei." The whole context makes clear that it is courage which Nietzsche prefers.

moral objections raised by Nietzsche are transformed into ontological distortions. For Nietzsche, we recall, the projection of an ideal, supersensible world as the locus of value serves to drain the physical or physiological world of its creativity. Recognition of the worthlessness of the world in an ontological sense is the necessary condition for the creation of vital human values. Heidegger, accusing Nietzsche himself of Platonism or Humanism, reverses the terms of the issue. The creation of human values is itself a nihilistic interference with the "values" presented to man as gifts of Being. Hence a recognition of the worthlessness of human values is an essential part of the necessary condition for the revelation of the world as the horizon of ontological value.

Despite this radical difference between Nietzsche and Heidegger, they share the view that Socrates or Plato is responsible for the emergence of nihilism in the western world. They also agree that this responsibility emerges from a misunderstanding of man or Dasein. To this extent there is agreement between the ancients and moderns in question; the former believed that it is insufficient for the philosopher to look only at the things above and beneath the earth. In order to see the whole, it is necessary to study the intermediate things as well. And it is necessary to grasp the consequences of the fact that the activity of looking is itself intermediate. As the later Heidegger might partly agree, the daimon of philosophy, standing midway between the human and the divine, links the things of the earth to the things above and beneath the earth; it links earth and heaven by linking men and gods. Heidegger's criticism, of course, amounts to the contention that Plato's daimonic vision manufactures or projects its links, which are things among things, and human rather than "divine," or ontic rather than ontological. Even in his attention to the intermediate, Heidegger sees it as finally neither human nor divine, and hence as finally not intermediate. Such distinctions are merely ontic and thus obscure the one thing that matters—the ontological difference. Heidegger's celebration of facticity, as we have seen previously at some length, is directed simply toward uniqueness (the Being-process), rather than toward unique things. In Platonic language, one might say that Heidegger ignores the danger implicit in the marvelous powers of the daimonic. By linking earth and heaven, it may lead certain daring mortals to quit the earth, or the cities of the earth, and to strive, whether in the absence of the gods or through their destruction, to become gods themselves. The problem then arises of how, in the absence of the genuinely divine, divine madness may be distinguished from mere madness.

It should be unnecessary to repeat here the various ways in which Heidegger's Being resembles a god. The crucial point is the impossibility of distinguishing between this god and man. This impossibility, however, does not give divine status to human values; rather it robs them of all value. Attention ostensibly directed toward the intermediate is reinterpreted as an attendance upon Being. In this respect, there is a curious resemblance between Heidegger and the young Socrates, who, as we know from the Platonic dialogues and Aristophanes, was himself a "pre-Socratic" or natural philosopher. Prior to his discovery of the intermediate, Socrates understood nature in terms of the divine, or as the mathematical order underlying corporeal motions. In the *Clouds,* we see the young Socrates, studying the things above and below the earth and, suspended in his balloon, looking down upon the gods as well as the cities of men. This Socrates, we may assume, is still ignorant of, and defective in, the human eros. He has not yet received, or at least absorbed and been transformed by, his training in eros and political rhetoric from Diotima and Aspasia.[2] His hard, masculine nature has not yet been softened, and so completed, by the feminine. As the *Parmenides* indicates, his failure to "love" the intermediate still prevents him from comprehending the divine as well.[3] No doubt Socrates, in this stage of his career, would apply to humans the same methodological techniques by which he measures the jumping of a flea. From this "mathematical" perspective, there is no essential difference between the art of

2. Aspasia is portrayed in the *Menexenus* as Socrates' teacher of rhetoric. For the relation to the *Symposium,* see my *Plato's Symposium.*
3. *Parmenides* 130c5.

generalship and that of louse-catching.[4] Thus Aristophanes portrays Socrates as teaching his pupils the arguments of the unjust as well as the just *logos,* but not how to choose between them.

Aristophanes in a way anticipates the charge of Nietzsche and Heidegger by implicitly accusing Socrates of nihilism. But he does so for reasons which would apply more readily to Nietzsche and Heidegger than to the mature Socrates or his pupil. As we would now express it, Aristophanes condemns pre-Socratic philosophy, at least in that version which identifies ontology with mathematical physics, as nihilistic. The identification between divinity and number has the same disastrous consequences for the relation between reason and the good as does contemporary ontological nihilism. We cannot, of course, provide a complete interpretation of the foundation of Platonic thought. Nevertheless, we must try to understand how the mature Socrates of the dialogues attempts to provide a steadfast refuge from the timeless negations of time. If the good is the One,[5] it can be in neither an Eleatic nor a Pythagorean sense. The music of the spheres, even though composed from ordinal rather than cardinal numbers, cannot in itself account for those who count and measure it.

II.

According to Heidegger, "Being" in the original and authentic Greek teaching is understood as the presence of visibility, in the dual sense of "sprouting" or "opening forth" (φύσις) and "gathering together" or "collecting" (λόγος).[6] Heidegger thus

4. Cf. *Sophist* 227a4 ff.

5. Aristoxenus reports Plato as having said in his famous lecture "On the Good" that ⟨τ⟩ἀγαθόν ἐστιν ἕν (quoted in K. Gaiser, *Platons ungeschriebene Lehre* [Stuttgart, Ernst Klett, 1963], p. 452). This means literally that "[the] good is one," and not that it is the One.

6. *Einführung in die Metaphysik,* pp. 11, 131–34, 142; *Vortrâge und Aufsätze,* pp. 269 ff. At p. 274, Heidegger says that φύσις means the same as ζωή: "life" is here defined as "stepping out" or emerging into view. In *Einführung,* p. 11, however, he states that φύσις includes as instances the course of the heavens, the waves of the sea, etc.

emphasizes the priority of motion and development to rest and completion.[7] The appearance or presentation of beings within the openness (*Lichtung*) of Being is a process, happening, or eventuation whereby Being both diversifies itself by spilling out from an unknown and silent source and also collects or gathers itself together in the common bonds of sight and hearing.[8] When man is enmeshed in these bonds or distracted from the presentation of the process by its collected components, when he becomes absorbed in the technical activity of sorting and measuring these components in accordance with kinds, then Being is forgotten. In its place arises a world of "kinds" or "forms," namely, how things look to man;[9] this "look" is transformed into an independent, objective, and fixed or eternal paradigm. Man forgets that he has made these paradigms in his own image and thereby maims the *that* of manifestation by sundering the shape in which it has gathered itself together; this shape is now conceived as a *what*. Plato has divided λόγος from φύσις, the shaped process from the processive shaping; he thereby veils Being with the two artificial domains of the supersensible and the phenomenal.[10] Whereas previously "truth" or "uncoveredness" was the same as "Being" or the process of sprouting forth and gathering together in the openness of

7. For some representative passages, cf. *Die Frage nach dem Ding*, pp. 33 ff.; *Nietzsche, 2,* 13, 485, 489; *Der Satz vom Grund,* p. 144; "Vom Wesen und Begriff der Physis Aristoteles Physik B1," in *Il Pensiero* (May-August, 1958), Pt. I, p. 138. In *Unterwegs zur Sprache,* p. 213, Heidegger says: "Die Zeit selbst im Ganzen ihres Wesens bewegt sich nicht, ruht still." But *Ruhe* is for Heidegger self-constraining motion.

8. "Process, happening, and eventuation" translate *Bewegung, Geschehen,* and *Ereignis.* For the unknown and unthought character of the source, cf. *Identität und Differenz,* p. 44; *Nietzsche, 1,* 471, *2,* 484; *Unterwegs zur Sprache,* p. 31, and the discussion in the preceding chapter. For the common root of sight and hearing, *Der Satz vom Grund,* pp. 86 ff.

9. *Vom Wesen des Grundes,* p. 41; *Was ist das—die Philosophie?* (Pfullingen, G. Neske Verlag, 1956), pp. 16, 24–27; *Platons Lehre von der Wahrheit,* pp. 34, 46; *Einführung,* p. 139.

10. *Nietzsche, 2,* 430 ff.

presence, it is now conceived as a property of statements *about* beings. "Truth" is now defined as "correctness" in the sense of similarity or correspondence between propositional speech and the separate Ideas.[11] Man is thus sundered from lived intimacy and integrity with Being. Truth is no longer an activity of manifestation or uncovering in which man participates, and by which he is "in touch with" what presents itself.[12] Wisdom no longer retains its authentic meaning of "knowing one's way about in that which is present as the uncovered and which is the continuous as that which appears." [13] Philosophy is no longer life, but a preparation for dying; or more accurately, it is the death of φύσις through the instrumentality of the sundered and so altered λόγος.

Plato reinterprets Being as ἰδέα, that is, as the paradigm which defines beings in terms of their calculative, categorizable attributes. Hence the significance of his conception of these paradigms as τὸ ἀγαθόν, the good, namely, "that which makes the thing (*das Seiende*) useful or capable (*tauglich*) to *be* a thing. Being shows itself in the character of making possible and conditioning. Here the decisive step for all of Metaphysics is taken." [14] Being is conceived both as pure presence and as the condition for the possibility of pure presence.[15] The condition for the possibility of a thing is the primitive version of what Nietzsche calls "value," namely, what permits things to be. The priority of the condition to the thing amounts to its identification as ὄντως ὄν, whereas the thing is reduced to τὸ μὴ ὄν.[16] This is the basis for the development, in the history of western philosophy, of Being as a system of necessary conditions with which man as subject must calculate in advance. It is the basis for the development of *values,* and so for the "devaluation" of

11. *Einführung,* p. 142; *Platons Lehre,* pp. 41–42, 49; *Humanismusbrief,* p. 106.
12. *Einführung,* pp. 134, 146; *Was Heisst Denken?* pp. 73–74, 122–26; *Vorträge,* pp. 208 ff.
13. *Platons Lehre,* p. 47.
14. *Nietzsche, 2,* 226.
15. Ibid., p. 229.
16. Ibid., p. 227.

what is posterior to, dependent upon, brought to light by, these anthropomorphic value-paradigms.[17] This is the classical origin of nihilism, or the view that things as a whole are worthless.[18]

Nietzsche and Heidegger in effect accuse the Platonic Socrates of a lack of existential courage and a consequent failure to attempt a direct encounter with Being. Whether this failure is one of human morality or ontological destiny, it leads to the effort to domesticate Being, to make it useful and so (as becomes especially clear with Descartes) secure. Socrates himself touches upon the danger of a direct encounter with things ($\tau\grave{\alpha}$ ὄντα) in the *Phaedo,* while discussing the development of his own philosophical views. He warns against the lack of caution that leads some to look directly at the sun during an eclipse:

> the eyes of some are destroyed, if they do not look at its image (εἰκόνα) in water or in something else. I had something like this in mind, and I feared lest I might altogether blind my psyche in looking at things with my eyes, trying to grasp them with each of the senses.[19]

This warning, of course, applies immediately to the procedures of those natural philosophers like Anaxagoras, who take their bearings by bodies. But as the reference to the sun suggests, it applies also to those who strive for a direct encounter with Being. The issue is that of the safest access to visibility, and hence to the source of visibility. Mathematical physicists and fundamental ontologists share a disdain for icons; they are iconoclasts, who in their eagerness to see the divine disregard the merely human. This onto-epistemological daring has its practical counterpart in a resolute, even ruthless "sincerity" concerning what Socrates calls πίστις, or, as we may translate it, belief in icons. Socrates, on the contrary, just as he is cautious with respect to looking at the sun, also practices a prudential irony in the domain of human opinion.

The iconoclasm of physicists and ontologists is itself shat-

17. Ibid., p. 230.
18. Ibid., pp. 282, 313.
19. *Phaedo* 99d4 ff.

tered on the problem of speech. Physics and ontology are both speeches, or icons of things as manifested in the human psyche.[20] The attempt to purify speech of its human or iconic content is obviously necessary, if in different degrees, for both physics and ontology. In the case of physics, the result is mathematics, and so long as mathematics remains an instrument of human speech, the results are salutary. But when mathematics itself becomes the paradigm of speech, the result is paradoxical and destructive. Speech purified of iconic content deteriorates into a most peculiar icon—a silent image of speech, very much like the silent speech of fundamental ontology. The pure speech of non-iconic εἰκασία is silent because it has altogether forgotten about its origin in the human psyche. This radical self-forgetting, which leaves speech uprooted, is an optical hallucination caused by excessive daring. In other words, the act of looking directly at things is in fact an act of looking at speeches about things. Whatever else it may be, looking is for man also speaking; hence the inseparable connection between theory and logos. To see is to see something—in the language of sense perception, to collect (or re-collect) the sensuous qualities in a spatio-temporal field into a determinate shape. The process of col-lection, as the etymology indicates, takes place *with speech*. Logical collection, in this fundamental sense, is the process by which the psyche identifies to itself unities within the perceptual field. To keep silent about a present unity would be to fail to identify it to oneself, hence to render it invisible, or nothing.

A resolution to look at things rather than at speeches about things amounts to being blind to things. Here the analogy with sense perception is possibly misleading, since we do not or may not notice, in looking at a flower, a sunset, or what you will, that internal speech makes visible "the thing itself" toward

20. Consider *Republic* 596c4 ff. In comparing the mimetic artist to a mirror, in which one may reflect the whole, Socrates is obviously employing an icon of the psyche, as the context makes clear; cf. 588b10 ff. He uses the term εἴδωλον to designate the inferior images of the mimetic artist (e.g. 598b8, 600e4). See also Jacob Klein, *A Commentary on Plato's Meno* (Chapel Hill, University of North Carolina Press, 1965), pp. 112 ff. and my *Plato's Symposium,* pp. 294 ff.

which we are maintaining an external silence. If words interfere with, or cannot do justice to, the visual impact of a given scene, this impact nevertheless depends altogether upon the previous collective function of the psyche, which presents to some other function the scene being admired. In the case of thinking, Being presents itself in the shape of beings, apart from which (as the fundamental ontologist apparently agrees) it is nothingness. The visibility of Being depends not upon a prior recognition of its absence, but upon the accessibility of the shapes of its manifestation to the logical function of the psyche. Thinking is seeing made articulate, speaking vision, hence, to be sure, not just speech, but col-lection. Therefore, to think about the silent aspect of thinking which accompanies speech is analogous to looking at the presentation of things which accompanies sense perception. We can do this, but *through* the sense perceptions, not independently of them. Similarly, we can think about silent thinking (νόησις), but *through* speaking thought (διάνοια); this is one way of understanding why Socrates calls the highest philosophical activity *dialectic*.

In the passage of the *Phaedo* previously cited, Socrates goes on to discuss his own transition from looking directly at things to "taking refuge with speeches (λόγοι), so as to see in them the truth of things." [21] At this point, one must make a distinction between the procedure of Socrates and that which is common to Husserl and Heidegger. Entirely apart from the many differences between the latter two, they share the conviction that the significance of a thing is inseparable and unintelligible apart from our intentional consciousness of that thing. This is perhaps more obvious in Husserl than in Heidegger. But even for Heidegger, the "sense of Being" is constituted in the open horizon of Dasein's project of Being. After *Being and Time,* this point is transformed into the manifestation of the truth of Being to itself as the gift of man. But this change in emphasis (from Being as man's project to man as Being's project) only exaggerates the unity of thought and thing. In both Husserl and Heidegger, the essence of this unity (thought and the sense or being of the

21. *Phaedo* 99e5-6.

thing) is Historicity. The problem of Historicity is displaced in Husserl from the noetic *eidos* to the nature of subjectivity. In Heidegger, however, the intention is to avoid subjectivity as well as objectivity; this more radical self-forgetting serves to suppress the spoken element in the unity of thought and Being. Both thing and thinker, both col-lection and col-lector, are subordinated to the "and" or "col-" by virtue of the ontological difference.

From this contemporary perspective, we may say that Socrates turns to speech in an effort to avoid the twin dangers of Historicity and silence. Socrates looks through speech as the icon of things (in his example, the sun) [22] to the sense or truth of the things as independent of, though revealed by, the activity of looking. He is led through speech beyond thought to the "safest" or "steadiest" hypothesis of the Ideas, or "the beautiful in itself, good, great, and all the others." [23] Let us observe immediately that this does not result, as Heidegger claims, in a limitation to the "correspondence theory" of truth, namely, to truth as a property of the correspondence between speech and things. To be sure, there is in one sense a correspondence between speech as icon and the shapes (or, indirectly, the horizons) which accompany speech; but in this sense, there must be a correspondence between what the Being-process uncovers and the thought in and before which it is uncovered. But more fundamentally, the function of the icon (in dianoetic *eikasia,* as Jacob Klein calls it) is to manifest or un-cover ($\dot{a}$-$\lambda\eta\theta\epsilon\hat{\imath}\nu$) the truth as the sense of the being of the thing spoken. There is a difference between the speech and the form revealed by the speech. Truth in the fullest sense is not a property of propositions or icons, but is the being reflected within the icon.[24]

In the *Phaedo,* the "safety" of the Ideas lies in their steadfast

22. 100a1-3: a λόγος is no more an εἰκών than τὸν ἐν ἔργοις, or, as Aristotle might say, the things qua being-at-work. Therefore, it is either as much or less an icon, but still an icon.

23. 100b5. Socrates says that it is "safest" (ἀσφαλέστατον) to refer to these as the sources of qualities within genesis.

24. Cf. *Republic* 506e3, 508d4 and e1. From 522 ff., Socrates uses οὐσία and ἀλήθεια interchangeably.

endurance against the motion of bodies (physics) and the glare of the sun (ontology). The connected notions of reliability, safety, and steadfastness play an important role in the discussion of the Ideas throughout the Platonic dialogues.[25] The simplest way to appreciate the significance of these terms is by considering the insecurity, perpetual motion, and destructiveness of genesis. The transition from genesis to the safe domain of οὐσία, from bodies to speeches reflecting the truth about bodies, is especially apparent in the *Republic*. Socrates begins to emphasize the safety and steadfastness of the noetic domain after discussing the ambiguities of sense perception.[26] Mathematics (counting and logistics) serves as the transition from these ambiguities to the certitude of dialectics: we can "count upon" the numerological structure of the perceived thing in two different senses. Mathematics also functions to unite the soldier and philosopher in their common war against the destructive uncertainties of genesis.[27] Thus steadfastness elicits the courage of the soldier and the dialectician, depending in both cases not on existential resolution, but on knowledge. Socratic courage is inseparable from knowledge, and therefore from prudence and moderation: one must not mistake rashness for steadfastness, nor a blind hope for synoptic vision. The Ideas thus protect us against two forms of blindness, one due to an excess of darkness (the blur of motion), the other to an excess of light (the sun).

As justice, its main theme, suggests, the *Republic* is a dialogue devoted to the moderate aspects of philosophy. It therefore abstracts for the most part from eros, mania, and poetry, all of which are related to the body or genesis, and which are criticized throughout the dialogue.[28] Mathematics, the most sober of sciences, is an especially appropriate ally in the presentation

25. See the entries under such terms as ἀσφαλής, βέβαιος, and μόνιμος in Ast, *Lexicon Platonicum*.

26. E.g. 533c7; 535a10, c1; 536e3; 537b8.

27. 525b3 ff., 533b1 ff.

28. For the necessary qualification, see my article, "The Role of Eros in Plato's *Republic*," *Review of Metaphysics, 19* (March 1965), 462–75.

of the sobriety of philosophy. The public atmosphere and theme
of the *Republic,* when contrasted with the private atmosphere
and themes of the *Symposium* and *Phaedrus,* suggest that divine
madness is permissible and safe only after the polis has been
made sober and steadfast. At this level, the fundamental problem of the *Republic* is how to construct, albeit only in speech,
the form of man's life within genesis, while at the same time abstracting from or restricting genesis as much as possible. The
impossibility of justice is due precisely to the nonmathematical
character of political existence. From this viewpoint, there is a
disproportion between the courage of the soldier and that of the
dialectician: the upward ascent of mathematics terminates in
radically nonpolitical universality. Thus the dialectician returns
to the polis through external constraint, forced, so to speak, by
the soldier whose spirit he has himself politicized. The courage
of the soldier is enlarged or ennobled by the knowledge of the
dialectician, whereas the knowledge of the dialectician is restricted or vulgarized by the courage of the soldier. We may recognize here an implicit version of the dialectic of master and
slave.

Socrates' final word on the possibility of the just polis is to
deny the relevance of its actuality in history:

> perhaps it is a paradigm set up in heaven for him who
> wills to see and, seeing, founds a polis within himself. It
> makes no difference whether the polis exists somewhere
> or ever will exist. He will do only the deeds peculiar to
> that polis, and none else.[29]

These lines express as well as any the trans-political infrastruc-
ture of the *Republic.* In the present context, they show how the
philosopher responds to the insecurity of genesis, or of bodies,
by turning away toward speeches. His political responsibility is
determined by the polis of logos, not because of an "idealistic"
incapacity to face or grasp political reality, but because reality
can be faced or grasped only through speech. The "real" polis
of historical existence is in itself as impossible to grasp by a di-

29. *Republic* 592b2 ff.

rect encounter as is the coincidence of long and short in a single finger by immediate sense perception. The fact that we speak about the motion of bodies cannot be explained as a direct encounter with bodies or things themselves;[30] words and numbers intervene between us and the bodies or mediate between the strange mixture of excessive light and darkness that constitutes the nature of bodies. The double mediation of words and numbers, however, is again not visible or intelligible in its own terms, since it too participates in the motion and glare of genesis. The visibility or intelligibility of words and numbers as icons of things apparently depends upon their also being icons of the visible and intelligible simply or in itself.

The hypothesis of the Ideas is suggested to us primarily by reflection upon the fact of speech, or the utility of words and numbers in our various encounters with things. Their utility includes the power of self-reference, so that we may encounter them too, albeit not without paradox. But the paradoxical instability of words and numbers arises from their eikastic nature, not from the intelligible shapes of which they are icons. The capacity to distinguish the terms of a paradox, for example, or to uncover stability in the pattern of motions, cannot be derived from the destructive negations of the contradictory or totally moving. The paradoxical co-presence of stability and instability in words and numbers is a direct exhibition of the co-presence of the dimensions of genesis and *ousia*. In short, logos is both good and bad or, as Aristophanes expressed it, both just and unjust. The logical icon is reflected upon the "surface" of genesis, in whose darkness or "evil" it necessarily shares.[31] But that which is reflected in the icon does not share in the evil of genesis, any more than a body shares in the distortion of a warped mirror. To repeat, the manifestation of the Idea in the logical icon is different from the manifestation of the logical icon in

30. Consider here *Timaeus* 49c6 ff. and esp. the use of ἀσφαλέστατα at 49d3.

31. Cf. F. M. Cornford, *Plato's Cosmology* (London, Routledge and Kegan Paul, 1948), p. 184: "The qualities do not belong to [the Receptacle]; they only pass in and out, like images crossing a mirror."

genesis. Therefore the "goodness" of the Ideas is different from the "goodness" intrinsic to the correlatives "good and evil" or "just and unjust."

Words and numbers share in the deception of genesis because they are the most characteristic product of the continuous motion of the psyche.[32] The Ideas (and Ideal Numbers), on the other hand, are not speeches. When Socrates refers to the Ideas as a "hypothesis," he does not mean that they are projections or a "project" of the human will. The Ideas stand beneath the corporeal motions in such a way as to make them stand forth or acquire and maintain visibility. In this sense, perceptible bodies are "projects" of the Ideas. The projective or hypothesizing capacity of logos is thus a response to, rather than a creation of, the silent stability of the Ideas. The persistent silence or indifference of the Ideas is precisely what renders them steadfast, safe, reliable: we can count upon the Ideas precisely because they do not care about us. Lacking in care or eros, the Ideas neither approach nor recede; they have no intentions, no will, no perspective, and no history. As a result, they are "beyond good and evil," or like perfect judges. They cannot err because they do not move; they make no decisions, never "take a stand" because they have always been standing.[33] The Ideas are that by which man takes his stand, through the mediation of words and numbers. And, like perfect judges, they make it possible for each man to take an equal stand: all men are equal before the Ideas.

III.

In the previous section, I have tried to suggest a way of approaching Plato's Ideas that illuminates their function as the source of goodness in the political as well as the mathematical

32. *Phaedrus* 245c5 ff. Cf. 247d1 ff. The divine psyche never leaves the cosmos of genesis, but goes round with it while standing on its surface.

33. I am here referring to Heidegger's question-begging interpretation of οὐσία as *Verweilen*.

sense. The key step is to recognize that political stability depends upon the stability of logos. The distinction between the just and the unjust logos is derived from the stable or self-transcending dimension of words and numbers. If men cannot give an account of their deeds, they will never be able to measure the relative value of those deeds. The perception of nobility is thus the first premise of Platonic pragmatics or the human interpretation of divine measures. Man achieves justice by measuring his deeds in accordance with logos or eidetic speech. The difference between the indeterminate psyche and the determinate Ideas makes this measure of political music both possible and difficult. Without measure, speech becomes self-contradictory or is reduced to silence. If the act of speech must project its own measures, the result is ultimately the same, postponed only by the degree of tenacity with which the resolute speaker clings to his integrity. It is especially important for us to observe that political music does not exclude human freedom, but gives it coherence and articulateness. A freedom which cannot give an account of itself is indistinguishable from slavery.

The only discussion in the Platonic dialogues of the goodness of the Ideas is presented in terms of three icons—the sun, the divided line, and the cave. In the dramatic structure of the *Republic,* the divided line is itself the dividing line between the icons of sun and cave. One might infer from this that the divided line represents the ordinary surface life of man, as the sun stands for heaven and the cave for hell. This inference, of course, can be easily exaggerated. To mention only the obvious difficulty, the cave represents the polis and would therefore include the domain of ordinary terrestrial existence. Nevertheless, and with all due caution, I believe it is helpful to think of the divided line as a sort of ladder suspended between noetic and political existence. In modern terminology, the divided line is an epistemological icon, intermediate between noetic vision and political praxis, hence pointing in both directions, and therefore indeterminate (if not altogether meaningless) in isolation from the sun and cave. This indeterminateness is indicated by the fact that the section marked off on the line itself for the domain of

icons is insufficient in two different ways: first, it does not account for the fact that the geometric arts of the dianoetic section
use the bodies of the visible world as icons; and second, it does
not explain the sense in which the entire line as well as the sun
and cave are icons. This is further emphasized by the fact that
Socrates does not speak of the good in describing the divided
line, as he must when discussing the sun and the cave.[34]

One cannot understand the discussion of the good in terms of
modern epistemological procedures. The icons employed are
part of the teaching, and not a superfluous medium of transmis-
sion. Otherwise stated, the mode of exposition followed by Socrates is downward rather than upward—from the sun down to
the cave by way of the ladder of the divided line. The "released" cave dweller, like the young guardian, may then be conveyed upward in the opposite direction, thanks to the prior
manifestation of philosophy or noetic vision. In sum, mathematics and politics are both subordinate to, and illuminated by,
philosophy. The way up, contrary to the assertion of Heraclitus,
is not the same as the way down; it merely seems so from the
perspectives of mathematical physics and fundamental ontology. Finally, the discussion of the good in the *Republic* is an
icon in a sense which conforms to the demand made earlier by
Socrates and Glaucon on the poets: only those are to be permitted to make poetry in the just polis "who have impressed the
icon of the good character onto their poems."[35] Socratic
speech (and Platonic writing) is poetry of this kind, namely,
speech exhibiting the psyche as the ground of unification of
mathematics and politics. But this is another way of saying that
man's freedom lies in the recognition of his need for delimita-
tion, precisely because this need is unlimited.

The Ideas, then, are not, as Nietzsche thought, a "moral"
hypothesis; Plato's moral teaching is a consequence rather than

34. The good is discussed in conjunction with dialectic at 534b8 ff.
after, but not as a part of, a reminder of the classes designated by the
segments on the line. Cf. O. Utermöhlen, *Die Bedeutung der Ideenlehre
für die platonische Politeia* (Heidelberg, C. Winter, 1967), pp. 42 ff.

35. *Republic* 401b2-3.

the condition of the goodness of the Ideas. The more serious question is whether the teaching of the good is a kind of onto-logical utilitarianism, as Heidegger maintains. We recall that, in his interpretaton, the good, through the instrumentality of the Idea, makes the thing "useful or capable (*tauglich*) to *be* a thing." This in turn means that Being, or the lighting-process, is ignored in favor of the determinate shapes collected through the agency of the process.[36] Plato is said to define as Being that aspect of the whole which makes it serviceable for man; this is his prototypical subjective Humanism. Thus Heidegger says of Plato's emphasis in the *Republic* on fire, firelight, shadows, day-light, sunlight, and sun:

> Everything turns upon the shining of what appears (*am Scheinen des Erscheinenden*) and upon making possible its visibility. Uncoveredness is indeed named in its vari-ous stages, but it is thought there only for this: how it makes accessible what appears in its aspect (εἶδος) and [how it makes] visible this self-pointing-out (ἰδέα).[37]

It would seem that Heidegger, even in calling attention to the complex structure of Platonic eikasia, assumes that Plato is conscious only of the words spoken by Socrates. That is, he accuses Plato of missing the significance of his own light imag-ery by subordinating truth in the sense of uncoveredness to the Idea as the standard of correct speech. In sum, Plato is accused of suppressing or forgetting Being in favor of an anthropo-morphic perspective or interpretation of Being. If Nietzsche is the last Platonist, Plato is apparently the first Nietzschean.

In order to ascertain the validity of Heidegger's analysis, we must inspect the most important details of Plato's own presenta-tion. Let us begin by reminding ourselves of the general inten-tions of the *Republic,* and then of the immediate context of the discussion of the good. Henceforward we shall restrict ourselves almost exclusively to the *Republic,* which is permissible because only there does Socrates speak at length of the good, and be-

36. *Humanismusbrief,* p. 77.
37. *Platons Lehre,* p. 34.

cause it is the subject of Heidegger's most influential attacks on
Plato. The dialogue has as its explicit guiding thread the question, what is justice? This question very soon merges into another, is justice in itself, independent of reputation or external
rewards, desirable or good? In other words, does it bring
εὐδαιμονία (literally, a good daimon) or blessedness to the individual psyche? The investigation of the polis is thus a digression from the main issue, introduced for purposes of clarification.[38] Similarly, the discussion of philosophy is a digression,
intended as a clarification of the political investigation.[39] Let
me emphasize this most important fact. *The icon of the good is
a digression within a digression from the primary question of
whether justice is good, i.e. desirable in itself.* But justice in itself is the Idea of justice; the task is to see whether we can gaze
upon the goodness of the Idea of justice by looking exclusively
at it, not at its lower and concomitant epiphenomena.

The dramatic center of the dialogue, often characterized as
the peak of Socrates' dialectical ascent, is thus shown by the
most elementary observations to occupy a peculiarly oblique
position within the total scheme. This observation may be
solidly reinforced by noting the various ways in which Socrates
explicitly calls attention to the tentative and incomplete nature
of his eikastic remarks about the good.[40] We have, at the
center of a dialogue which abstracts from poetry and genesis, a
poem or prophecy, the key to which (the sun) is expressed in
terms of genesis. The mode of speech appropriate to a description of the good character is thus evidently appropriate to a
description of the principle of the good character. The "ethical" or humanistic aspects of Socrates' prophecy of the good
would seem to be intentional dramatic accommodations to his
central thesis, namely, that justice is good in the sense of desirable for itself alone. Even further, these aspects are accom-

38. *Republic* 368c8 ff. and 369al ff.
39. 543c4 ff.
40. Socrates refers to the incompleteness of the treatment at 506e1,
509c7-10, and 517b6. His speech is characterized as "prophetic" at 505e1-
506a5 and 523a8; it is called a game at 536c1.

modations to Socrates' intention to transform this investigation from the private to the public domain. Entirely apart from whether the logic of the analogy is sound, Socrates' claim that we can understand the order in the psyche only by studying the order in the polis is obviously designed to convince his interlocutors that happiness, the highest good for the individual, depends upon justice in the polis.

In view of Heidegger's tendency to read the image of the cave as though it were a meditation on Being, it seems desirable to remind the reader that the discussion of the good has a political context. However, merely to repeat this platitude would be more confusing than illuminating. One reason for this, which Heidegger does not seem to have grasped, is that the cave itself is a political rather than an ontological metaphor. The significance of the overall political context is to tell us something about Plato's ontology; the key to that ontology is not the cave, but the sun. Let me make a general remark here about the confusing character of the political context. Perhaps the two central difficulties in the obvious plan of the *Republic* are the relation between the individual psyche and the order of the polis and, within the polis, the relation between the philosopher and the soldier. There is nothing in the explicit argument of the *Republic* to show why the blessed or internally harmonious (and in that sense just) individual is, by virtue of his internal harmony as distinct from external compulsion, identical with the just citizen of the just polis.[41] In other words, if it were Plato's goal to give his answer to the problem of political justice, philosophy would seem to be not merely a digression, but an insuperable impediment. If, on the other hand, he wished to demonstrate that individual happiness or blessedness is accessible only

41. Cf. 519d8 ff. and 520a6 ff.; the philosophers are constrained to enter politics, either out of self-protection or to pay a debt. This issue is well stated, within the conventional perspective, by A. W. H. Adkins, *Merit and Responsibility* (New York and London, Oxford University Press, 1960), esp. pp. 249, 253, and 288–91. Socrates' remark at 592a7 does not contradict the conventional interpretation, since it refers to the polis in philosophical speech, and not to the incarnation of that speech in deed.

through philosophy, then the political analogy seems an unfortunate superfluity.

The connection between politics and philosophy becomes genuinely clear only when we remember the point made at the beginning of this section: order and stability in speech and deed depend upon what Socrates calls the Ideas. But speech and deed are not themselves Ideas; they are functions of the human psyche. The difference between the psyche and the Ideas, which is not present in Heidegger, is sufficient evidence of his error in asserting that Plato replaces Being by the eidetic "looks" of what is. This amounts to the assertion that Being in Plato is, or is represented by (the Idea of), the good, in the sense of the goodness or essence of the Ideas. But this is to identify the whole with the domain of the Ideas, or to forget about the psyche (and the receptacle). The goodness of the Ideas rather would seem to be but one manifestation of the good itself; intelligibility does not account for life or intelligence. A further peculiarity of the *Republic* is that, although its main explicit intention is to study the psyche, or what is intrinsically good for the psyche, the discussion of the good seems to be conducted in terms of the Ideas rather than the psyche. Can this be due to the fact that an abstraction from the body is necessarily also an abstraction from the psyche?

In any case, the icons employed in describing the good are surely unintelligible except as speeches about the process by which the psyche sees the Ideas, and hence the good. If I am not mistaken, it is our ontological or epistemological prejudices which often obscure our perception of the importance of the psyche to the discussion of the good.[42] The nihilistic consequences of these prejudices lead finally to the complete suppression of the psyche. In the final noetic vision of the Ideas (and of the good), the seer would no longer be cognizant of his psychic individuality, and blessedness would be indistinguishable from death. If philosophy aspires to godhood in the Aristotelian sense of pure noesis, then it is radically disconnected from

42. At 578c6, Socrates points out that knowledge is necessary because περὶ γάρ τοι τοῦ μεγίστου ἡ σκέψις, ἀγαθοῦ τε βίου καὶ κακοῦ.

human or political existence. If, on the other hand, this aspiration is an "Idea" in the metaphorical sense of a standard or measure by which to impose stability on the indeterminate psyche, then an inner harmony between philosophy and the polis becomes intelligible. Its intelligibility resides in the fact that the philosopher is also a soldier or citizen; that is, the human psyche is not coextensive with the Ideas, and it cannot be restricted to vision of the Ideas without undergoing suppression or destruction. But this is scarcely a reason to repudiate the "restraining" measure of the Ideas, since the psyche, when left to its own indeterminate devices, is necessarily vitiated by its own chaotic exuberance.

IV.

The immediate context of the icon of the good is a discussion of the philosophical nature. Just as the divided line mediates between sun and cave, so the abstract content of philosophical study, or mathematics and dialectic, mediates between philosophical and political existence. The philosophers are "saviors of the regime"; a rare combination of steadiness and quickness, they stand to the polis as do the Ideas to logos.[43] In other words, it is the human psyche, conceived as a whole, that unifies philosophy and politics. Man is the principle of his own unity because he is able to measure himself by the Ideas. Plato's solution to the problem of the disjunction between private blessedness and public justice is to sublate it in the dialectical development of man's Protean nature. His solution to the problem of the indiscriminateness of Proteus is contained in the hypothesis of the good, which becomes accessible to us in the vision of the Ideas. This means that the good in the ordinary sense of useful and helpful, although itself useful in pointing toward the good in the highest sense, is too unsteady to serve as a basis for hap-

43. 502e1-504c8. Note that justice and moderation, attributed to the philosophical nature at 487a2-5, are suppressed in the revised list of philosophical qualities at 494b1. At 503a1, Socrates ambiguously asserts as their previous conclusion that δεῖν αὐτοὺς φιλοπόλιδάς τε φαίνεσθαι.

piness and blessedness. Ordinary language is certainly an icon of truth, but one in which the reflection is blurred by history, as reflections in water are blurred by the rippling of the waves.

Socrates, of course, does not speak of history, but rather of the body. He divides the education of the guardians into gymnastics and learning; the pursuit of courage, justice, and temperance belong to the former, or to cultivation of what is today called "the lived body." It is in connection with this cultivation that the nonphilosopher, even one so austere as Adeimantus, supposes "the greatest study" to be found.[44] He is mistaken; there is a study "still greater than justice" and the other virtues, and one about which he has often heard, namely, that "the Idea of the good is the greatest study . . . through the use of which, just things and the others too become useful and helpful." [45] Adeimantus can scarcely be presumed to be an expert on the theory of Ideas: ἰδέα undoubtedly conveys to him the sense of shape, pattern, look, or nature. He is, however, familiar with discussions about how things become useful, or with commonsensical opinions about the good. Even from the vantage point of common sense, Socrates indicates, just things are not useful in themselves, and hence are not good in themselves. They become so through μάθημα—study or knowledge (from which the word "mathematics" is derived). The utility or helpfulness of human goods is dependent upon the intelligibility or order of beings, and so upon intelligence.[46] To this extent, it is already evident, Heidegger is correct: the good confers utility. But as

44. 504c9-e6. Socrates says that the previous discussion of the virtues has been sketchy and implies that, from now on, they must proceed with greater precision. Yet this is followed by the tentative prophecy of the good. Perhaps the prophecy is more precise in its way than the discursive ascent which preceded it.

45. 504e7-505a4. One may suspect that the "always most courageous" Glaucon, who first questioned the intrinsic desirability of justice, would not have been as puzzled as Adeimantus to hear that it is not the greatest study.

46. Cf. 518e4: when Socrates returns to the distinction between the corporeal and psychic virtues, he once more characterizes the latter as χρήσιμόν τε καὶ ὠφέλιμον.

Socrates immediately notes, we do not yet understand the true meaning of "useful" because we are normally oriented by the body rather than by the psyche.

In everyday discourse, "good" means useful, helpful, or beneficial. But ordinary understanding is defective or unstable; it does not tell us what is truly useful, helpful, or beneficial. The many, for example, define pleasure as the good, and so by implication the useful is the pleasant. Those who are more clever, namely, those who understand the commonsensical distinction between good and bad pleasures, define the good to be φρόνησις, or intelligence.[47] This distinction is parallel to the previous distinction between gymnastics and study, and so between the body and the psyche. The result is to suggest a correlation between gymnastics, the noncognitive or political virtues, and pleasure. It is obvious that what is useful for the psyche is not necessarily useful for the body. More fundamentally, to call the good useful is circular or question-begging, since, if asked what we mean by "utility," or why we value it, we would have to reply, "because it is good"—that is, we would assume that pleasure (let us say) is good and would define the useful on the basis of that unstable hypothesis. Socrates repudiates this ordinary hypothetical reasoning about the good. He insists that if we cannot discharge our hypotheses, or identify the good in a sense which unambiguously defines what is truly useful, helpful, or beneficial for man, then nothing is truly, or can truly be called, useful.

For all we know so far, Socrates could easily mean by "the good" a manifestation of Being in its openness or uncoveredness, in a way similar to, if not identical with, Heidegger's conception of "the one thing needful." To say that the good is the source or the ground of the utility of things is very much like saying that Being makes a gift of itself to man via the intelligibility of beings. But there is another difficulty, more trivial and consequently much more influential, that needs to be dissipated at this point. I refer to the widely held view that Socrates is guilty of "naturalism," or the logical fallacy of inferring from a

47. 505b5-7. Cf. 518d9 ff.

factual description the value or desirability of a given factual condition. I have already had occasion to comment on the untenable nature of the post-Humean distinction between "facts" and "values." Here it must be observed that Socrates does not identify a factual condition with a moral value. On the contrary, factual conditions possess for him no intrinsic value whatsoever; they are contingent for their value upon whether and to what degree they contribute to blessedness or wisdom. It should also be clear that the value of blessedness or wisdom is not intelligible in terms of a conception of morality derived fundamentally from the Judaeo-Christian Scripture. As I noted in a previous chapter, there is a close historical connection between the Judaeo-Christian religion and the modern mathematical epistemology which severs facts from values. In addition to what was previously said, let me add here that the dilemma of the difference between facts and values arises from accepting the view that value is trans-rational, while at the same time denying the trans-mathematical unity of the human psyche. Socrates is guilty of neither of these views. What we today call a "fact" is for him rather a moment or phase in a dialectic between the psyche and the domain of intelligibility. Our "facts" represent an unanalyzed historical synthesis of nature and history. Socrates, on the contrary, does not identify nature with history, nor does he restrict it to the subject of the mathematical sciences.

Plato, using the "arguments" of Socrates as one element in the exercise of his complete dialectical skill, uncovers the intrinsic meaning or directedness of human desire (often called "eros"). Like the great founders of the modern world, he agrees that "good" is, in the most fundamental and comprehensive sense, what men desire. He differs from them, however, in his analysis of desire. I shall return to this point in the next chapter. For the present, this much may be said: Plato maintains that the true object of every desire, when properly understood, is and can be nothing less than perfection, blessedness, or the satisfaction in a comprehensive rather than numerically particular sense of every desire. On the basis of this contention, since the useful is the desirable and the good is the useful, there cannot be any other standard of goodness than wisdom. Plato's analysis of desire may be mistaken, but it has nothing to do with subjectivism, humanistic relativism, or the mystical attribution of value to facts. The good as the source of intelligibility is necessarily the source of the good as the useful or valuable, because the satisfaction of desire in both the vulgar and the philosophical sense always depends upon knowledge, and so upon the knowability of the kinds, shapes, or Ideas of things. To say that the Ideas measure desire is also to deny Heidegger's assertion that possibility is higher or more illuminating than actuality. The psyche acquires knowledge of itself by the intentional activity of desiring, which is always for this or that thing or condition. We know what we can be by an actual investigation, through the instrumentality of logos, of what we do.

The good, then, is the goal of every human act, whether in speech or deed, without in any way compromising the difference between one particular good and another. With respect to justice and beauty, men will often rest content with opinion; but in the case of the good, everyone looks for "the real thing." [48] In everyday life, the useful is closer to truth (true being) than justice and beauty, and for two reasons. First, in using things, we necessarily discover something reliable about their natures. Second, we are less likely to deceive ourselves about what we desire than about what we admire. This commonsensical distinction, incidentally, reflects the "ontological" superiority of the individual to the polis and casts doubt upon the analogy between the two. It is no accident that the digression about the good, despite the political environment, takes its bearings by selfishness rather than justice. Needless to say, Socrates does not remain at the commonsensical or everyday expression of desire for the useful.[49] He claims that selfishness, in its own best interests, is

48. 505d5-10.

49. As is obvious from 505d11-506a3: without knowledge of the good, i.e. wisdom, the psyche is doomed to incertitude about the utility of whatever it desires. It is restricted to prophetic intimations rather than the stability of *logos* measured by Ideas.

forced to transcend itself by the very process of true self-gratification. This thesis is closer to Hegel's notion of "the cunning of reason" (though not in its historical sense) than to the Kantian community of enlightened devils. What Hegel makes a necessary historical result of the development of Absolute Geist is for Socrates contingent because accessible only to the philosopher, and only as philosophical knowledge of the significance of human nature.

A word should be said here about the connection between the noble or beautiful (τὸ καλόν) and the good. It is correct to assert that a good speech or deed may also be beautiful, but from the opinion that X is beautiful, it does not follow logically or truly that X is good. The perception of beauty is more closely conditioned by the body than the perception of the useful. A judgment is theoretically verifiable in terms of the universal goal of desire. A judgment of beauty is an expression of sense perception, historical aesthetic taste, political opinion, and the like, none of which need be useful truly or theoretically. There is no inconsistency between the facts that X seems beautiful to Y and that X is harmful to Y. In fine, it is meaningful to speak of "true beauty" only on the basis of knowledge of true utility. But one may speak of true utility even with respect to the ugly. The conjunction "noble and good" (καλὸς κἀγαθός, also the phrase for "gentleman") is narrower in its scope than "good," because "good" and "noble" are not synonyms. To repeat, one cannot distinguish between the seemingly beautiful and true beauty except by knowledge of truth. And it would be difficult to maintain that such knowledge always dispels the appearance of beauty in conjunction with the false. One has only to think of Socrates' admiration for Homer to grasp this point. In sum, "true" and "false" apply to the noble or beautiful only with respect to the final goal of human desire, or wisdom.[50]

Throughout the early books of the *Republic,* the good is regularly identified with, or in terms of, the useful.[51] As we move

50. Consider 400d11 ff., 452d6-e2.
51. Examples: 333b1,   339b3,   349e6,   367d3,   379b1 ff.,   408a1, 412d2 ff., 424a4 ff., 438a2-3, 457d5-7.

toward and into the discussion of the philosophical nature, this identification ceases to appear with the same regularity or explicitness, although one might say that, even when the useful is not mentioned, it is implied in the context.[52] The movement toward philosophy is a movement beyond the commonsensical understanding of the good as the useful.[53] Or rather, there is within common sense itself a movement by which the good separates itself from the useful. As we have just seen, the fundamental stratum of meaning in the term "good" is "useful, helpful, beneficial." But it is obvious that some useful things cannot be called good in the ordinary sense of the term. This difficulty arose with respect to the noble or beautiful; it is also apparent in the case of the just. It may be just to sacrifice oneself in war, for example, but it can scarcely be good in the sense of useful. Self-sacrifice may also be noble or beautiful, but the term itself explicitly rules out utility or satisfaction of a personal desire. In ordinary discourse, we attempt to reconcile these disproportions by speaking of "a higher good" with respect both to noble sacrifice and to the sometimes necessary utility of injustice, ugliness, or falsehood. But this expression contains two ambiguities. First, if "good" is measured by some standard which divides it into "higher" and "lower," is not the standard itself higher than the good? Second, how can the use of the low (e.g. injustice) be as "high" as the surrender of utility in noble sacrifice?

Consideration of ambiguities like these leads us sooner or later to recognize that the good simply cannot be reduced to the useful in the ordinary sense of the term. It leads us to see that "utility" is an equivocal term; the utility of the "higher good" cannot be the same as the utility of the necessary but base action (and this is, incidentally, one reason why the attempt to re-

52. Examples: 470e7 ff., 484d2, 489e4, 493c1 ff., 501c8. In these passages, the good is linked to the institutions of the just polis, which in turn owes its existence to Socrates' attempt to prove that justice is useful in itself. See n. 46.

53. After the philosophical digression, the good is again linked explicitly with the useful, e.g. 607c3 ff., 608e3.

duce all conduct, even that of self-sacrifice, to the motive of selfishness in the sense of pleasure is altogether unsuccessful). The utility of what in moral (and probably also aesthetic) terms we call the "good" and the "evil" is thus revealed as a derivative consequence of the intelligibility of the world. The light exhibited in the heterogeneous forms of the world enables us to see how necessary evils may be subordinated to, or made useful for, the good, in the sense of the noble and the just. Things become useful because of their visibility within the order of the whole, but the visibility of the ordered whole is not the same as the usefulness of its parts. The order of the noetic whole never changes, whereas utility and harm do change. What is useful in one context may be harmful in another, because of the infinite variability of the human psyche. This variability makes it impossible for the psyche to define the good exclusively in terms of its own desire or will. Taken as autonomous psychic motions, one desire contradicts another, and the result is chaos, or nihilism. The intelligibility or measurability of desire arises from the distinction between intention and object. The sense of the object is not the same as the sense of the object constituted within the act of intentionality. This is evident within everyday experience by a simple analysis of the phenomenon of utility.

The distinction between intention and object, or between thought and form, certainly raises a serious difficulty for the explanation of *how* we know, but none at all for the fact *that* we know. On the other hand, to unite the essence of thought and form enables us to give a monistic account of knowledge, but it leads to the negation of standards or values, and so to the human significance of knowledge. As I have argued throughout this book, a monistic account terminates necessarily in silence, because it is unable to speak of itself as other than the silent manifestation of Being. In the Platonic analysis, the silent manifestation of beings provides a measure of coherence for the incoherent, because indeterminate, function of speaking desire. This manifestation is the source of the utility of things to man, or the basis for the establishment of a hierarchy of degrees of utility. But it is not, and cannot be, itself grasped as "useful" in the same sense as the utility derived by man from the intelligibility of the heterogeneous world. Use is measured by the goal of wisdom, which is not in turn useful for something else, but an end in itself, or rather *the* end. If wisdom is knowledge of the whole, and the intelligibility of the whole is the good, or more precisely the ground (αἰτία) or form (ἰδέα) of the good, then the good, whether as the perfection of psyche or the order of the noetic cosmos, can no longer be called "useful."

To summarize, the useful points to the good in a way which is at first more stable than the way of the beautiful or just. But reflection upon the difference between the useful, on the one hand, and the beautiful and just, on the other, renders unstable the preliminary comprehension of utility. This stability may be recaptured only if we divine what the good is, that is, thanks to a "divine gift" which is separate from and higher than "whatever the advantageous component might be of the other things," i.e. of things other than the good as a whole.[54] Socrates says we must divine what the good is because the question, what is X? (τί ἐστι) can be answered only with respect to a determinate something, or what Aristotle calls a τόδε τι. It refers to, or can be answered about, a *what* within a *that,* or a specific form. But the good as the whole, or form of forms, is *a* form only in a metaphorical sense, certainly in a sense which could never be expressed in a determinate speech (compare recent mathematical demonstrations of the impossibility of a complete mathematical language). One cannot give a logos of the good, and this is why Socrates calls it sometimes the good and sometimes the Idea of the good. We see wisdom or wholeness as the goal and basis of our desire, but we do not know it in the technical or determinate sense.[55] By calling such a vision divine, or asso-

54. 505d11 ff. Cf. n. 49.
55. This seems to be contradicted at 534b3 ff. But in fact Socrates states there what will be the case *unless* we have a *logos* of the good. The "case," as the whole corpus shows, is particular knowledge mixed with particular and general opinion in a vision of the whole which is neither knowledge nor opinion.

ciating it with prophecy, Socrates here, as in other dialogues,
indicates both the absence of determinate knowledge and the
presence of the vision which makes determinate knowledge possible.[56]

Socrates claims that the best men in the just polis must not be
unenlightened concerning the good, for "if a man is ignorant as
to how just and beautiful things are ever (ποτέ) good, he will
not be a very worthy guardian of the things about which he is
ignorant. For I divine that no one will know them sufficiently
before he learns this." [57] If we in the unjust communities cannot
gain access to knowledge of the good (whatever may be the
case with respect to the philosopher–kings), is there available
in our ordinary experience an icon of what Socrates means by
the "vision" or "prophecy" of the good? I believe that there
is—the good man. A good man, as we observe him within our
daily lives, is not "useful for . . ." in the same sense that
tools, food, acts, even just and beautiful things exhibit utility.
Entirely apart from the happiness which may justly accrue to
the good man because of his consciousness that he is good,
there is a certain fulfillment, completeness, or perfection which
shines forth from such a man, and which we too admire, even
perhaps without envy or desire, because of its splendor. This is
what we mean by "genuine goodness" or "purity of character."
The shining of the good man's splendor may illuminate and help
to complete our own lives, whether by virtue of its nobility, or

56. It can only be misleading to say, as does Heidegger, that "Seit
der Auslegung des Seins als ἰδέα ist das Denken auf das Sein des Seienden metaphysisch, und die Metaphysik ist theologisch" (*Platons Lehre*,
p. 48). The significance of the identification between τὸ ἀγαθόν and
τὸ θεῖον can scarcely be understood in terms of what Aristotle meant by
θεολογική, let alone in terms of Christian metaphysics. It has considerably more to do with the criticism of the poets, and so with the political
context of the discussion. The word θεολογία is used in the *Republic* by
Adeimantus (379a5), where it refers to the myths spoken of the gods
by the poets (379a2: μυθολογεῖν τοὺς ποιητάς), or rather of such myths
as corrected by founders of a just polis. In this early context, the good
is said to be useful (379b11) and the cause not of all things, but only
of good things (379b15-16).
57. 505e4 ff.

because we are able to see better what to do ourselves when that noble light permeates the otherwise dark contours of our lives.

However "useful" the splendor of the good man may be to those who observe it, would we not agree that we have ceased to discern it in the moment that we identify it as the principle of utility? As a mark of the difference between the good and the useful, we may note that the vision of the good man is not in fact useful for persuading those who cannot see him in his own nature. There are no tools by which to persuade the bad; more generally, the just polis does not exist by nature (other than in the speech of the good) because there is no knowledge, and so no τέχνη, of the good, but only divination on the part of inspired or blessed individuals.[58] The essentially private act by which an individual divines the good does not restrict the splendor which emanates from his character, but rather its power, utility, or function as a cause.[59] The weak and even the bad may admire the splendor of goodness without being transformed by it. The divine nature of the vision of the good, then, is what we may call its internal appropriation. This is the reason why Plato distinguished between the demotic and philosophical virtues, while referring to the latter as divine. Even though it may be difficult or impossible for us to be good men, it is not impossible for us to admit that we have seen a good man. And those of us who have been vouchsafed this sight have an icon of the good in itself.

58. Cf. Leo Strauss, *The City and Man* (Chicago, Rand McNally, 1964), pp. 92, 109–10. See also *Republic* 489b6 ff.: it is not natural for philosophers to seek to rule. My statement that there is no τέχνη for seeing the good seems to be contradicted at 518d3, one of the most difficult passages in the *Republic* which has already demanded our attention. But the τέχνη is mathematics, and its function is to turn the psyche round and lead it upward, but not to enable it to see the good. Also, the capacity to see is not obtained by τέχνη (518d5-6).

59. Cf. 438e1-3: the ἐπιστήμη τῶν κακῶν καὶ τῶν ἀγαθῶν is not itself κακή καὶ ἀγαθή. The goodness of the knowledge of the good comes not from the knowledge, but from the vision of the sun.

V.

The dialectical unity of the objects of desire and the existential coherence or visible splendor of the good man prepare us for the icon of the sun. The corporeal icon of the sun refers to a noetic relationship which is itself described in visual terms. All discourse about thinking is conducted in language derived from the senses, usually sight, hearing, and touch. For this reason, a complete abstraction from the body would be equivalent to silence. One function of the dialogue form is to underline the eikastic nature of speech, or to preserve the harmony of body and psyche, without which human speech would be impossible. We have to see what we are speaking about; otherwise, our speeches are opinions and, whether true or not, necessarily blind. In this icon, Socrates communicates his point by allowing us to "see" the blind men on the right road; this is immediately deepened by his next question, in which the opinions, rather than those who hold them, are presented as blind.[60] To be aware of one's own ignorance is already to see something comprehensive about human life, as for example when we say, "I am moving in the dark." The icon thus illustrates how, in everyday experience, we have divinations of unity or wholeness which are not determinate speeches or rational accounts, but about which something crucial to reason may be said.

Adeimantus chides Socrates that it is not just to express the opinions of others while suppressing one's own, but he seems to be succumbing to Socrates' evasions.[61] He is then rescued by the more daring Glaucon, who insists that Socrates must "traverse" the road of the good, presumably whether the opinions encountered are blind or not. Socrates agrees to speak about the

60. 506c6-d1. Socrates also speaks of *hearing* "shining and beautiful things," which I take to refer to a divination of qualities which are not visible in the sense of being capturable by discourse or knowledge.

61. 506c2-5. Perhaps Adeimantus' lack of firmness here is due to his belief, indicated at 382a3, that there is nothing unjust about the association of lying (a form of suppressing one's opinions) and ruling.

good as he has already done about justice, moderation, and other matters. But he now indicates that the previous discussions, although "sufficient," were incomplete.[62] "Let us relinquish for now what sort of thing the good is itself—it seems to me too much to reach my current opinion about it by means of the present march." [63] Socrates does not admit to knowledge of the good itself, but only to opinion, and one more adequate than the one he is about to relate. The stability of this opinion is evidently great enough to permit him to honor the demands of justice; Socrates' "business," in accord with the definition of justice as "minding one's own business," is to provide a steady foundation for the just polis. It is obvious that Socrates knows more than he is saying. But we ought not to assume too quickly that what he says is insufficient to indicate to the careful auditor what he knows. We have already learned that divination concerning the good is not quite the same as knowledge or opinion.[64] The same point seems to hold true of Glaucon and the other members of the party. Socrates warns them to guard against being deceived by his account of the good.[65] This warning would be superfluous if his interlocutors were altogether in the dark concerning the good. Socrates seems rather to assume, as the previous transference of blindness to opinions implies, that Glaucon will be illuminated by the very discussion of the good, as is altogether appropriate in the presence of a sun.

Socrates desires to reflect his stable opinion of the good, which the present company at least cannot safely look in the face, in an icon: "I desire to speak about what seems to be a child of the good and most like it, if it is agreeable to you; if

62. Cf. 612a5.
63. 506d8 ff.: note that ὁρμή (march) is not the same as ὁδός (road). Perhaps a different march along the same road would achieve superior results.
64. Consider in this connection the myth of Er, or a prophecy about the psyche's crucial choice of a good life. As is noted within that myth, there is no τάξις (determination) in the psyche itself, which differs depending upon which life it chooses (618b2 ff.). This lack of order can be circumscribed only in a prophecy.
65. 507a4-6.

not, I will let it go." [66] Socrates, the father of the logos about
the just polis, uses the language of generation to introduce the
principle of the good, and in a most intricate sentence. To begin
with, Socrates seems to have no desire to speak of the good itself and will speak of the icon only if Glaucon approves—
literally, if he is "friendly" (εἰ καὶ ὑμῖν φίλον). There is a
radical difference between a description of how to found the
just polis and the training of the philosopher–kings within the
polis. The latter must see the good itself, whereas it is evidently
not strictly necessary for Socrates' interlocutors to see the icon
or child of the good. The important point here is that the earlier
claim of justice is insufficient to make Socrates speak; agreement or friendship is also necessary. As Aristotle later makes
explicit, friendship is higher than justice.[67] Only those who are
by nature friendly to the good will be illuminated by its image.
This is the same point I made in the previous section about the
sight of the good man. We may admire the good without desiring it, or be affected by it without admiring it. Second, Socrates'
speech shows or presents itself (φαίνεται) as a child of the
good. At the peak of the abstraction from the body and genesis,
we find an icon of a body and genesis. Again Socrates is appealing to the visibility of bodies as mediated by speech; more concretely, it is the generative or biological powers of the sunlight,
rather than the mathematical or astronomical aspects of the
sun's motions and substance, which Socrates employs to illustrate the good. Of the many implications this raises, I shall mention only one. The significance of the good is to unify life and
formal structure; we can infer the mathematical properties of
form from biological visibility, but we cannot infer life from
mathematical properties of form. This is perhaps the greatest
defect in all attempts to provide an exclusively or even primarily
mathematical version of the principles of Plato's teaching. Finally, Socrates says that the sun icon is "most like" the good
(ὁμοιότατος ἐκείνῳ); in other words, it corresponds to, but
does not contain, the τί ποτ' ἐστί or "whatness" of the good.

66. 506e3-5.
67. *Nichomachean Ethics* 1155a22 ff.

Correspondences (ὁμοιώσεις) are not the same as what they resemble—in this case, true being. It is therefore false to say, as does Heidegger, that truth is for Plato a correspondence between speech and thing. On the contrary, speech is an icon of things.[68]

Before the discussion of the good or its child can proceed, there must be agreement and recollection.[69] Agreement establishes a community of friendship or harmony, a re-collecting of the unity of goodness from the diverse instances of its manifestation in everyday life. The harmonious completeness of the good man, which stands to his good acts as the sun stands to generated things, is the existential paradigm for this dialectical exercise. The unity of the existential paradigm may perhaps be called the existential monad. It is closely related to, indeed inseparable from, the unity of perceived bodies or the aesthetic monad. The splendor of the existential monad shines forth through the body and the body's modifications as its intrinsic or psychic coherence, significance, shape, or form. These beautiful visions may then come to be loved, honored, and observed as somehow independent of the bodies through which they shine—like the gods.[70] The visibility of the homogeneous mathematical monad is thus posterior to the visibility of the internally articulated aesthetic and existential monads. We cannot count what we do not see, but we may see without counting. As soon as we begin to reflect upon what we see, of course, counting begins; more accurately, we come to see that, even in gazing upon beautiful unities, we were already implicitly counting. And we realize the difference between the immediate sense of utility and the beauty of goodness. The beauty of goodness attracts our attention to the unity of the source of utility. From this it does

68. The financial metaphors of principle and interest (506e6-507a6) may also be related to this point. Money is a ὁμοίωσις of the value of things, as speech is a ὁμοίωσις of truth. Also, if the polis of the *Republic* is grounded in a vision of the offspring of the good, does it not stand to the truly just polis as the sun stands to the good itself? For speech as an icon, cf. the *Cratylus*.

69. 507a7: Διομολογησάμενός γ᾽, ἔφην ἐγώ, καὶ ἀναμνήσας ὑμᾶς.

70. Cf. Strauss, *The City and Man*, pp. 120–21.

not follow that the good is identical with beauty or utility, as to some extent we have already seen.

There are many beautiful things and many good things; Socrates distinguishes the two kinds in asking us to define the one shape underlying each manifold, which designates the "what it is" ($\hat{o}$ $\check{\epsilon}\sigma\tau\iota\nu$) of the units in the manifold.[71] This identification is possible because pre-dialectical perception distinguishes between individuals and kinds of individuals, or between the one and the many. The distinction between the one and the many is not exclusively or even primarily mathematical, as it may sound to our ears. It is rather the basis for the possibility of counting; for the Greeks, we recall, one is not a number, but the unit for measuring numbers. There is, then, a kind of collecting that makes use of numbers but does not count: the preliminary sensory–noetic act of grasping formal unities within a manifold. On the basis of this distinction, we are able to see that the one within a manifold is the measure by which we answer the question, what is it? The "whatness" of unity is the measure of the "thatness" of the many. This whatness is called by Socrates an Idea. The etymology of this word is both revealing and ambiguous: it means literally "look" and thus refers to the primary appearance of heterogeneity in bodies. On the other hand, we cannot literally see a *what,* and many *thats* are neither bodies nor (in any evident sense) modifications of bodies, for example, numbers, geometrical forms, the virtues, theoretical definitions. The word "Idea," as a term designating whatness, cannot be reduced to the look of a corporeal *that;* in addition to the distinctions between one–many and what–that, it calls our attention to a third distinction, between two kinds of perception, or what we call seeing and thinking.

Each of the three distinctions we have just noted arises from thinking about seeing, which by and large has priority among the senses in Plato and Aristotle.[72] One might paraphrase the

71. *Republic* 507b2 ff. Note that we are said to distinguish this $\tau\hat{\omega}$ $\lambda\acute{o}\gamma\omega$.

72. Cf. my article, "Thought and Touch," in *Phronesis, 4* (1961), 127–37.

reasons for this priority as follows. In vision, we combine discrimination of form with detachment from body. Touch is an excellent discriminator of shapes, but only through immediate corporeal contact. Hearing, on the other hand, is restricted in its kind of discrimination because it is too detached from the corporeal. We can see both silent and speaking shapes, and the vision of tactile forms does not depend upon a distorting contiguity with the shaped body. In addition to variety and presence, vision gives us detachment or perspective. Of course, one may interpret the visual perspective as a subjective distortion of the thing in itself. But Socrates' point is that the thing in itself is not and cannot be the same as the object of sense perception. A visual perception of X is perspectival or partial in a sense that includes the possibility of distortion, because there is no visually perceptible difference between the "subjective" and "objective" (non-Socratic terms) aspects of that perception. How the thing visually looks is identical with how the thing visually looks to us. Even here, however, a given view of X may be supplemented by others from a different perspective, as well as by perceptions from the other senses. But this is not the crucial point. The cooperative and in part self-correcting activities of the senses take place only under the unifying direction of thinking.[73]

So far as the activity of thinking is concerned, one might object that it is prey to the same perspectival ambiguities as sense perception. But there is this radical difference: thinking is reflexive, whereas sense perception is not. Thought is capable of "detaching" itself from the united results of its efforts combined with those of sense perception, or of regulating its collective perspective in terms of a measure or standard that is not integral to the aforementioned union of sensory–noetic perspectives. For example, we criticize the results of a given set of perspectives as inferior to another set ("that looks like a man, but it can't be, because . . ."), and, in the last analysis, this criticism occurs by means of a standard which itself cannot be reduced to still another set of sensation-bound perspectives

73. Similarly with the κοινὴ αἴσθησις in Aristotle's *De Anima*.

without committing an infinite regress. The objection to an infinite regress is not logical, but empirical or perceptual. *Noetic criticism works.* The form of a "set" of sense perceptions cannot be grasped in the same way that we grasp the sensory content of that set. In looking at the looks of things, thinking grasps a pattern which cannot be reduced to the looks without blurring, and even negating, them. This is true in every instance of mental work, from sense perception to logical or mathematical inference. Every "nominalistic" attempt to reduce form to a set of corporeal or epi-corporeal individuals fails for the simple reason that the visibility of the individual within the set is differently grasped from the fact that it is an ostensibly corporeal individual; and the individuality of the individual is different from the individuality of the set of individuals. I add here parenthetically that the nominalist effort is misconceived because based upon an erroneous conception of the position it is attacking. To say that form is different from its instances is *not* to say that form "is" or "constitutes" a separate world from its instances, if by "separate" is meant spatially or temporally separate.

To repeat, every mental act of any kind of intentionality is held together, and so exhibited as what it is, by a noetic shape which cannot be reduced to the mental act itself (let alone to the "external" content of that act). This noetic shape (not to be confused with Husserl's eidetic constitution within the flow of subjectivity) *is* the thing in itself, or the Idea. It is not, of course, the Kantian *Ding-an-sich,* because, unlike the latter, it manifests itself in the act of making visible its instances. Let me emphasize: Socrates does not claim that thinking as a psychic activity is free from perspectives. Instead, he claims that thinking works because, in each of its perspectives, it apprehends the source of those perspectival illuminations.[74] Thinking is a "looking at" (in the sense that we are considering it here) which differs, from the ground up, from *what* is looked at, whereas

74. This apprehension is often compared to prophecy by Socrates, which has something to do with the doctrine of recollection. Consider *Theaetetus* 178b2 ff., esp. 179a2.

seeing is a "looking at" which cannot distinguish itself from *what* is looked at. To speak of the *what* is to go beyond seeing to thinking. It is also to look beyond perspectives to *what* we see perspectivally. To see that these perspectives must necessarily be of a *what* is, of course, not to see what it is. The perspectival nature of thinking prevents a complete, determinate, synoptic vision of the Idea, but from the perspectives accessible to us, we infer or divine its necessary presence. This is as true of hardheaded nominalist epistemologists as it is of perspective ontologists.

A noetic divination of the principle of unity stands to the perspectival apprehensions of that principle as does our vision of the unity of a thing to the perspectival visions or looks of that thing. However perspectival sense vision may be, it carries with it, in each of its perspectives, the awareness that they are perspectives of a single thing or unified manifold—what I previously called an aesthetic monad. The aesthetic unity of the corporeal object may be added, then, to the existential unity of the good man as icons within genesis of the ungenerated Ideas. Heidegger's interpretation of an Idea is therefore as inadequate as, and related to, his interpretation of the good as the useful. The Idea is what we look at, but it is not the act of looking. Similarly, the good is the source of the useful, but it is not the use to which we put its gifts.

According to Socrates, there are three "kinds" or elements involved in the act of vision: the eye, color (by which the object is visible), and "a third kind, peculiar by its nature to this very function"—light. The light is thus distinguished from the sun and is called an Idea (οὐ σμικρᾷ ἄρα ἰδέᾳ) which yokes together vision and the visible.[75] The sun, as the source or cause of the light,[76] is different from it; the term "Idea" is not applied

75. 507d8–508a3.

76. Because so much stress is laid on the term αἴτιος by interpreters, it is important to notice that it is used unqualifiedly at 508a4 ff. and 508b9 of the sun as cause of sight. At 508e3 ff., when the discussion turns to thinking, αἴτιος is used as part of a right supposition; at 516b9 it is an inference (συλλογίζοιτο) about the sun's relation to the shadows

to the sun, as it was to the light. In other words, the sun as the good is (at least in this passage) not the same as the Idea of the good. In noetic terms, the Ideas stand to the good as the light stands to the sun: they light up the shape of the object, which corresponds to the color of the visible body. Furthermore, the good stands to the mind as the sun does to the eye: both noetic and visual perception occur through the mediation of a third or binding element (Ideas, sunlight) which not only is different from, but draws our attention away from, its source. In order to see an object, we do not look at the sun or even at the light, but at the illuminated object. The sun, when looked at directly, blinds us, and the light, considered apart from all visible bodies, is itself invisible or homogeneous. If we translate this result into the noetic realm, we discover a crucial restriction in the icon of the sun, which, by focusing its illuminative powers, teaches us an essential element—perhaps the essential element—in Socrates' opinion about the good.

In the visible realm, light is not the same as color or, more accurately, as the colored body. Hence the structures of the body are heterogeneous, although they depend upon the homogeneous capacity of the light in order to become visible. From this it follows that the eidetic light of the good is also homogeneous. The homogeneity of the eidetic light of the good is the noetic visibility or intelligibility of "what is thought" (τὰ νοούμενα). Therefore the light of the good does not designate, and is not in itself the cause of, the noetic heterogeneity of the domain of thought. The good does not cause things or beings in the sense of instances, but is the ground or principle of their intelligibility. The Ideas, then, in accordance with the present icon, cannot be altogether separate from things or beings, even if the good, in whatever sense, is different or separate. *Heterogeneity is in the things themselves.* To say that the light makes intelligible "what is thought" is not the same as to say that what is thought is totally separate from the things or

___

in the cave; and at 517c1–2, it is an inference (συλλογιστέα εἶναι) about the relation of the good to right and beautiful things (ὀρθῶν τε καὶ καλῶν αἰτία).

beings we think. As Plato himself pointed out in the *Parmenides,* this makes no sense whatsoever.

We may now translate what is identified by Socrates himself as his summary concerning the good:

> "This then," I said, "you may say is my speech about the offspring of the good, which the good has generated analogous to itself, so that, as it stands in the noetic domain to mind and what is thought, thus the offspring stands in the visible domain to sight and what is seen." "How?" asked Glaucon. "Give me further details." [77]

We note in passing that Socrates, not the good, generated the icon of the sun, thanks to his logos. The sun generates sight in the eye, which is then the "mother" of vision; similarly, the mind or psyche is the "mother" of intelligibility. The psyche stands apart from all other beings in a special relationship to the good, just as the eye is "most sun-like" of the corporeal organs. Furthermore, just as the sun does not generate the eye (but is at most a contributory principle to its generation), so nothing is said here of the mind's origin. To say that the mind sees in the light of the good is not to say that the mind has been generated by the good. Finally, the power of illumination is not equivalent to the power of generation. In the visible domain, the sun illuminates the living and nonliving alike, which are thus yoked together by their visibility, not by common parentage. So too in the noetic domain, difference in kind (heterogeneity) is not the same as common intelligibility.

The sense in which the good is "separate from" or "beyond" the things of the visible world is not, as we may now realize, one which deprives those things or that world of their goodness or value. On the contrary, it is the necessary condition for goodness to be manifested at all. As the opinion is presented in the *Republic,* goodness emanates into the world of speech and deed like light emanating from the sun onto the colored surfaces of bodies. The homogeneous light illuminates the heterogeneity of these bodies but does not contribute heterogeneity to them. Sim-

77. 508b12-c3.

ilarly, the light of the good is rendered visible thanks to the heterogeneous shapes of things: the things "articulate" the light, which is visible only in and as a specific intelligible form, a *what,* or in a pattern of *whats.* If the good were a *what* or an Idea in the same sense as, let us say, the Idea of a man, a horse, or justice, then it would be a determinate shape or form, heterogeneous with respect to the other Ideas; there would be no way to explain how such a determinate Idea transmits intelligibility to the others. The good is "beyond" the Ideas in the sense that it is not a determinate form, but the intelligibility shared by these Ideas. If "being" (οὐσία) is used to designate the Idea, then the good is "beyond being." [78] On the other hand, to the extent that goodness may be identified as intelligibility, it has a kind of reflexive visibility, shape, or look and, in this sense, may be called an Idea. Hence Socrates' fluctuation in terminology.

The goodness of this world, then, depends upon the difference between the cause or ground of goodness and the good things in the world. One might illustrate Socrates' view by saying that he denies the contention, common to Husserl and Heidegger, that man is *radically* a being-in-the-world. This doctrine of man is equivalent to a denial of transcendence in any but a temporal sense, which cuts with equal force against the status of the meaning or sense of the being of the world itself, or, in other words, of Being. It therefore unites the sense of Being to a subjective or noetic activity, which, as altogether worldly, shares in the defective attributes of genesis, now called Historicity. The least, and perhaps the most, one can say of the Socratic good is that it preserves the sense of the world as the permanent intelligibility of the being of the world. As always, for Socrates, "to be" is to be intelligible. Paradoxically enough, intelligibility is itself indeterminate, which permits it to be shared by heterogeneous forms, and which also makes it like the mind, the indeterminate capacity to see, and thus to assume, all formal determinations. Intelligence and intelligibility are thus both "beyond" being because both contain nonbeing or "other-

78. 509b6 ff., where the good (and not the Idea of the good) is said to be ἐπέκεινα τῆς οὐσίας. I shall return to this sentence shortly.

ness," as the Eleatic stranger calls it in the *Sophist*. But the
Ideas are not beyond being, because "to be" is to be an Idea.

VI.

Thus far we have subjected to fairly close scrutiny a small
section of the *Republic,* about three pages of the Stephanus
edition. And yet I believe that this section contains the essence
of Socrates' teaching about the good. What follows is an ex-
pansion and clarification, part of which we will study closely,
and a large part of which, important though it undoubtedly is
for any exhaustive study of Plato's thought, we will merely
summarize for our own purposes. Socrates rephrases his speech
about the good as follows. When our eyes look at things illuminated by night light, they very soon become dull and nearly
blind, as if pure sight were not present within them at all. What
the sun illuminates, however, they see clearly, and pure sight is
itself manifestly present (ἐνοῦσα φαίνεται). So too with the
psyche: "whenever it fixes its eyes upon what the unity of truth
and being (ἀλήθειά τε καὶ τὸ ὄν) lights up, it grasps noetically
and knows it, and is manifestly in possession of reason
(ἐνόησέν τε καὶ ἔγνω αὐτὸ καὶ νοῦν ἔχειν φαίνεται)." [79] In this interesting sentence, the unity of truth and being stands in the thing
known as does the unity of noetic vision and knowledge in the
mental activity. "Truth plus being" here replaces the sun as the
source of illumination, one of the many passages that make it
impossible to identify "truth" as the correspondence between
propositions and Ideas. If "to be" is to be intelligible, the source
of being must also be the source of truth. The "truth" of a
proposition is thus not the same as the truth of being, but an
icon or reflection of it. After identifying the dark as "coming to
be and passing away," Socrates continues: "this then which
presents the truth to the things known and gives back the power

79. 508c3–d10. Cf. 518c9, where τὸ ὄν καὶ τοῦ ὄντος τὸ φανότατον designate what is here called ἀλήθειά τε καὶ τὸ ὄν. I understand τοῦ ὄντος τὸ
φανότατον to refer to truth, not a particular being like a sun, which shines
brighter than, and so illuminates, the other particular beings.

[of knowing] to the knower, you may say to be the Idea of the good." [80] Apart from the substitution of "Idea of the good" for "the good," the main feature of this sentence is the contraction from "truth plus being" to "the truth." There can scarcely be any doubt that, according to Socrates, truth, being, intelligible visibility, and goodness are all approximately equivalent in his icon.

The term ὁμοίωσις, we discovered, applies to the relation between icons and noetic beings. "Truth" is not a relation of correspondence to being, but (in its fundamental sense) being itself. The principal icon by which man "mirrors" and so gains access to truth is dianoia or discursive speech—logos. A logos is "true" if it mirrors or exhibits the unity of truth and being. If we refer to the mirror image in the logos rather than to what it mirrors, we may say that the mirror image "corresponds" to the original,[81] or is "correct" (ὀρθότης, or correctness). "Correctness," then, is a secondary term referring to the truth of dianoetic icons, in the sense that we speak of a "true copy." [82] In terms previously employed, there is a difference between the "look" of an Idea and the act of "looking at" the Idea. Having established the primary unity of truth and being, Socrates now uses the term ὀρθῶς ("correctly") for the first time with reference to the good,[83] and precisely in the manner I have indicated: "it is the cause of knowledge and truth, and you may discursively grasp it as known, but whereas knowledge and truth are both beautiful, if you suppose [the Idea of the good] to be other and still more beautiful than these, you will suppose correctly." [84]

80. 508e1–3: I suspect that the difference between the two verbs (παρέχον, ἀποδιδόν) means something like this: the sun gives being to the thing known, but not to the mind. Instead, it restores the previously quiescent power of knowing by the manifestation of visibility.

81. The image of the "mirror image" contains the problem of the reversed image. Correspondence would seem to be a reversal of truth in the ontological sense.

82. This distinction is suppressed by Heidegger, who makes "correct vision" central to Plato's conception of truth: *Platons Lehre*, pp. 41–42.

83. At 506c8, ὀρθῶς is used to describe a journey of blind men on the road of δόξα.

84. 508e3.

This sentence, with the possible exception of the opening
clause, is an accommodation to Glaucon's inability to grasp the
earlier cryptic formulation. A correct dianoetic supposition is
not the same as a noetic apprehension of truth. The accommodation is also indicated by the attribution of beauty or nobility
to the dianoetic supposition. Beauty is a characteristic of the
eikastic re-presentation of truth, or an attribute of the look of a
what which is indeed dependent upon its being looked *at*. If
there is an Idea of beauty, as Socrates claims, it is not in itself
beautiful in the way that a dianoetic representation of the Idea
is (and the same applies to the other Ideas: they are not "self-
predicative"). Being as truth manifests itself as what it is, but
the manifestation to the human psyche thereby serves as the
stable foundation for dianoetic judgments of beauty, justice,
utility, and the like. One cannot infer the latter from the former
alone, but the former manifests itself not alone, but to the
psyche. "Values" are thus intelligible only if we take both components, Ideas and psyche, into account. They emerge from man's
vision of the Ideas, or from the measurement of desire by that
vision, hence not simply from a harmony between mind and
being, but from their difference. In other words, the transition
from theory to practice is not intelligible solely on the basis of
the Ideas, but rather on the basis of the unity of the theoretical
and practical psyche. It is not the unity but the measure of the
psyche's differentiated activity which the Ideas supply.

The ambiguous status of beauty is shown by Glaucon's response to the sentences just analyzed. The attribution of sur-
passing beauty to the correct supposition of the good is taken by
him to refer to the good itself, which leads him to wonder
whether the good may not perhaps be pleasure after all. "Don't
blaspheme," Socrates replies, "but look again at the icon of [the
good] rather in this way." [85] Socrates thus reminds Glaucon
that the dianoetic vision is an icon, and not the good itself. The
blasphemy originates in confusing these two, not in associating
beauty with pleasure. The connection between beauty and intelligibility is rooted in the unity of body and psyche; dianoetic
thinking is eikastic because that unity necessitates a thinking in

85. 509a6-10.

conjunction with sense perception, as is obvious from the root metaphor of vision. The beauty of eikasia, as linked to the body, is necessarily pleasant. What Socrates claims is that, by reflecting upon dianoia, hence inescapably by employing dianoia itself, we can divine or surmise the noetic ground "through" or "by means of which" (διά) discursive thinking occurs. This noetic ground is not pleasant and, in any ordinary sense, not beautiful, because it is neither speech nor speaker, neither corporeal nor psychic. We can speak about it, but we cannot bespeak it. But the difference between Socrates and, say, the early Wittgenstein is that Socrates regards dianoetic thought as adequate to the task of speaking—through the supplementation of discursive logos by myth—about what cannot be spoken. These speeches are the waking dreams or serious games of the Platonic dialogues.

The second look at the icon of the good, taken by Socrates on Glaucon's behalf, is ostensibly a clarification of a clarification. The sun, Socrates begins, furnishes visible things with their visibility, genesis, growth, and nourishment, although it is not itself genesis (οὐ γένεσιν αὐτὸν ὄντα). After Glaucon has agreed to this by no means obvious remark, Socrates adds:

> Then say too about the things which are known that not only do they receive the capacity to be known from the good, but their presence united to whatness (καὶ τὸ εἶναί τε καὶ τὴν οὐσίαν) comes from the good as well, which is not a whatness, but goes beyond even whatness in dignity and power.[86]

Glaucon's response, in which he jokingly identifies the sun with Apollo, shows that he has not understood the clarification of a clarification. And indeed, Socrates' language is considerably

86. 509b2-10: I translate ὄν as "being," hence prefer different terms for οὐσία and εἶναι. The former expresses the formal capacity of any being to identify itself, or to serve as a measure of its instances: I call this "whatness." Εἶναι is the way in which an ὄν "presents" itself as "what it is," thanks to its οὐσία. Needless to say, Plato is not consistent in his terminology, but he is absolutely precise in communicating different shades of meaning. Note that οὐσία replaces ὃ ἔστιν, a preliminary formulation used at 507b7.

more obscure here than it was in the initial statement. One would need the prophetic powers of an Apollo to decipher it upon first hearing.

In a previous passage, Socrates replaced the good by truth plus being. He now says that the good, or truth plus being, is the source of presence plus whatness in knowable things. There are two difficulties here. Let us try to resolve them in order. First, why is the participial form "being" (ὄν) made to stand for an essential aspect of the good or source, whereas the more abstract verbal noun "whatness" (οὐσία) is used to designate the eidetic structure of illuminated shape? The good is active and concrete in comparison with its eidetic consequences. By "concrete," I mean here that, as the source of good things, the good must somehow contain them all; it is undifferentiated goodness, whereas the Idea, as a determinate *what,* in abstracting from concreteness, fixes its identity by separating itself from all other determinations.[87] On the other hand, τὸ ὄν primarily means "the thing," namely, a specific thing, and so an instance of a determinate *what.* My suggestion is that Socrates plays upon the ambiguity of ὄν to indicate the ultimate unity of the good, even though the latter is other than every specific whatness, with the phenomenal world of individual things. The vividness of the spatio-temporal world is the bloom of being, in a way that pleasure, according to Aristotle, is the bloom of activity. And this bloom is the manifestation of the presence of the good in the world, even though not as a being-in-the-world. In other words, my suggestion is that the Aristotelian conception of ἐνέργεια, or "being-at-work," renders explicit an implication of Plato's use of the participle ὄν.

If this suggestion is acceptable, it serves to reinforce what

87. Is the separateness of the eidetic monad the same as the nonbeing in the undifferentiated good and mind? I do not believe so. In my opinion, which I can only mention here, the former separateness is due to reflection of the eidetic monads within the Idea of matter, in other words, to the fact that forms are indeed forms of things in this world. Here I would say only that Plato's fidelity to the difference between form and mind leads to a parallel difference between otherness and nonbeing. This is certainly never adequately discussed in the dialogues, any more than are the Ideas themselves.

has already been established on other grounds, namely, that Plato did not empty the phenomenal world of goodness. The second difficulty concerns the attribution of "presence" (εἶναι, to be) rather than "truth" to the eidetic structure. In trying to remove this difficulty, we may take a hint from Heidegger. If "truth" means "uncoveredness" or "uncovering," it is clear that the good uncovers or discovers by its illumination what is standing present within the light. The truth of the presence of a thing originates in, and in that sense belongs primarily to, the good. It is the counterpart, in its reference to activity and undifferentiated concreteness, to the participial ὄν. Again we find reinforcement for a previously established conclusion: the truth of a logos is the analogy in speech to the vividness in deeds and things. It is the bloom or the manifestation of being, as the uncovering or discovering of things, through the mediation of their whatness or intelligible shape. Socrates' concentration upon speech about whatness, or determinate accounts about Ideas, is thus due not to his having forgotten Being, but to the fact that he proceeds in two different ways on his philosophical march. The dianoetic way, which attracts the almost exclusive attention of the epistemologically inclined reader, treats of whatnesses, or discursively describable, intelligible patterns. The noetic way cannot proceed by discursive logos, since it attempts to exhibit the conditions of speech. This it does by icons, both as explicitly labeled by Socrates and as furnished by Plato in the total dramatic structure of the dialogues.

The good, then, is beyond οὐσία, or whatness, because it is the visibility of "whatever" we see. It is present in the noetic world without delimiting itself as the class of all *whats,* or as a specific *what,* just as the sun is present in the world of genesis without (in Socrates' phrase) itself being genesis, or an element undergoing genesis. *There is nothing in Socrates' description of the good, up to and including the passage traditionally cited to prove the radical separation of the noetic from the visible domain, to substantiate that interpretation.* In general, the same may be said of the two icons which will not be studied here in detail. A divided line is a continuous magnitude; too many readers have been distracted by its internal articulations from observing that they are united by the continuity of the line (and that the infinite divisibility of a line would seem to affect the domain of intelligibles as well as the domain of sensibles). Probably the main reason for this distraction is the erroneous attempt to grasp the significance of the line in isolation from its position between the sun and the cave, and to use it as the key to the entire discussion of the good, if not of Plato's teaching altogether. In somewhat different terms, the cave is the "interior" of the same earth upon whose surface the sun shines. The light, or illuminative capacity, however weaker in the fires of the cave than in the sun, is homogeneous in kind.

Without in any sense wishing to denigrate its own function or importance, I have referred to the divided line as an epistemological or mathematical icon, designed to facilitate Glaucon's understanding of the ontological icon of the sun. As his responses from 506d2 to 509c6 reveal, Glaucon has not understood that icon.[88] He begins to say "I understand" as soon as Socrates introduces the divided line, and his last statement in Book VI begins with that word.[89] The pedagogic power of mathematics is already mirrored in these responses by Glaucon. The cave image, on the other hand, is neither an ontological nor an epistemological icon, but a pedagogic one, as Socrates explicitly asserts.[90] In general, the function of this

88. His most positive answer in this section is at 507e5, Ἀληθῆ . . . λέγεις, which refers to light as necessary for the process of vision; he never responds so confidently to questions or statements about the noetic process.

89. 510a4, d4; 511a2, b1, c3, and e5. Cf. also 510a7 and b1. At 510b10 he "does not sufficiently understand" Socrates' first account of the division corresponding to dialectic; it is the hypothetical method, rather than the classification on the line, that puzzles Glaucon. Similarly at 511c3.

90. 514a1: Μετὰ ταῦτα δή, εἶπον, ἀπείκασον τοιούτῳ πάθει τὴν ἡμετέραν φύσιν παιδείας τε πέρι καὶ ἀπαιδευσίας. Glaucon at first finds it an ἄτοπον εἰκόνα (515a4), but he soon becomes adjusted to it. Cf. 517c6, where, after Socrates restates in summary the connection between the cave icon and τοῖς ἔμπροσθεν λεγομένοις (517b1), Glaucon says, Συνοίομαι . . . καὶ ἐγώ, ὅν γε δὴ τρόπον δύναμαι.

pedagogic icon is to show the possibility and necessity of a "conversion" ($\pi\epsilon\rho\iota\alpha\gamma\omega\gamma\dot{\eta}$) of the potential philosopher's psyche from pre-philosophical opinion toward the pursuit of dialectic.[91] That is, it prepares us to look for the technique ($\tau\dot{\epsilon}\chi\nu\eta$) by which a psyche in possession of naturally good vision may be trained or converted for or toward the philosophical vision of the good.[92] This technique, which is distinct from dialectic, is mathematics.[93] Shocking as it may seem to contemporary admirers of mathematics, the greater comprehensibility of the divided line is a sign of its lower philosophical status. As I suggested at the beginning of section III, the divided line is actually closer to the cave than it is to the icon of the sun. Mathematics (Socrates claims) is necessary to get us out of the cave, but it is insufficient to enable us to see the sun.

In my opinion, this casts considerable light on the accounts given by Socrates of his youthful studies, which I have discussed elsewhere. The sum of the discussion may be plainly stated. The young or "pre-Socratic" Socrates emerged from the cave of opinion through the study of mathematical physics. But then, thanks to the instruction ironically attributed by him to Parmenides, Diotima, and Aspasia, he realized that his exit had not been properly or completely effected. It was necessary for him to return to the cave, or to bring philosophy down from the heavens to the cities of man, in order to discover the complete dialectical method for achieving a vision of the good as the source of justice and beauty in addition to truth. In order to avoid nihilism, the philosopher must both exit from and return to the cave. It is, however, important to observe that just as mathematics is inadequate to achieve dialectic, so nothing is said about the nature of life within the cave to explain how the potential philosopher is released from his chains and "forced

91. 518d3 ff., 521c1 ff.
92. 518c4-d1, d3-7.
93. 521c10-522c8. Cf. 533b1 ff.: the function of mathematics is to remove our attention from genesis; in itself, however, it is merely a dream about being.

instantly to stand up and turn his head"; this is merely called by Socrates a "natural happening." [94] If mathematics is the art employed to purify the vision of the cave dweller, there is also a kind of constraint which must be applied to the released student, who is not merely forced to stand up and turn round but is also "dragged forcibly" up into the sunlight.[95] This constraint obviously represents the political art of the guardians and, ultimately, the philosophical legislation of Socrates, whose speech founds the just polis. This art cannot be deduced from mathematics. The source of philosophical enlightenment is to be found neither in the divided line nor the cave, but in the sun.[96]

VII.

I have now accomplished the main purposes of this chapter, and it remains to summarize the results and their connection with the previous stages of our investigation. The contemporary nihilist situation is essentially a mood of boredom with the tradition of western European rationalism. It arises from a tendency implicit in the origins of the modern revolution against the classical Greek conception of reason, as is obvious in the existential and ontological attacks against "Platonism" mounted by Nietzsche and Heidegger, and which also motivates the ostensibly anti-metaphysical or even anti-philosophical teachings of Marxism and positivism in its various contemporary guises. Nihilism as a political or cultural phenomenon is a consequence of philosophy in two senses. First, it is a consequence of the transformation of nature and eternity into history and temporality fundamentally to advance human mastery, freedom, autonomy, or creativity, to mention the most important terms that have been employed in this connection. But second, it is a

94. 515c4 ff.

95. 515e6 ff. Cf. 516a4: the releasement is instantaneous, but not the actual vision of the good. As 516e5 suggests, the return to the cave *after* the vision of the good is also instantaneous.

96. Cf. 520b2, where philosophers are said to grow up automatically in corrupt, i.e. historical, polities (αὐτόματοι γὰρ ἐμφύονται), that is, like plants in the sunlight.

consequence of the at least partial failure of this revolutionary transformation. The destruction or exclusion of nature and eternity, intended to regain for human appropriation the value implicit in this world and mistakenly alienated or projected into another, supersensible, trans-historical world, has instead resulted in the dissolution of value in the world of concrete history. The destruction of the past, very far from freeing our creative will for a new stage of positive human or superhuman existence, seems rather to entail the destruction of the present as well.

Whatever our hope may be for the future, and however much we may endorse the modern project to make man free, or the master of the fruits of his own labor, we do no service to humanity by failing to see the thorn within the rose of the modern conception of reason. In the preceding chapters of this book, I have tried to lay bare the thorn without ever insisting that the rose be discarded. My discussion of Plato was necessitated by the logic of contemporary nihilism, or rather of contemporary philosophy, and not by a reactionary preference for the past. I make no effort to provide a complete defense, or even interpretation, of the Platonic teaching. My purpose was to determine whether the extreme criticism of Plato as the father of nihilism, best represented today by Heidegger, is valid. As a corollary, I wanted to show by my refutation of this specific criticism how Plato actually furnishes us with a defense against the emergence of nihilism. Before I summarize the results of this discussion, let me add one crucial remark. The Platonic conception of reason is a defense against the emergence of nihilism, but not an infallible preventive or cure. Nihilism is a fundamental danger of human existence. I shall return to this issue in the next chapter.

According to the charge of Heidegger, Plato is responsible for the division of nature into the two realms of the Ideas and the phenomenal (historical) world. Instead of recognizing the unity of truth and being as the manifestation of openness, Plato concealed that process of illumination by mistaking the "looks" of things for their being, and the correspondence of propositions to

those looks for truth. The good, or the cause of the Ideas or
looks of things, was understood by him as the principle of utility
—what shapes things in such a way as to render them accessible
or useful to man. Hence the importance of technique, mathematics, and logic: by these tools, man was enabled to manipu-
late beings, to impose his perspectival intentions and calculations onto the Being-process. This obscuring or forgetting about
Being was thus accompanied by the creation of an anthropomorphic world of Ideas as the ostensible locus of truth, and
so of value. A human interpretation of Being was mistaken for
Being itself, an interpretation which removed significance from
the world of actual human existence. Plato is the source of the
dehumanizing, devaluing, or "reifying" of human existence,
thanks essentially to his mathematical conception of reason,
which treats man in terms of calculation, utilitarian manipulation, or things, rather than as the locus of the manifestation of
Being.

In the preceding pages of this chapter, I have tried to show
that Heidegger's charges, in view of the text which is the basis
for his own analysis, are not merely unsubstantiated but false.
By implication I am accusing all those who follow him in their
denunciation of "Platonism" of lacking an accurate grasp of the
teaching they denounce. Socrates explicitly identifies truth and
being in a way similar to, although of course not identical with,
the teaching of Heidegger. He carefully distinguishes between
the "looks" of things and the activity by which we "look at"
things. Propositions are dianoetic icons of the being of things;
hence the correspondence between speech and things is an
image of truth as uncoveredness or intelligibility, and not truth
itself. The good is not the principle of utility in an anthropomorphic sense but, as the visibility or intelligibility of the
world, the donor of utility in all senses of that term. It may be
called "cause" in dianoetic speech, but only as a conjecture or
inference.[97] Technique and mathematics serve to purify our pre-
philosophical conceptions of utility but cannot in themselves
achieve the synoptic vision of dialectic, or what Heidegger
97. See n. 76.

might call "genuine" or "foundational thinking." Of course, Plato does not understand Being as a process, but, if as anything, then as the intelligibility of the world manifested in extra-historical shapes as whatness,[98] and as the intelligence, manifested as psyche, which grasps the world. The world of Ideas is not another, separate world, but the whatness of this world. The visibility of the eidetic monads, which serve to measure speech and desire and so furnish the basis for value as well as for truth, is thinkable only because of the otherness of visibility from any or all of its specific determinations. This otherness does not lead to the creation of two worlds but serves as the bond that holds together, and so accounts for the appearance of, the one world of nature, understood as both οὐσία and γένεσις. The noetic and the visible places are both places in this world. The transcendence of the good, however impossible to describe discursively or to mirror adequately, is thus analogous to the difference between Heidegger's Being and beings, but with the crucial qualification that the good is neither sentient nor historical. As the source of intelligibility, it does not include or account for the origin of the psyche. There is, then, no concept of "Being" in Plato, identical to that of Heidegger, which encompasses mind and form, but only the incompletely analyzed conception of nature, cosmos, or the whole. The unification of the internally discontinuous nature in a principle of Being is, I suggest, impossible for philosophy because life is not the same as form. One can speak of the "whole" of life and form but never give a logos which serves to exhibit the ground from which the two are derived. This is the task attempted by religion.

The unity-within-difference of nature is symbolically manifested for Plato in the existential unity of a good life or character, in the aesthetic unity of the things in the world, and the dialectical unity of philosophy. The difference-within-unity of nature is exemplified fully by the aforementioned difference be-

98. Consider the summary of the comparison between sight and noetic thought at 532a1 ff. Dialectic gives a *logos* ἐπ' αὐτὸ ὃ ἔστιν ἕκαστον, but νοήσει λάβῃ what the good is itself. Cf. n. 55.

tween form and mind or psyche. But it is also present within man himself, in the difference between mind and desire, or thought and body. More accurately, the phenomenon of life itself manifests an inner dualism of rest and motion, contemplation and excitation, speech and deed, self-forgetting and self-obsession. Plato never attempts to suppress these differences within the unity of nature; he repudiates every form of monism as false to the phenomena and finally as unspeakable. Man exists as an icon of nature, both in its unity and its difference. As a microcosm, man possesses the capacity to "transcend" difference by a vision of unity, but this transcendence is constantly being suppressed by the difference it encompasses. To be a man is to be constantly falling apart and growing back together again. This means that nihilism is a perpetual danger, rooted in the very divisions which make speech, thought, and so completeness possible. One does not, then, overcome nihilism by understanding the errors of modern philosophy (and I am concerned here only with its errors, not with its virtues) or by refuting the contemporary interpretation of Plato. Instead, one hopefully acquires theoretical tools for a study of the dialectical nature of the human psyche. In my final chapter, I shall attempt to give a synopsis of that dialectic.

Chapter 6

Wisdom

I.

It is more than possible to maintain that nihilism arises not from the absence of truth, but from its tedious presence. Man is a creature of change, who prefers novelty to truth, and so poetry to philosophy. The philosopher learns eventually not to be disconcerted by the fact that last year's truths are this year's platitudes.[1] Whereas we may read and sometimes enjoy last year's poems, we cease to be poets if we do nothing more than repeat them. But if our preference for poetry over philosophy leads us to transform philosophy into poetry, if even the truth of novelty is seen through poetic eyes, or itself understood as only a poem, then our impatience with whatever endures too long deprives the principle of its charm and finally negates altogether its impetus, if not its truth. The truth of novelty does not become less true, but less novel.[2] This phenomenon is obviously not peculiar to the contemporary situation. In all ages, cultivated men have suffered from "world-weariness," or the loss of interest which comes from unending repetition. The fruit of the tree of the knowledge of good and evil decays with time. The process of decay accelerates, however, when time is transformed into historical sophistication, or the experience of communal old age. Historical consciousness, at the moment of ripeness, becomes the poet who is fatigued by his poems, and so by his poetic activity. In this context, the question is not whether poetry is "true," and not even whether it is "good," but whether

1. Cf. Xenophon, *Memorabilia* IV. iv, 6 ff. with Plato, *Republic* 557c7-9, *Laws* 658a4 ff. and Nietzsche, *Jenseits,* ed. Schlechta, *2,* 604 (43).
2. "La varietà è tanto nemico della noia che anche la stessa varietà della noia è un rimedio o un alleviamento di essa . . . All' opposto la continuità della stessa varietà annoia sommamente" (Leopardi, *Zibaldone, 1,* 78). Cf. Kierkegaard, *Either/Or* (New York, Anchor Books, 1959), *1,* 36, 282–87.

we understand any longer what it would mean to call poetry "good" or "evil."

The two most important figures in the attempt to transform historical decadence into a doctrine of human creativity are Nietzsche and Marx. Despite the many differences between them, both men were inspired by an essentially theological vision of the human spirit (Geist), in which freedom and creativity are synonyms. Each labored to free the spirit by advocating a return to the body as the locus of generative power. Each in his own way attempted to shape or contain history by a conception of nature as corporeal genesis. Neither may be said to have resolved the problem of the relation of spirit to body within genesis; that is, neither succeeded in distinguishing between nature and history. We have already studied these difficulties in the case of Nietzsche: the identity between nature and history makes every instant both unique and eternally determined. Man's "free creations" are then an expression of his perpetual historical enslavement; the creation of value is negated by the worthlessness of the ground of creation.[3] Without a standard for distinguishing between noble and base creations, the advocacy of creativity is itself debased. Having already conceived of standards as creations, and of creations in terms of physiology or corporeal genesis, Nietzsche was led to distinguish the noble from the base in terms of "power" or "life-enhancement." Since the root of spiritual power is the body, elegance is from the outset compromised by bestiality. Nietzsche's aristocratic tastes are thus contradicted by the principles from which they are deduced. His immediate disciples still preserve something of the master's taste, but their message for the next generation is evident. The Nietzschean creator turns inevitably from the intangibility of thought to the tangibility of the flesh; in Gide's words, "The sensation is always sincere; it is the only guarantee of the authenticity of our sentiments; our sentiments are guaranteed by their physiological repercussions." [4]

3. There is an echo of Spinoza in Nietzsche's conception of freedom; see his letter to Overbeck of July 30, 1881 (Schlechta, *3*, 1171).
4. *Journals* (August 8, 1905), tr. J. O'Brien (New York, A. A. Knopf,

The authenticity of physiological sentiment leads not to an aristocratic aestheticism, but to egalitarian democracy—exactly the reverse of Nietzsche's intentions. One man's sensations are exactly as "sincere" as another's; to replace the church by the body is simply to make a church of the body. A free man's worship then becomes identical with the worship of his own physiological appetites. The difficulty in Marx is fundamentally very similar. Creativity depends upon a nature which is itself a product of human creativity. In the manuscripts of 1844, Marx identifies nature as the "sensuous external world" of real physical objects, among them man.[5] Man is thus said to live "in" nature, as part of a continuous process which he reproduces in himself, or in his work.[6] But there is a dualism within nature, represented by the difference between man and his external world. Whatever may be the case with the objectivity of the external world, man makes his own nature and, by extension, the objective social world within which his natural work takes place. Man generates himself not just sexually, but spiritually: his work generates human nature as political or social history.[7]

> History itself is a real part of natural history, of nature becoming human . . . . Man is the immediate object of natural science; for the immediate *sensible nature* for man is immediately human sensibility (an identical expression), immediately sensible as the *other* man, present to him; for his own sensibility is first [accessible] to himself as human sensibility through the *other* man.[8]

1949), *1,* 146. Cf. D. H. Lawrence, *Women in Love* (New York, Compass Books, 1966), p. 72: "Pure culture in sensation, culture in the physical consciousness, really ultimate *physical* consciousness, mindless, utterly sensual. It is so sensual as to be final, supreme." For relevant texts from Nietzsche, see *Der Wille zur Macht,* p. 47, par. 54; *Jenseits,* pp. 569 (3), 571 (6); *Antichrist,* Schlechta, *2,* 1164 (2): "Was ist gut? —Alles, was das Gefühl der Macht . . . erhöht."

   5. *Ökonomisch-philosophische Manuskripte,* in *Werke,* ed. Lieber and Furth, *1* (Darmstadt, Wissenschaftliche Buchgesellschaft, 1963), 562, 650.

   6. Ibid., pp. 566, 568.

   7. Ibid., pp. 600, 607, 652.

   8. Ibid., p. 604.

In this revealing passage, Marx speaks of nature as itself historical. Man first has access to nature through recognition of his own humanity, which in turn is revealed to him by the presence of another man. Nature is perceived through, and consequently objectified by, politico-historical human nature. The similarity to Nietzsche is unmistakable, although Marx speaks of social work rather than unique creativity. The contradiction is equally obvious: if natural objectivity is a product of politico-economic work, then it is as inaccessible as Kant's thing-in-itself. Man in effect creates himself *ex nihilo*. And since this creation depends upon society, or the perception of another man, Marx must explain how men are, and perceive each other to be, men, prior to the social labor which this perception engenders.[9]

On the basis of Marx's analysis, men cannot come into being, since they must first exist in order to create themselves. If, on the other hand, the human species is eternal, then man does *not* make himself but at best only fulfills his nature in an Aristotelian sense. The ostensibly objective, external nature out of which Marx says men create themselves, since it is in fact inaccessible, is effectively equivalent to nothingness. It is impossible for Marx to overcome the dualism or contradiction between man and nature because he does not, as he believes, end with Humanism as the conclusion of work upon nature; he begins with it.[10] If nature is the product of human work, namely, of thought or speech, it cannot serve as the principle, standard, or objective measure of human speech. According to Marx, Geist is speech, but "the element of thinking itself, the element of the externalization in life of thought, *speech,* is sensuous nature."[11] Spirit then arises from the exchange of goods in the satisfaction of material needs; but material needs depend upon the sensible world, which is itself a product of industry and social

9. The same problem is unresolved in the best Marxist interpretation of Hegel, by A. Kojève. Kojève does not explain how animal desire first becomes human desire. The animal ostensibly becomes human by risking its life for recognition, but could only desire to do so if it were already human. See *Introduction à la lecture de Hegel,* p. 14.

10. *Manuskripte,* pp. 593–94.

11. *Manuskripte,* p. 605; *Die Deutsche Ideologie* (Berlin, Dietz Verlag, 1960), p. 27.

conditions, i.e. of *speech*.[12] For Marx as for Nietzsche, things are interpreted as speeches, which are in turn paradoxically created by corporeal desire. Both men fluctuate irresolvably between onto-poetic historicism and positivistic materialism; the result is not coherent speech, but silence. Both understand nature as the body but make the significance of the body a historical poem. In both cases, the desire to transform man into a god is contradicted by the conception of man as a creation ex nihilo. The failure to distinguish between nature and history, or God and genesis, is reflected in the unintelligible relation between body and spirit in man. Hence the incoherence among contemporary Marxists concerning the status of freedom and creativity in the domain of historical materialism.

For reasons of this kind, it has become next to impossible to distinguish between ontological and Marxist nihilism in our time. The Marxists are prepared to destroy the present through negation of the past, on the basis of a hope for the future that does not permit rational articulation. Nevertheless, there is this difference between Marxism and existential ontology: the former, despite a theoretical incoherence at which we have just looked, is positively related to the great tradition of European rationalism from Plato to Hegel. Marx's virtues are essentially those of Hegel; his incoherence stems from the mistaken belief that he has made a theoretical *Aufhebung* of, or advance upon, the Hegelian teaching. In fact, Marx, like Kierkegaard, Feuerbach, and Nietzsche, is a post-Hegelian whose thought proceeds from a fundamental *narrowing* of the Hegelian horizon, namely, from the acceptance of history and the repudiation of wisdom. Differently stated, the post-Hegelians replace theory by practice rather than reconciling the two. This is radically more marked in Kierkegaard and Nietzsche than it is in Marx, who remains closer to Hegel. Marx's conception of the mastery of nature through work and the subsequent development of the free human spirit ought to terminate in a completely rational speech about the world (a *mathesis universalis* that is not merely mathematics), a speech in which the prima facie difference be-

12. *Deutsche Ideologie,* pp. 17, 24, 27, 41.

tween man and nature (alienation) is overcome. Despite his circular derivation of spirit from corporeal desire, Marx understands that human work is fundamentally rational or discursive. Strangely enough, what he does not seem to understand is that the division in nature between spirit and body cannot be overcome except by the reinstitution of monism, whether it be called Idealism or Materialism. We see here again the problem of the two motions, discussed in Chapter 3. Whereas Rousseau, to take a proximate example, conceived of history as a consequence of nature, Marx is unable to conceive of nature as independent from history, and so from human creation. There can be no speech overcoming the alienation of man from nature, because Marx's nature can never be spoken of or conceived as independent of man.

If the modes of economic production are the key to the understanding of man's historical nature, they must themselves be subordinate to his biological nature and can have only a contingent bearing upon the post-historical world. We see here the same problem as was discovered in Nietzsche and Heidegger— the dislocation or disjunction of the temporal dimensions. In Marx, the post-historical world is the future, the physical world of biological nature is the past, and the world of economic history is the present. Presumably we are moving toward the future, within the present, by way of a creative transformation of the past. But this is to say that biological nature, very far from explaining the appetites or desires which give birth to the present, is in fact conceived as an extension from the present superimposed onto the past. The past is in fact a speech, e.g. the science of biology, which is itself explicable only as the work of the human spirit, and so in fundamentally economic terms. The past-in-itself does not exist: it is nothingness. But the future has no more intrinsic solidity; it is either a wish or a prediction based upon, and so again a projection of, the present. It is a *silent* projection, since the categories of economic explanation are not appropriate to post-revolutionary, post-historical man, freed from alienation for the autonomous exercise of creativity. Just as Nietzsche can say nothing about the creations of the superman, and Heidegger can say nothing about the gifts of the next epoch of the history of Being, so Marx can say nothing about the future.[13] Marx's philosophy of history reduces to an interpretation of the present as what may be called the economic monad. The validity of this interpretation has exactly the same status as a poem or projection of the historical consciousness. It is self-certifying or self-asserting—a manifestation of the will to power.

The self-assertion of Marxism lacks the persuasiveness of Hegel because it is a claim to wisdom, expressed as an interpretation of history, which denies the end of history and therefore the possibility of wisdom. As a poem about completeness, however, it is preferable to the sterile and fragmentary poems of logical epistemology or the gnostic epics of existential ontology. In the remaining sections of this chapter, I shall discuss the phenomenon of nihilism as an ingredient in the dialectical pursuit of completeness by the human psyche, and the sense in which that pursuit is capable of achieving its goal. The attentive reader will observe that my discussion of this dialectical process is itself conceived in terms of a dialectical confrontation between the Platonic and the Hegelian conceptions of wisdom. My study of nihilism, taken as a whole, may then serve as an introduction to the reader's own investigation of the most serious version of the quarrel between the ancients and the moderns— the choice of a good life.

II.

Marx criticizes Hegel for having reduced life to abstract dialectic or thought. Since abstraction does not know itself as such, we must return to nature in order to discover the natural man who performs these abstractions.[14] This criticism is in principle the same as that raised against Hegel by Schelling and Kierkegaard, namely, that the existing individual, the real source of unity between thought and form, cannot be derived from the

13. Other than romantic predictions about the omnicompetence of communist man: cf. *Die Deutsche Ideologie*, p. 30.
14. *Manuskripte*, pp. 655–60.

universal categories of logic. Whatever the defects of Marx's own conception of nature, the sense of the criticism is very close to the Platonic–Aristotelian teaching in an important respect. For Plato and Aristotle, it is also impossible to deduce the phenomenon of life from the logical or dialectical analysis of intelligible form. However, it is not possible simply to begin with the fact of the existing individual, whether in an ontological or scientific sense, because the "natural" individual is not directly accessible, whether to himself or others. The "immediate" in Plato and Aristotle is not nature (and certainly not sense perception), but opinion. Philosophy begins in the attempt to distinguish between nature and convention, or opinions about nature. A failure to begin in this way raises the danger that we will replace nature with an opinion, that our ontological analysis of human existence will produce an analysis of a historical stage of opinions about human existence. From here, it is a short step to the view that the sense of human existence is a matter of opinion, or that man is a radically historical animal.

The Hegelian response to this difficulty is to claim that the truth may be ascertained from a dialectical study of all fundamental opinions, which are identified with the history of philosophy in one sense, and with human or world history in another. Of the many problems which this approach raises, I mention only two: first, the need to demonstrate that every fundamental opinion about the world *has* in fact been manifested, and so that history (in the special Hegelian sense) is essentially complete. The Hegelian cannot offer an opinion, or even a myth, about wisdom as the essential completeness of opinions; he must demonstrate his wisdom in a perfect, and hence self-explanatory, speech. The second problem is a corollary to the first: in the course of identifying wisdom as the encompassing speech about opinions, nature has been replaced by history. As we saw in the case of Marx, the Hegelian begins from the assumption that nature is accessible only through an opinion or spiritual modification. This is not the same as the Socratic contention that things become visible to men in speeches, although at first glance the views are identical. The difference lies in the fact that

Socrates claims access to noetic entities which are neither things (in the colloquial sense) nor speeches about things. Socrates claims that speech is possible only on the basis of silence, but that silence is indirectly accessible to speech. Hegel claims that silence is impossible for thought, or that Socrates' noetic entities are in fact primordial, historically undeveloped speeches, which have achieved articulate fulfillment in his own logic.

Hegel does not simply attempt to derive the existing individual from speech, but more fundamentally every possible speech is derived from the fact of speech, which is thus shown, when fully developed, to be Absolute Spirit. There is no noesis in Hegel, but the claim of a complete dianoia. This claim is open to serious formal or dialectical difficulties, which I shall examine at length later in this chapter. At the moment, I want to observe that there is another line of argument in Hegel, subsequently revised and developed by Marx, which has its roots in the Socratic conception of eros and the Aristotelian doctrine of "being-at-work." I refer to the argument from human desire, which is related to Hegel's understanding of work as negation. Parenthetically, I may observe that Socrates and his students, instead of referring to history, conceive of the polis as the informal structure of human opinions (including, at least indirectly, those which transcend the polis). Man's political nature is due to the fact that he is a talking animal: his desires may be satisfied only through speech (διὰ λόγου: this is the root meaning of man's "dialectical" nature). Reflection upon political speech gives us access to a distinction between nature and opinion which does not depend upon the presence of every opinion, but upon the logical consequences of the fact of desire. Put very crudely, man's desire for things can be satisfied only through the medium of speech. Desire in its most characteristically human form is soon deflected from (external, objective) things to speeches about things, and finally to speech about speech.

Nihilism is a permanent danger to the human condition because negation or silence is present in the difference between desire and things and in the problems connected with our desire for a complete speech. Hegel and Marx are correct in speaking of the negativity of work, but wrong in thinking that negativity is itself negated by the completion of work in speech or in deed. Their error is essentially discursive: they cannot discover a natural terminus or measure for speech, because they make the scope of speech total. In the absence of a total speech, we are left with partial and mutually contradictory speeches with no criterion by which to measure their relative merits. The wise man would seem to be indistinguishable from the sophist. As Plato might put it, the sophist and wise man become blurred together because neither can escape from the necessity of non-being. We must therefore discover a kind of speech which, in the absence of a complete speech, nevertheless serves to distinguish philosophy from sophistry. Our search will begin in a way that owes something to Hegel but more to Plato—with human desire. The kind of speech we need will become visible only by means of a consideration of the dialectical nature of the psyche.

Every desire, however humble, implies in addition to its immediate object the conditions which guarantee the accessibility of that object. For the most part, we have only a vague awareness that this is so; the implications of a desire are not the same as consciousness that I desire X. But even in ordinary experience, we frequently subject our desires to analysis or render them articulate by asking questions such as, what must I do in order to obtain X? Again, for the most part, these reflections are of minimal extent, whether because the object is readily accessible, or because the life of heterogeneous desire leaves little time for reflection, or for some other reason. Suffice it to say that reflection tends to be silenced by a minimal degree of satisfaction. But life soon teaches us, even if we are incapable of benefiting from the lesson, that the conditions upon which the secure satisfaction of a desire for X rests are manifold. We learn that one desire leads to another, that an instance of satisfaction is soon followed by the same desire that preceded it, that the experience of satisfaction is itself a stimulus to new and more complicated desires. The previously acceptable minimal degree of satisfaction sooner or later becomes unacceptable;

even the moderate man is forced to take into account or to
desire security concerning the many contingencies upon which
the pursuit of moderation depends. Desire for the absence of
desire is still a desire, and one which finally implicates the
whole of experience, just as does the desire for desire. The
desire for X is always the desire for Y; an infinite regress is
avoidable only by the complete satisfaction of desire. If desire
remains content with its immediate object, it preserves silence
but thereby ceases to be human, not to say secure. But if it
reflects upon the conditions for satisfaction or mediates its object by speech, it is necessarily inflected toward the desire not
for this or that object, but for speech about desire. The immediate and silent desire for X is always a desire for speech about
the whole.

We may call this self-transcending characteristic of desire its
rational nature. I am not speaking here of individual desires, the
passions, mutilated or deprived of their rationale by having
been ripped from the context of desire altogether. Nor do I refer
to a discontinuous multiplicity of individual desires, which lack
the reflexive connections by which men are able to arrange their
activities in a hierarchy of excellence or desirability. A single
desire, considered in itself, is no more (and no less) reasonable
than a single axiom or argument. And a multiplicity of discontinuous desires is indistinguishable from a single desire, because
the principle of distinction, the coherence of desire, what provides ultimate or secure satisfaction, or speech, is absent. Of
course, we may say, "I want X, and I want Y, and I want Z."
But if we cannot speak of the relations between X and Z, or say
why Z is better than Y in the sense of bringing us closer to the
ultimately desired speech about desire, then we have said nothing worth saying, or have been silent. Finally, I am not suggesting that the rationality of desire altogether makes it rational to
attempt to satisfy each single desire in its own immediate terms.
Individual desires or passions, if all are given their head, soon
come into conflict with each other and thereby prevent the satisfaction of all, or contradict the nature of satisfaction altogether.
Indeed, the term "satisfaction" has no more significance inde-

pendent of the recognition that desire is directed toward completeness, than an argument may significantly be called "rational" independent of the function it plays in the complete speech of the wise man. Desire, although not the same as speech, is completed by it; completely satisfied desire entails the complete speech. However, the completion of speech and the complete satisfaction of desire define a god rather than a man. To achieve godhood is to cease to be a man, and so not to speak, but to be silent. In this crucial respect, it is virtually impossible to distinguish between a god and a beast (or even a less articulate natural "force"). We can make this distinction only by asking the ostensible god to exhibit his divinity, in other words, by engaging in dialogue with him. Whether the god simply acts or also speaks in response to our questions is irrelevant. For the response of an act to a speech is equivalent to a speech; and in speaking, the god ceases to be a god and becomes a man. Even further, gods cannot keep silent without thereby suppressing for themselves the difference between divinity and bestiality. The only evidence a god can have of his own divinity is or includes speech, and this is evidence of his humanity. In other words, there is no complete speech (since it would then be the same as, or indistinguishable from, silence), but only speech *about* complete speech, or speech which articulates, renders intelligible, and is accompanied by desire. Again, this does not mean that desire is the same as speech, but only that it is rational, i.e. capable of explication by speech. Desire is a mark of imperfection; "satisfaction" does not and cannot mean simply "the fulfillment of this desire or that," but makes sense only when applied to the fulfillment of desire altogether. A desire may therefore be defined as "base" when it interferes with the goal of complete satisfaction, and "noble" when it advances that goal. A base desire stands in essential contradiction to the ultimate object of every desire, and so to itself. Unfortunately, a correct distinction between base and noble desires is as difficult as self-consciousness about desire altogether, or the construction of an adequate speech about the complete speech. Hence the difficulty of distinguishing between the philosopher and the sophist. The speech of the philosopher is an anticipation of, but not the same as, the complete or circular speech of the sage or god; as an anticipation only, it is easily confused with the infinite chatter of the sophist. In sum, one might well claim that philosophy is as dangerous as, or for all practical purposes indistinguishable from, sophistry, and this is to say that speech is as dangerous as silence, or that man's natural condition is nihilism. The standard of a permissible speech is then the warning against the dangers of speech. Unfortunately, as we have seen, such a warning is pointless if taken as an invocation to silence, since it then becomes indistinguishable from an invocation to bestiality, or the impossibility of satisfying our desires as men. The most one can say is this: man is by his nature forever intermediate between speech and silence. As a consequence, he must conform to his nature by engaging in an intermediate or moderate speech, one which says enough to preserve his humanity, but not so much as to obfuscate the difference between the human and the divine. Speech which preserves the difference between the human and the bestial by a recognition of the difference between the human and the divine is *prayer,* or the speech of religion. Nihilism, as has been frequently asserted, would then be understood to be due to the breakdown in traditional "values," or essentially to the cancellation of religious faith by the notorious pride of the philosophers. If we must have philosophy, let it at least take place privately, behind closed doors; public speech must be *ad captum vulgi,* or accommodated to the political necessity for the sovereignty of a god or gods.

But can nihilism be contained by keeping philosophy out of the marketplace? The radical defect in the religious solution can be easily stated as the problem of the false prophet. The natural diversity of man leads inevitably to disagreement as to the correct version of prayer, or the true interpretation of Holy Scripture. Since gods can communicate with men by speech alone (if at all), the meaning of that speech is open in principle to as many interpretations as there are human partners in the divine dialogue. Of course, one interpretation may be enforced on all members of a community, at least for a given period of time; but the appeal to force is an admission of the failure of interpretation, and so of speech. In admitting the insolubility of the meaning of the divine difference by speech, one admits the desirability not of a moderate speech, but of silence (and thus force is a silent immoderate speech which negates itself by its excess). However this may preserve political stability in one sense, it cancels it in another and deeper sense; only human beings can dwell in political stability, but human beings are characterized by speech, not by silence. The stable city is no longer a city of men, but, to borrow a phrase from Plato, it is a city of pigs. The attempt to satisfy desire by recourse to prayer, if followed consistently, leads to the suppression of the difference it was designed to preserve. In order to safeguard their humanity, men must allow the false prophet to be heard; that is, they must dispute with him, thereby submitting and resubmitting the Holy Word to human interpretation. And if they are not to be duped by a pseudo-piety into accepting a shoddy defense of the traditional teaching, or in effect mistaking silence (and so bestiality) for speech, then they must call forth the philosophers from their studies and unseal their lips or permit the most fluent speakers to engage in a testing of the faith. Anything less than the best, most fluent test of the faith leaves one a prey to the teaching of the false prophet. Yet to combat the false prophet, we must submit prayer to philosophy, or the word of god to the word of man. Is not the inevitable result of the necessary turn to a philosophical defense of the faith the destruction of faith? For, apart from the pride of the philosophers, how can they be distinguished from the sophists by the simple man of faith?

Whether we speak of false prophets or base desires, it would seem that man is doomed to nihilism, not simply because of an encounter with nothingness or silence, but by virtue of the nature of speech itself. Man preserves his humanity by speech; yet in speaking, he destroys it. Whereas it may be true that the unexamined life is not worth living, the same is apparently the case with the examined life. We seem to have arrived at the modern formulation of the human dilemma: desire is the desire for speech, but speech "alienates" us from our desires. Whether or not we can finish speaking, we are in either case subject to the danger of boredom, and so the truth of what we say may at any moment become irrelevant. If, dazed by the infinite chatter of philosophical and theological interpretations, we escape from nihilism by a return to the earth, is this not itself recourse to a negative interpretation? The fear of death, the instinct of self-preservation, intermittent pleasures and joys, whether in the flesh or in the mind, all amount to nothing more than recourse to silence, or a forgetting of one's own humanity. In the dimension of silence, man preserves enough of his humanity to replace the desire for completeness by the desire for complete bestiality. But man is not even a beast; the beast possesses a coherence or completeness that is the mark of his naturally finite desire. Human desire is infinite; when speech is suppressed, it becomes incoherent and discontinuous. An escape to desire from the alienation of speech becomes an alienation of desire from itself. Without speech, one cannot tell the presence or absence of desire, which has replaced consciousness as the essence of human nature. Nihilism again presents itself as the disjunction between speech and desire. Nihilism is an expression of the impossibility of human perfection. But how can we avoid the conclusion that it is also an expression of the impossibility of being human?

The danger of nihilism is inseparable from the nature of speech because speech is a mark of imperfection. Men speak because they are partially detached from things and try to overcome this disjunction with a bridge of language. I have put this point very generally by attributing to speech the function of articulating desire, and so of explicitly acknowledging this detachment or disjunction. Since words, however remarkable, are not things, the disjunction between the two can never be entirely overcome. The very remarkableness of words serves to charm us away from things (as the remarkableness of numbers and symbols charm us away from words), away from the unity desired, and into the lonely splendor of speech unrestricted by things, or poetry. It is therefore essential to acknowledge desire in order to combat the human inclination toward solipsism. Desire rather than speech joins us to things and so provides the medium which gives substance to language, whether we call it eros, hope, wonder, or some other name. At the same time, it is not enough for a man merely to be joined to things, or to elude the terrors of speech in unrestricted desire, since the result would be to cancel out desire, or to turn man into a thing. Desire, in order to preserve its nature or to achieve its intentions, needs speech to provide it with a sufficient "distance" from things, within which it may begin to practice the discriminations, restraints, or evaluations upon which its satisfaction depends.

Human existence is a harmony of desire and speech, or of union with and distance from things. This does not necessarily mean that too much speech will dissolve the harmony, but rather that nihilism is the result of two kinds of disharmony. From two primarily "theoretical" errors, which finally amount to the same, comes the "practical" obliteration of mood known as nihilism. Either we assume that speech is independent of desire, or we assume that desire is independent of speech; the results are equal, and equally disastrous. I call these errors "theoretical" because they take place only after considerable experience, or reflection upon experience, and so primarily through speech. The most radical form of these errors occurs after that peculiar reflection upon experience by old age, which generates "history" in the modern sense of the term, or the "historical consciousness." For what I have just referred to as our disjunction from things is also the origin of human temporality: we experience time as the activity of "running after" things in dis-cursive thought. When the pursuit of discourse comes to be regarded as vain (because theoretically detached from desire), the result is Historicity and finally nihilism. The nihilist is not susceptible to reason because it is precisely reason which he holds responsible for his "detachment" or boredom. One may therefore say that the nihilist does not and cannot

understand his dilemma by speech; if he is to be cured at all, it
will be by mood, by the excitation of desire, by rhetoric rather
than by logic, and, if you will, by magic rather than by science.

III.

Nature furnishes man with desire, but it also furnishes him
with speech, or the means of satisfying desire in such a way as to
threaten it constantly with extinction. Man is that paradoxical
being, unique so far as we know, who strives for a perfection
which, if attained, would altogether deprive him of his nature. If
there is dignity in the human condition, it lies in the recognition
that to exist is already to be in danger not simply of death, but
of consciousness as boredom. We preserve our dignity by pur-
suing the implications of this shock of recognition, both helped
and hindered by nature, and so preserve ourselves as we seek to
overcome ourselves. Discursive thought is thus like fire: it purifies, but it also destroys. The legend of the phoenix is in fact the
legend of man. At least so far man has continuously reemerged
from the ashes of his self-immolation. This process of reemer-
gence is called "history": literally, an inquiry into human acts
and speeches. When, however, man becomes detached from
things, or lost in speech, he comes to think of himself as a
radically or exclusively historical being, a being who is nothing
but self-inquiry or, more accurately, self-interpretation. But
logical solipsism provides no criteria to evaluate speeches other
than the rules of logic. When speeches become distinguishable
only on formal criteria (e.g. style in art), they are indistinguishable with respect to their content. It no longer matters what we
say, so long as we say it "correctly." In the most fundamental
terms, desire ceases to be articulate. At first, this lack of discrimination is taken to be freedom: every desire is permissible
(and this is why "moral experimentation" always accompanies
formalist or stylistic overemphasis). But as we have seen, freedom in this sense leads to incoherence or self-negation, and so
to the absence or alienation of desire—to nihilism.

"History" in the sense just defined (the post-Hegelian conception of "historicity") is then not simply change, not mere process, not even most essentially actions, but speech in the sense of self-interpretation.[15] History begins from a memory of the past, or the self-interpretation known as "tradition." Tradition in itself, however, is only potentially history which is actualized by the critique or reinterpretation of tradition. I referred to this process previously as the problem of the false prophet, which was easily seen to be identical with the problem of philosophy. What we may call the "conservative" solution to this problem is to distinguish between private and public speech, if not to suppress philosophy altogether, in order to keep it out of the marketplace, which is reserved for prayer, including its most obvious "political" form, patriotism. But this is no solution, because prayer is as diverse as philosophy. For this reason alone, an intelligent or articulate conservatism is constantly (if slowly) transforming itself into "radicalism." If it attenuates this process too sharply, conservatism ceases to be articulate and deteriorates into bestiality. Nevertheless, the intelligent conservative has rightly perceived the danger of speech; his defect lies in the fact that he does not know how to respond to this danger. Hence he tends to vacillate in the privacy of speech as concealed by irony, which, as Hegel wisely observed, contains an absolute negativity,[16] or, as we may say, is all too close to the nihilism it seeks to avoid.

The radical's response to the problem of the false prophet has been to "let a hundred flowers bloom," as it were, or, in a more appropriate metaphor, to found the republic of letters. But the republic of letters does not simply emancipate speech from itself; it is a republic of "mere letters," sundered from things and desires rooted in things. The emptiness of the republic of letters is a consequence of the excessive acceleration by radicals of the process of self-interpretation. The radical correctly sees

15. Hence the popularity of "hermeneutics" among the followers of Heidegger. See esp. H. G. Gadamer, *Wahrheit und Methode* (Tübingen, J. C. B. Mohr, 1960), e.g. pp. 323 ff.

16. *Ästhetik*, ed. F. Bassenge (Frankfurt, Europäische Verlagsanstalt, 1955), Bd. I, pp. 73–74, 161.

that man, as a speaking animal, retains his humanity only by continuing to speak, or that the goal of speech is completeness, i.e. a complete self-interpretation. But he does not see the danger in continuous speech, no doubt because he has not fully grasped the danger of silence as already implicit in the goal of the complete speech. The radical is characterized by the mood of daring or excitement, not so much with respect to deeds as to speeches or interpretations about deeds. When through excessive speech he becomes enamored of words apart from deeds, his excitement begins the process of deterioration into boredom. If this process is arrested before its final stage (and sometimes even if it is not), the radical is slowly transformed into a conservative. In the last analysis, the radical and the conservative are scarcely distinguishable from each other, as is especially clear in the contemporary political sphere, where "radicalism" often seems to mean a combination of Stalinism and anarchism. Neither the radical nor the conservative represents an adequate confrontation of the paradoxical dialectic of human nature. Neither is adequate because each is a single term, isolated from the dialectic within which alone he finds his meaning. The radical and conservative, apart from this dialectic, are indistinguishable because equally meaningless, equally fragmentary, and so equally fanatical. Each attempts to force a simple solution onto a complex problem. Each is operating with an altogether inadequate model of coherence and completeness.

In presenting this sketch of the dialectic between the conservative and the radical, I do not mean to imply that the solution to man's problems lies in the process of joint evolution or development toward union between the two. Of course, under specific circumstances, and to alleviate a specific difficulty, one may have to act rather more conservatively, or rather more radically. But everything I have said is intended to show that there cannot be any final solutions to man's problems, that man *is* a problem (or paradox), however little this may appeal to common sense, and that to "solve" the problem would be to dissolve man. This dissolution, or nihilism, arises precisely from the exaggerated attempt to enforce a simple solution, or to reduce complexity to unity in opposition to a more or less unstable harmony. Unity, or a nonarticulated monad, is unspeakable and unthinkable. It is therefore true that, in order to exist, man must successfully combine the traits of conservatism and radicalism, but not that he must unify them. As both radical and conservative, man is neither one nor the other. In this vein, it makes sense to say that man is a harmony of opposites. Thus man can know the truth about himself with respect both to his end and his incompleteness, but he cannot, by virtue of the nature of that truth, possess a "systematic" or "complete" account of it. The truth is that, instead of solving his problems and thereby incurring the disaster of a "final solution," man must reconcile himself to a perpetual process of approximations, of prudential adjustments and accommodations, sometimes in the direction of daring, sometimes in the direction of caution. But these approximations are not directed toward an infinitely distant, and so infinitely inaccessible, goal of progressive perfection, for that would amount to having no goal at all, and so to approximating nothing, or to nihilism. The goal is accessible but unaccomplishable; man can understand that his nature would be fulfilled in a completely rational speech satisfying his desire as such, if it were not the case that such a speech, when completed, would destroy his nature.

Speech qua speech is partial, or testimony to the fact that man stands apart from (although connected to) those things in and through which he must find his completeness, provided only he could at the same time remain himself, that is, conscious of the difference between himself and things, and speaking of that difference. To be complete, man would have to be simultaneously partial. If this is impossible, there is nevertheless an imitation or surrogate form of completeness available to him, namely, to speak in the light of, and so about, completeness. Speech that is genuinely about completeness and not about something else—that is, speech which has grasped the truth about human nature, and so which functions in a healthy or sane way to articulate desire, guided by the ideal of perfection, but which, for that reason, avoids pressing any element in the situation beyond what it can bear, or which is guided by the ideal to avoid all unbalanced attempts to achieve it—is *philosophy*. Other modes of speech, such as art and science, are reasonable or unreasonable, and so "good" or "bad," as they do or do not participate in philosophy in the genuine sense of the term. It is therefore nonsense to judge philosophy in terms of art, science, political ideology, or any other secondary (because detached) form of speech, which itself implies prior philosophical decisions, whether known to the speaker or not. Philosophy can submit to no judge but itself, which is of course to say that it submits not to self-indulgence or pride, but to the standard of things, desires, and fundamentally to the desire for a complete interpretation of things, desires, and speech, or itself.

To speak, then, is to philosophize, although we reserve the name "philosopher" for those who understand, and can therefore give an account of, the nature of speech. The philosopher is the man who can speak about the complete speech (as opposed to the linguistic theorist, who speaks about complete speech as an abstract form in terms of mathematics, rather than about what is said by that complete speech). If it is not the complete speech about or toward which we speak, we are not philosophers; if our speech is the complete speech, then we are not men, which is to say that we are not speaking. To be quite accurate, there are not several or indefinitely many "philosophies" or "conceptions of philosophy," but only one. There are, however, indefinitely many philosophical speeches, certified as philosophical by the criterion just mentioned, indefinitely many because coextensive with human existence, or with "history" in the vulgar sense of the term. Philosophy is always the same, but circumstances vary constantly, as they must by the nature of temporality and so of the dialectic between memory and forgetfulness. Every new circumstance demands a new philosophical speech. But just as memory provides the thread of continuity to circumstance, so the nature of desire and speech provides the double-thread of continuity to philosophy. Those who forget too much, and specifically this, break the thread of continuity, and of circumstances as well as speech. Speech becomes unending chatter, however analytically proficient, since the principles of analysis are themselves discontinuous speeches, beautiful perhaps, but like scattered pearls when the string of a necklace snaps.

If speech radically understood is philosophy, it follows that men lose their roots when they cease, or attempt to cease, to philosophize. The unphilosophical and so nihilistic temper of our own time is most clearly visible in the anti-philosophical speeches of recent spokesmen for philosophy. This in turn stems from the historical development, or rather the development of "history" in the modern sense, as disaffected speech. In terms of the present chapter, we may say that disaffected speech takes essentially two forms: solipsism and communism. It is not necessary to repeat here a dialectic which was sketched out in terms of the conservative and the radical. Suffice it to say that, in the same way, the solipsist and communist, because standing for two isolated elements whose meaning depends upon their position in the whole, are finally indistinguishable from each other. Of course, in immediate, daily life, there are no "pure" solipsists or communists, any more than there are "pure" conservatives or radicals. I have purified these types in order to facilitate comprehension of the motives that determine an individual's character when one or another achieves dominance therein. The types correspond to isolation from deeds in speech (solipsism), and to a loss of self, and so of speech, in deeds (communism).

To descend to a level of greater immediacy, these two types share a propensity to excessive speech, and so to rapid deterioration into ideologies, whether of the academy or the marketplace. One may suspect that philosophy, when removed from the marketplace to the academy, degenerates into an ideology of solipsists that is the inverse form of political ideology as it springs up in the marketplace to fill the void left by philosophy's departure. This observation must be modified by the further comment that, since the ideology of the academy is a more fluent expression of man's nature as the speaking animal, whereas the ideology of the marketplace springs from the love of justice, which is like mathematics (in its abstraction from circumstance and desire for equalities or tautologies) and so is a form of relative silence, it often happens that the academicians are stirred once more to desire by the deeds (if not the speeches, or the incoherence of the speeches) of the marketplace. In attempting to accommodate their verbal solipsism to the relative silence of communism, which is intentionally directed toward the unspeakable, because unarticulated, monad, they succeed only in reinforcing by combination the two separate inclinations toward nihilism. The result may be (as in the case of Nietzsche and Heidegger) infinitely more interesting than the sterile speeches of the apolitical "logicians," but, for that reason, in the long run infinitely more dangerous. The logicist ideology leads so quickly to boredom that it is easily absorbed by the ideology of the academicized marketplace. The specific terms of that absorption, as well as the specific cast of the academicized marketplace's ideology, obviously vary from age to age and country to country. Once the essentials of the process are grasped, it is relatively easy to understand and describe the variations.

IV.

The desire for things moves man to speech; the negativity of work, by which man appropriates his physical environment, is at a deeper level a war against the silence of the world. And yet, as we have seen, speech is itself permeated by the very silence against which it struggles. The voice of man seems to be muffled by the silence of Pascal's two infinities. One need be neither a mystic nor a romantic to feel the pressure of, and sometimes even the need for, silence. Not infrequently, silence, our ambiguous enemy, seems to heal the wounds of futile chatter. The relief we experience in these cases is a symbol of the ultimate silence in which a completed speech would terminate. But it is a spurious remedy, purchased at the cost of our birthright. Silence is not the explanation man desires, but the negation of explanation. With respect to intelligibility, silence is subordinate to speech, since speech points out silence, points to the silence within itself. Without speech, silence would be invisible; it would be nothing, and even if our goal is an identification with nothingness, a total self-cancellation, we can achieve this negative condition only by first defining it in discursive thought and then proceeding, again through discursive thinking, to negate each of the logical determinations that make us something rather than nothing. "Nothing" is intelligible only in contrast with something, or it is intelligible only if it is "Being." [17] The intelligibility of Being = Nothing depends upon the manifestation of (negative) characteristics which can only be communicated to oneself (to say nothing of others) through thinking the (negative) form of these characteristics. To think even negative form, however, is to think positively, or concretely, to think a content by duplicating it; and this formal duplication is logical or spoken in the most radical sense. Thinking away thought is nevertheless thinking, and thinking toward even total negativity is nevertheless identifying our goal as *something,* identifying silence by and through speech.

In the two preceding sections, I discussed the nature of wisdom as completeness, or the fulfilled intention of every finite human desire. Philosophy is thus speech in the light of wisdom, which is formally or ideally visible as the necessary model of the complete speech within which everything is essentially explained, and in terms of which philosophically partial speeches are distinguished from unphilosophically partial speeches. The ideal visibility of wisdom is both the beginning and the end of philosophy. Philosophical speech, as the reflection of wisdom, must therefore be both archaeological and teleological. [18] The *archē* and *telos* of the part illuminate the place of that part within the whole which is itself the structure of beginnings and ends, and indeed their identity. The intelligibility of a part, or of a partial speech, cannot be identical with that part *as* partial, for if it were, there would be as many principles of intelligibility as

17. Even Hegel, in his *Logik,* although he identifies abstract Being and Nothing, begins his presentation with Being rather than Nothing.
18. Cf. Aristotle, *Metaphysics* 981a30–982a4, 982b5, 1050a8.

there are parts, and these would be mutually self-contradictory. To be radically partial is to be unintelligible, or not even an identifiable "part." For example, the intelligibility of a sentence in some formal language derives from the exhibition within its structure of the systematic or ordered totality of the principles of that language. The same is true of sentences in so-called ordinary or natural languages: it is true of speech as such. One cannot chatter "aimlessly" (i.e. to no end, in the denial of teleology) without implicitly aiming at the ideal conditions of intelligible interminability, which, as intelligible, cannot themselves be interminable. And this is to say nothing of the subservience, even of chatter, to syntax. In other words, it is a denial of philosophy to regard languages simply as artificial systems which are themselves interminable, and each of which is partial. For no partial system can be identical with the principle of its intelligibility without making these principles infinite, and so indeterminate, or unintelligible, and mutually self-contradictory.

It therefore seems to me that either each part is in principle unintelligible (and hence a part in name only), so that what we at any moment think of as intelligible is merely local superstition, a kind of epistemological patriotism, or else the intelligibility of any part, even the most ordinary one, is a manifestation of the accessibility or intelligibility of the whole—of the ideal condition for the possibility of partial intelligibility, a condition which is evident in, inferable from, but necessarily independent of each and every part.[19] This condition is the archē and telos by which and toward which philosophical speech is directed. As for the first alternative, the radical skepticism or systematic agnosticism implied by the denial of the intelligible is not only formally self-contradictory, since it depends upon an ideal of intelligibility, but perhaps even more immediately and simply an unnecessarily elaborate form of metaphysics or mysticism which denies the direct accessibility of formally heterogeneous phenomena, that is, the immediate form of experience. We ought to mistrust attempts to deduce an inner unity from outer variety,

19. Cf. ibid., 1025b ff., 1061b4 ff.

attempts which lead necessarily to the destruction of that outer variety. Since the starting point of every argument is intelligible variety, no argument can intelligibly deny the beginning (and the end) condition of its own intelligibility. And this is as true for the ostensibly "realistic" skeptic as it is for the "partisans of the One."

The initial heterogeneity of experience as the given and necessary condition for philosophy understood as the question, what is being? means that the answer to this question must also be heterogeneous. As a question about what is heterogeneous, philosophy asks about each element of the whole. The structure of the question, if it were fully visible, would exhibit fully the structure of the whole; therefore, it would be identical with, or indistinguishable from, the answer. In other words, those who define philosophy as the comprehension of the fundamental questions are faced with the same difficulty that Hegel poses. To speak of philosophy as knowledge of the fundamental questions and ignorance of the fundamental answers seems to be like saying that one loves wisdom but does not know what it is. Again, how can we know the fundamental questions without knowing their essential structure? And if we know this, how can we be said not to know the essential structure about which the questions are asked? If we cannot know what to ask unless we know that about which we are asking, then either we are wise and so ought not to ask questions but give answers, or we are so ignorant that we cannot ask *the* questions: we cannot distinguish between the fundamental and the accidental questions. And so we may ask any questions with equal legitimacy or lack of legitimacy, which is to say that philosophy is reduced to an infinite interrogative chatter.

But is infinite interrogative chatter possible? I do not believe so, for the following reason. The intelligibility of a single or finite question depends upon the intelligibility of criteria for determining intelligible questions, criteria which are separate from the questions themselves and so are not themselves questionable. If the criteria were questionable, we could not identify a question as determinate or as distinct from other questions, whether intelligible or nonintelligible; and so we could not know it as itself. All questions would blur together, and instead of chatter, we would have noise or silence. If the meaning of a question is itself unintelligible, then we do not know what we have asked, which is the same as saying that we have not really asked anything. Furthermore, we should have to possess unquestionable grounds for knowing that everything is questionable, or that the unending procedure of questioning can in principle never be terminated, either temporarily or permanently, by an answer. We must know the answer to the question, why can we do nothing but question? Whatever the answer to this question may be, when we answer it, we have terminated the merely interrogative; we have circumscribed the domain under interrogation. We possess an ideal of interrogation which regulates, rationalizes, renders our questions intelligible, but which is not itself a question, is not itself questionable.

If, then, the concept of speech as chatter, whether interrogative or declaratory, is self-contradictory, we are forced to conclude that the whole is at least partially intelligible, as the necessary condition for the possible intelligibility of any question or answer. This conclusion establishes the validity of what Plato means by "the good" and provides those who are accessible to reason with a basis for the refutation of nihilism (although it is perhaps worthless in combating the presence of the *mood* of nihilism). But let us examine one more case. Suppose that the difference between philosophy and wisdom is this: the philosopher knows both the fundamental questions and the possible or fundamental answers to each of these questions, whereas only the wise man can know which of a plurality of possible answers to each fundamental question is the correct answer. This position is merely a more complete statement of the view that philosophy is knowledge of the fundamental questions. It should be evident by now that we cannot know a question to be fundamental, nor can we know that we know *the* (or all) fundamental questions, without knowing the foundations, the beginnings and ends, whose aspects are reflected within the structure of those fundamental questions. Exactly the same is true with respect to the possible answers to these questions. They cannot be fundamental answers unless they "answer to" the foundations. But even more "fundamentally," we cannot know that the possible answers are actually exhaustive, that they exhaust all the possible ways in which the foundations could be, without having circumscribed those foundations, as for example in repudiating all those ways in which they could not be, or ways which are ostensibly but not actually possible fundamental ways of being. And what way is there to compare and evaluate possible answers, except by comparing them to and evaluating them in term of the foundations themselves? Therefore, if we know the fundamental questions or the fundamental questions and answers, then it seems that we must know the foundations as well. But if we know the foundations, we are wise and have no need of questions.

For reasons of this kind, together with those which were presented in the earlier sections of this chapter, I am led to two conclusions. First, philosophy is an inescapable consequence of rational speech; every effort to prove that speech is irrational terminates necessarily in a self-contradiction or, perhaps more strongly put, in a self-cancellation. Second, the inescapability of philosophy means the accessibility or intelligibility (but not necessarily the achievement) of wisdom. That is, philosophy "begins" with the recognition of the accessibility or intelligibility of that whole within which we are but a part—a part, however, that is not merely "open" to the whole, but that in some sense circumscribes or reflects it. The sense in which we circumscribe the whole is itself reflected in the different conceptions of the determinate structure of the whole. The *difference* between those conceptions is intelligibility, that is, the common properties of each determinate conception, through which each is visible or intelligible, in and through which rational argument concerning these conceptions is possible. It is a failure to appreciate the force of this difference (which has nothing to do with the "ontological difference": see Chapters 2 and 3) which leads some thinkers to a doctrine of radical, and radically incompatible, Weltanschauungen, that is, of beginnings irrational because indefensible, each distinct from and excluding the others, among which no genuinely philosophical dialogue is possible. This doctrine, which even in its "historicist" form is closely related to the emergence of modern epistemology, results from a common human failure to remember that a refusal or inability on our part to discuss our presuppositions makes them neither secure nor undiscussible. If we can identify our presuppositions and thereby distinguish them from other presuppositions, then there must be a common environment of intelligibility within which this discrimination takes place. We must be able to understand the difference between our presuppositions and those of other thinkers, and the intelligibility of the differences is itself different from any of the presuppositions in question. That is, the intelligibility of the differences is independent of the adoption of any given presupposition. If it were not, if the differences were visible to us only from within and therefore as interpreted by our own presuppositions, then our conviction that ours differed from other presuppositions would be indefensible. For every presupposition ostensibly differing from ours would be merely an object determined by, and thus an object of, our own presupposition. As such an object, every "other" presupposition could be intelligently debated and evaluated from within the perspective of our own fundamental presupposition. But this would mean that our presupposition does not differ so radically from others as to make impossible rational dialogue among them. And so our presupposition would be no Weltanschauung in the sense of being radically distinct from other presupposition–Weltanschauungen, but rather would be the universal environment of intelligibility within which presuppositions (Weltanschauungen) are distinguished and so discriminated. This discrimination is necessarily an evaluation, or a rational argument about presuppositions, if only to the extent that it must decide which presuppositions actually are identical Weltanschauungen.

We cannot insist upon the irrationality of our presuppositions without at the same time making irrational the consequences of those presuppositions. By so doing, we make it possible for our opponent to reject our Weltanschauung without being required even to consider it. Why should he, if it is irrational? If whatever we say is irrational, then certainly we can say anything we like, including that we alone are rational. From such a viewpoint, he who pretends to deny reason is surely absurd. If there is any reason for us to think as we do, this reason must itself be reasonable: it must be intelligible. But if it is intelligible, one may discuss it rationally, which is to say that the conditions of its intelligibility are independent of its own jurisdiction. If they were not, then every Weltanschauung would define the intelligible, and there would be as many conceptions of intelligibility as there are Weltanschauungen. As a result, these conceptions would contradict each other (since for every A, one may posit non-A), or reduce each other to silence, to chaos or nothingness. Given the unlimited number of conceptions of intelligibility, there is no reason for me to accept my own. But this means that I cannot know that my conception is intelligible. It is not intelligible to me unless I have first understood and rejected all contradictory conceptions; therefore, it is not so much a Weltanschauung as a confession of ignorance. It does not illuminate the (my) world, but darkens it. The incompatibility of Weltanschauungen is therefore either intelligible or unintelligible. If it is intelligible, the theory is wrong, since this intelligibility must be shared by all and so be separate from each (again like Plato's good). If it is unintelligible, then no rational distinction can be made between Weltanschauungen, and it makes no sense to speak of their incompatibility or difference; thus they cannot intelligibly be said to be incompatible, and the theory is again wrong.

V.

Desire leads to speech, and speech is the desire for completeness. I now want to show how speech, precisely as necessarily partial, permits the exhibition of wisdom as the end of speech. The whole, because it is intelligible in and through the part, is partially intelligible. And this is so not because of the incompleteness of history, but because of the fundamental nature of rational speech. A speech is rational if it "measures" the form or structure of its object (whether in the sense of "corresponding to" or "disclosing"). It is thus necessary to see whether the speech has correctly measured that form. Let us suppose that we believe speech X to be the total speech, the fully developed concept or statement of wisdom. We therefore suppose that we have seen X′, or the totality of the fundamental intelligible forms or parts about which one could speak. Included in X′, however, is X, for a total speech must be about itself as well. It must explain not merely objects but also itself as the explanation of all objects. That is, X, as included within X′, is an object about which speech is possible. Indeed, it is the most important object; therefore, its form must be seen before one can speak about it, before one can say what one has seen. Yet, if X is total speech itself, this is impossible, for speech does not constitute a totality until *after* it has been finished. One cannot speak about total speech in the same sense that one can speak about some determinate or partial object. Consequently, X cannot be included within X′. On the other hand, if X is totally different from X′, one must be able to see the correspondence between the two, and the paradox of the "third man" is generated (X becomes equivalent to a supersensible *Jenseits,* the "alienated" essence of X′).[20] If X is identical with X′, then it is necessary to stand back from this identity in order to see whether it is actually a totality; but if we can stand back from it, then it is not a totality. On the first hypothesis (X is within X′), we cannot see X prior to saying what we have seen. On the second hypothesis (X is altogether different from X′) apart from the "third man" argument, the radical difference between X and X′ means that X is not the explanation of X′, nor (since what is radically different is unrelated) can X explain the difference between itself and X′. Therefore, it is not total speech (X′ might be Y and should perhaps be so designated here to indicate its total distinctness from X). On the third hypothesis (X is iden-

20. Attempts to obviate this difficulty by making speech the incarnation (disclosing) of Being lead to difficulties discussed in earlier chapters, turning on the impossibility of distinguishing man from Being.

tical with X′), the same difficulty arises as in the first hypothesis, in a slightly different form. $X = X′$ would have to be seen in advance of its own complete development (since now by hypothesis $X = X′$ is complete speech). Apart from the difficulty previously mentioned, the completeness of $X = X′$ could never be known by any speaker. No man could be wise, because the identity of speech with the objects of speech means that it is impossible to distinguish the two, which are not two, but one. And so, in effect, speech is equivalent to silence: this is the monism of fundamental ontology. The very conception of a complete speech is thus seen to be self-negating.[21]

In general, the difference between X and X′ (the ′) can never be so reduced as to make $X′ = X$ without at the same time destroying the existence and therefore the intelligibility of the ′. At the most, we could have not an identity, but an equivalence, which is based upon a difference and so upon a ground differing from either individually, from which the equivalence of differences can be expressed. If, then, discursive thinking is differentiation by limitation through the vision of form, then thought (and so speech) is always incomplete. But that incompleteness depends upon, and so in a secondary sense makes visible, completeness or the whole. Every attempt to bridge the gap between incompleteness and completeness succeeds only in destroying intelligibility. For the gap is itself the expression of a harmony between the two. Completeness or wisdom is only intelligible and therefore only accessible to incompleteness, to philosophy or rational speech. The intelligibility of the ideal of wisdom as the complete speech about the principles and causes, or beginnings and ends, of all things depends upon speech; and the intelligibility of each speech depends upon its own incompleteness. Incompleteness is indeed "completed" by its own intelligibility; to complete the uncompletable is to destroy it or render it invisible. In different terms, philosophy is "completed" by its own possibility, and this possibility depends upon the actual intelligibility of the whole. The whole is in principle the knowable, although we can never wholly know it. If it were not in

21. Cf. Plato, *Sophist* 244d3 ff.

principle the knowable, we could know nothing. Or again, whatever we know is made knowable by the intelligibility of what it would be to be wise. It is this, and this alone, which enables us to distinguish between true and false prophets, or sophists and philosophers. And so, no speech is philosophical which denies intelligibility, or the intelligibility of the whole as the heterogeneously articulated structure in and through which each part is intelligible. Philosophers have always disagreed, and they always will disagree so long as philosophy is present. But they cannot disagree on the intelligibility of their disagreements without ceasing to philosophize. In this sense, disagreement, alienation, and negation are tokens of the good. And so, strange as it seems, one must in a sense first be wise before one can be a lover of wisdom.

In this study, I have tried to show the nihilist consequences of the detachment of philosophy from wisdom, or rather of the reinterpretation of wisdom first as mathematical certitude and then as the experience of historicity. The paradoxes of mathematical logic symbolize the incoherence of historicism, or the misunderstanding of the nature of rational speech. Speech is rational only if it preserves the continuity between itself and will or desire. As is especially evident in our own age, the fundamental feature of nihilism is *discontinuity,* and particularly so in the efforts to replace speech by immediate ecstasy or symbolic abstraction. The two moments or phases of time, coming-to-be and passing-away, are disjoined from each other as is remembering from forgetting. Let me give one final illustration of this by a brief consideration of what is today the central experience of "creativity." One cannot create except by forgetting the authority of the past; at the same time, one must remember how to create, or what it means to be a creator, and therefore a certain memory of the past is indispensable. In a healthy or non-nihilistic society, the discontinuity of remembering and forgetting is overcome by *tradition.* Tradition (*traditio*) is the "handing over" from past to present of the basis for a significant projection into the future; underlying this temporal transfer is the "surrender" of temporality, that is, of creativity itself, to the ideal of the completely rational speech as the eternal foundation for the creative manipulation of time. A living tradition is possible only through this double transference, only where philosophy is the lifeblood of the spiritual activity; otherwise, the aforementioned discontinuity occurs. We see this today not merely in the so-called dissolution of formal structure which seems to be a characteristic of contemporary art, but in the attempt to suspend or replace form altogether by the spontaneity of "happenings." [22]

To take a still more specific example from painting, the Cubist, the Surrealist, the Dadaist, even perhaps the Abstract Expressionist may distort the traditional forms in a way that makes it hard for most of us to see the continuity with the past as a sign of the transfer of meaning from the eternal to the temporal. But this continuity remains, in the extreme case if only in the artist's intention to restate every perception by means of more valid formal matrices. To express a mood or perception abstractly is to adhere to the notion of intelligent coherence as present not simply in the artist's consciousness, but in the world he experiences. In at least some phases of so-called abstract art, we see the influence, perhaps the excessive influence, of geometrical perception and related modes of mathematical intuition. Elements of discontinuity, so-called quantum jumps, may be in the process of prevailing, as for example in the very turn to mathematical perception as dominant over natural perception. But continuity has not been suppressed. Or again, the artist may be communicating a perception of disorganization, but he does so with reference to criteria of order which may be seen, as it were, just outside the perimeter of the art work, and so as participating in its definition. Something quite different, however, is the denial of or indifference to order and organization, even as inversely reflected by a coherent portrait of disorder. People are not simply reduced to things, and

22. The impossibility, even the hypocrisy, of this search for sincerity is clear from the fact that "happenings" are planned or programmed.

human affairs to the contingent relations of things. Things
themselves are "dismantled" or deprived of causal connection,
and so of any rational significance.[23]

To substitute a shoe salesman for a prince as a dramatic hero
is one thing; to remove all perspectives by which we may see
the difference between them is another. Of course, the advocates of art as spontaneous happening will say, and rightly so,
that creative intention operates in the artist's selection and
technical presentation of discontinuous events, that he is por-
traying the contemporary world as it is, or as it is experienced
by an enlightened (or at least up-to-date) sensibility, or by one
which is free from the hypocrisy of dead traditions. But this is
merely to assert the artist's nihilism, either as a project of his
own will or as an acquiescence in the contemporary situation.
In the active or passive acceptance of nihilism, the world is
"held together" by nothing but man's refusal or inability to find
value in it. One could perhaps argue that this posture, if rigor-
ously maintained, is so contrary to our everyday inclinations as
to constitute in itself a highly abstract formalization of experience. I myself should be ready to suggest that we see in the
"adopted" nihilism of intellectuals a kind of erotic perversion
which is similar to the worship of machines. To the extent that
passion may be detected in either, we may still find at least a
negative taste for order.

Nevertheless, the artist or intellectual does not assume the
posture of nihilism as a special or esoteric mood, except in
response to, and as a defense against, popular or global
nihilism. In past ages, individuals who suffered from world-
weariness were immobilized by their condition and thus separated from normally functioning society. Only during the past
one hundred years or less has it become *fashionable on a
global scale* to say that it is abnormal to function normally.
Philosophers and prophets have of course always criticized
everyday, political, or "bourgeois" life, but always in terms of a
higher vision, not a lower one. And this is to say that, with

23. This is reminiscent of, and related to, Hume's denial that we perceive causal connections.

varying degrees of clarity, they have responded positively to the ever-present threat of active nihilism. Even in Dostoievski, the nihilistic protagonist is presented not as a hero, and therefore not as an anti-hero, but as a *victim*—one who has been disabled by the loss of vitality of traditional ideals. The remedy for nihilism is always evident: a restoration of the lost vitality, not an acquiescence in the consequences of that loss. By steady stages of decay, we have reached the present situation in which the nihilist protagonist is shown as the norm (even as an ostensible eccentric or instance of "black humor"), and indeed as the paradigm or ideal type for coping with discontinuous reality.

The discontinuity of reality, and so the irrational fluctuation of remembering and forgetting; the acquiescence in and glorification of absurdity; a fastidious attention to the bodily Eros in all its imaginable forms, first, as a consolation for the disappearance of the psychic Eros, then as a kind of applied mechanics of the technicist anti-mind; more generally, an obsession with technique, whether as applied to bodies or in the empty formal systems of logic and mathematics; the concomitant praise of intoxication and sobriety as themselves discontinuous or indistinguishable manifestations of chaos: these are the easily identifiable characteristics of the contemporary nihilist scene. But they in turn become intelligible only as consequences of a particular disproportion in the unending dialectic of the human psyche as desire articulated by speech. We might describe this disproportion by saying that man becomes discontinuous with nature, provided we add that the discontinuity is given by nature itself. It is true that, by nature, speech or reason is different from desire. But it is an error, and one which is basic to the modern world from its very inception, to attempt to suppress this difference. At first, the suppression takes the form of an identification between nature and desire, and freedom is understood as the freedom of reason to indulge in its highest desires. Unfortunately, the identification of nature and desire leads to the impossibility of distinguishing between high and low desires. It is then reinterpreted as the radical freedom or autonomy of human reason, or the replacement of nature by human work, through which the difference between the high and the low is reestablished. However, what reason gains in being freed from an external order is overcome by the negativity implicit in work or, more fundamentally, by time, which, as in the myth of Kronos, devours its own children.

The modern quest for freedom leads to the redefinition of man in terms of work or, its more recent name, creativity. But this in turn leads to the identification of man as a radically historical individual. The engine of work is negation; the fruit of man's labor, which depends upon its temporality, is also robbed of its stability and so of its significance by the very condition of its existence. The worker, or historical individual, alienated from the unchanging conditions which give significance to his essential condition, may be characterized by what Hegel calls the "unhappy consciousness," and which we might perhaps re-phrase as the melancholia attendant upon freedom in the sense of discontinuity. Hegel also links this condition with the recognition that "God is dead"; although he does not use the word, we have no trouble in understanding that we are here in the presence of nihilism. In Hegel's treatment, the self-alienation and self-trivialization of the sophisticated, skeptical individual, whose unhappiness is merely the opposite and completing side of his *comic* consciousness,[24] is overcome by the development from faith in the resurrection of God to the absolute knowledge of philosophical wisdom. In other words, the suppression of nihilism is equivalent to the suppression of man's merely historical individualism or uniqueness. The discontinuity of temporality is healed only by completeness in the sense of rational knowledge.

Hegel's analysis of nihilism, although it depends upon elements drawn from ancient thought, is given a thoroughly modern formulation. In effect, one may say that Hegel makes the suppression of nihilism dependent upon hybris, or the sanctioning of man's desire to be a god. In different terms, Hegel overcomes the defects of man's temporality by identifying eternity and time. I have already explained why I believe that this is

24. *Phänomenologie*, ed. Hoffmeister, pp. 523 ff.

an erroneous solution. Its instability is, to say the least, strongly confirmed by the actual course of philosophy in the 130-odd years following Hegel. The unhappy consciousness, having passed through the valley of existential dread, would seem to have lost consciousness, or at least to have deteriorated into the superficiality of the comic consciousness, into contemporary "black humor," or the ironical acceptance of one's own baseness and vulgarity. Under these circumstances, one thinks inevitably of Hegel's own observation that, in the dark, all cows are black.

Index